TALL LIVES

TALL LIVES

Bill Gaston

Macmillan of Canada
A Division of Canada Publishing Corporation
Toronto, Ontario, Canada

Canadian Cataloguing in Publication Data
Gaston, William Allen, 1953-
  Tall lives

ISBN 0-7715-9335-X

I. Title.

PS8563.A76T34 1990   C813'.54   C89-090673-4
PR9199.3.G376T34 1990

Jacket design: Leslie Styles

Macmillan of Canada
A Division of Canada Publishing Corporation
Toronto, Ontario, Canada

Printed and bound in Canada
First printing 1990
10 9 8 7 6 5 4 3 2 1

For Bob,
and the music since Pawnee Bay

Contents

TALL LIVES

Prologue

At dusk on January fourteenth, the anniversary of Albert Schweitzer's birthday, the brothers were herded to the barn again, to their father's homemade clinic. With no animals kenneled overnight, the heat was off and it was deathly cold. But since tonight's lesson had to do with self-sacrifice and hardship, it was fitting that while they listened they had to stomp their feet and grind their hands to urge the blood alive.

Facing his fifteen-year-old sons, who were newly taller than him, Dr. Baal clutched a tumbler of scotch in one hand and used the other to slash and stab urgent points of his philosophy. He staggered a bit, and slurred the usual words.

"I jus' wish I could show you how many flies wait there hungry on the screen in summer. The height of summer." He stared at a shuttered window and reflected a moment. "But of course you've seen that. Operations. Births. They smell the blood, oh do they smell the blood. And some get in." The veterinarian looked hard at his boys, who looked back at him, politely acknowledging the profundity taking place. "Little germ bombs. I try to keep 'em out. But I *kill* any who come in here. I *have* to."

Now the vet's look was imploring. One son, Del, who by nature grew nervous at times like this, stole glances into the dark rafters. As in a medieval dungeon, huge leather straps, chains, and machines of bondage hung, silently powerful, from hooks. The other boy, Frank, fixed blank eyes at his father's knees and made his teeth chatter a bit louder than they would have on their own.

"Fellas, it's so goddamned complicated. You can't be an absolutis' anymore."

Del's eyebrows rose and his father caught this, pleased.

"Absolutis', it's someone who is pure. In any sense. Never gives an inch. Schweitzer had to go all the way to Africa to do that. He was the las' absolutis' who was sane."

The brothers knew all about Albert Schweitzer, and about other absolutists as well. Years ago, their father had snapped off the TV one night and stood before it to tell them all about Mahatma Gandhi, and this was the third January fourteenth in a row they'd stood here freezing in this barn hearing about Schweitzer, the elaborate fly nets, the absolute decree of not-taking-any-life-even-tse-tse-flies, the vegetarianism.

"So there was Hitler . . . ," Dr. Baal was counting off on his fingers, "but he was nowhere near sane. Not even pure, really. Then the big fellas: Jesus, Epictetus, maybe Socrates. And God bless the men who were pure and died unknown. But today . . . it's so goddamned *complicated*. You'll find that out. I'm jus' trying to show you." He stood swaying, feverish, eyes not so much seeing as revealing pained thought.

"Here," he shouted, grabbing a huge scalpel, the kind used for livestock. "This is jus' what I'm talking about." He held the instrument aloft, like a ceremonial sword. The light from the operating lamp did not glint off the gunmetal gray but seemed absorbed by it. "Look a' this. It cuts, it tortures something godawful. In order to cure. That is complication at its simplest."

He breathed deeply and looked at his sons again. He smiled. He shrugged mightily. "Unless you're a saint, to save lives you have to kill flies."

Their father's famous little phrase. By now Del looked bored too, and Frank ventured beyond that into insolence by turning his back on his father to fiddle with a tray of ice-cold joint saws, pliers, braces.

"So I jus' want to say it's going to be hard, boys, it's going to get complicated for you. More in the future than now even. Tha's the way it's going."

It was hard to tell whether either boy, each one tall, angular, face cut with severe shadows, was listening at all anymore.

"Unless of course you're a saint. Unless you turn out to be Alber' Schweitzer."

This last statement was shaped through a smile, and the boys knew they could turn and leave, it was over.

Stepping quickly into the cold, ahead of their father, Frank and Del left the clinic. In the cavernous older part of the barn it was dark, and they made their way past empty screen cages toward the open double doors, which guided them with the faint purple of dusk. Their father's flashlight beam jerked in and out through their legs, making them stop short in front of sudden huge obstacles, which were, of course, their own shadows.

"Wait. Come here."

Frank and Del had to stop and go back. The vet was unlocking a storage locker in a corner.

"One last thing. You want to see a complication?"

Dr. Baal fumbled with the lock. The boys heard his empty glass drop, and the shatter was faint, almost playful, in the frozen air of the barn. The vet got the door open and shone his light inside. The boys bent forward. Hanging from a hook, the cut flesh red-black and smelling oddly sweet, was half a frozen horse. In places meat had been sawed from bone.

"Fellas, we've been eating this guy all winter."

Frank took a step back and frowned. Del leaned closer, eyes wide.

"Art Montague's quarter horse. Broke that leg, remember? I put him down. Art told me to bury him."

The vet paused to let the boys look and absorb the lesson.

"Now as far as a veter'narian goes, that's one fair complication, I'd say. And, fellas, it's going to get worse for you."

Snow fell heavily as they crossed the lawn to the house. Even though it was chicken for dinner, Frank didn't eat. He went out soon afterwards, tobogganing, he said. Del watched the last of the hockey game with his father, then Don Messer's Jubilee with his mother. That same evening, ten miles to the west, a vacant summerhouse was broken into and torn apart, all the windows smashed and the vilest imaginable words written with ketchup on the walls. There was no apparent motive, and the snow had covered all tracks. It was a complicated crime, people in this quiet community agreed.

CHAPTER ONE

Del

Gravity kills us all in time. But gravity is an
illusion, kept at bay by goodwill, and the posture
which springs lightly from that.
            —Felix d'Amboise

This tangled, lousy life—as his brother Frank described it—
was like living inside a vast paper bag filled with spiders and
broken glass. Every few days it gets grabbed and shaken stupidly
by some child brat-god.

His brother had a way with despair.

Today, as Del climbed into the shower, Frank's words didn't
seem so exaggerated for once. Del's bag had been shaken last
night. Turning on the spray, starting with cold, he stifled a yell.
He'd read in a self-help book that a shower was the best way to
combat sadness: get naked, step in, get clean, spray the devil out
of everything, it said. This was Del's third shower today.

Last night had started innocently, in murmured conversation
after sex. A sated temptress, smiling, Mary had asked, "So.
Would you still have been my best friend if I wasn't a woman? If
we didn't have . . . this?" She gestured back and forth from groin
to groin with a lazy hand.

Del hesitated. "Well yeah. Sure. I guess so. *I* don't know."

Now Mary hesitated. "Oh."

"Oh what?"

But his wife had rolled over, giving Del her back. Oh Christ,
she was mad again, at nothing. Del saw that his mistake had been
to give a coy love-quip something more than a coy answer.

"C'mon, Mare, what is it?"

"Del, after all these years I've been . . . hallucinating *friend*-ship, and for you it's just a case of tits and ass."

"Come on, Mary." Del laid a hand on her shoulder. "You serious?"

"I'm going to sleep." Mary got out of Del's bed, crossed the room, and climbed into her own. Del propped his head on his hand and stared at his wife's bare back. Across one shoulder blade were red marks, where his hand had just been, digging.

They talked on, the physical distance allowing anger and detachment, and the argument soon included all the familiar sore points of their marriage. They'd stopped growing, Mary said. Del's answer that they were "tall enough already" didn't help.

"There you go." Mary pointed a finger at him. "You know your stupid sense of humor hasn't changed in eight years? It's a cover-up."

"You married me with this stupid sense of humor. Did you hope it would go away or something?"

"I hoped mine and yours would grow more alike."

"My humor would have to disappear to be more like yours."

Et cetera. And sometime in the deep of the night Mary let fall, with no emphasis, no drama, the word "divorce." Del went cold at the word and stammered once, but otherwise pretended he hadn't heard.

Legs apart, all caution, Del pinned the bathroom mirror with those most sincere eyes in the world and tilted the buzzing razor to get at his nose hairs. Slow as a surgeon. Sometimes the razor pulled, bringing tears. You had to get the hair-ends up the slits just right. His body felt stupid and spongy from so many show-ers. But get clean, start fresh. The world will fix itself if you fix *your*self.

For two minutes Del didn't blink. He took this seriously, as he did all things, and he was extra self-conscious about the nostrils: they were huge, and all that hair didn't help. His nose he'd over the years grown to accept, almost admire, ever since a past girlfriend called it "so noble." For it *was* the Romanest of Romans, proclaiming itself in a grand arc, hump, and hang. But just as Rome had had its foul underbelly, so Del's nose had its nostrils. Nostrils that Del's friend Wally Kenny delighted in, declaring that if Tarzan ever found his way into one of them, he'd stand awestruck as in a bat-hung cavern, thinking he'd discovered a lost subterranean world. Wally would drawl the joke like a Texan, but at the same time lisp like the queen he was.

Del switched the razor off and leaned into the mirror, turning his face up, down, and sideways, checking his caves. Good job, and no tears. He stepped back, scanned his torso, his neck, his cheeks. Then, as always, to punctuate his mirror gazing he raised a skinny arm and flexed it. Suddenly he was staring at his eyes.

Del saw himself as if for the first time that day. He recognized the exact pose, the same childlike curiosity in the eyes. He was seeing himself at ten years old. More shocking still, he was seeing Frank.

They'd been, what, ten years old when the doctors had come again to measure them? Yes, about ten. Doctors who studied twins had come to Orillia from all over. That was when he'd gotten self-conscious about his nose, his nostrils, his feet, his height, and had taken to perusing himself in front of mirrors. Frank had simply gotten cocky and mean. Grown a shoulder chip. At ten, Frank had been a touch shorter than Del, and his nostrils probably a gnat's body not so large. Frank was two minutes younger.

According to their father the doctors had first swarmed all over them less than a week after their birth. Brampton, Ontario. August 8, 1954. Such an odd birth, such a bizarre circumstance, irresistible! And subsequently written up not only in medical journals but in the newspapers too. BAAL TWINS JOINED AT BIG TOE. Editors must have been in heaven. VETERINARIAN DAD SEPARATES SIAMESE SONS. They were on the *Brampton Times* front page for a week. DR. BAAL PARTS BOYS WITH WORKSHOP SAW. And TOWN VET MAKES PAINFUL CHOICE. Fearing for his family's peace of mind, Dr. Baal had declared it was time to move.

Sitting on the toilet now, elbow on knee and chin on fist, Del recalled the second time the doctors had swarmed, when he and Frank were ten, this time in Orillia, this time to measure their preadolescent growth spurt. And, yes, Frank had sprouted cockiness right about this time, a reaction to fame and humiliation. Del remembered one group of doctors—psychologists probably—running them through batteries of questions, some of which he could still hear. "If your mom were an animal, which animal would she be?" "When your dad hugs your twin brother, what do you feel?" "If your brother were a girl, would you like her?" The study of schizophrenia in twins was in vogue in the mid-sixties. When Dr. Baal discovered the nature of these tests he packed his family and moved once more. To the Fraser Valley, British Columbia, where there were lots of sick cows and so lots of business, and where under towering mountains you could grow as tall as a tree and still feel a dwarf. "Shrinks are crazy," Dr. Baal said, simply enough. And, as though to prove the vet's point, roughly half of the ensuing journal articles declared the Baal brothers sane as wheat, while the other half hinted darkly at shared loose screws.

Del stood in front of the mirror again, looking defiantly ruddy, feeling happily sane. He had decided to feel this. To brighten a dark world, one starts with oneself. He had decided to let simple goodwill overcome his rift with Mary, defeat that word she had spoken. To start, he would be happy with his nostrils, happy to be six foot five, happy to be skinny, happy even that his elbow joints were thicker than his biceps. Happy to be thirty-five. Happily employed. Happy . . . well, happily married. Happy to be partnered up with a woman of auspicious size, her five foot six an omen of opposites attracting, a yin-yanging of height, a sixty-niner of stature. Mary. He loved her body under his, her head cocked up to nibble his neck. But *happily* married? Del had to admit it. "Happily" was a word lazily chosen by couples lucky enough to enjoy a union devoid of too much pain.

He heard the kitchen door bang open and then Mary's chirping voice from the hall.

"Come in, people. I'll make tea. Everyone into the living room, sit up straight, and make conversation. Remember, Lulu, today is manners day. No name calling. Fraser, put that down."

Mary's chimps were here again. Eight of them crammed together for their class in "social normalization," which meant not drooling or slouching, and not spilling their tea. In other words, they were not to act like mentally handicapped teenagers, which is what they were. Del made it across the hall without being seen and locked himself in the bedroom. He'd join them all later. Mary wanted to discuss Wally's surprise party with him. And after all, the chimps (Del's secret term of endearment for them) were sometimes a joy.

Del lay spread-eagled on his wife's bed, masturbating, visualizing the iridescent blue necks of pigeons. His autoeroticism always started normally enough, a simple thickening lust, but when he put his mind to it he could get creative as hell. Lately he'd come to the accompaniment of images of rainbows, the conjured roar of a jet engine, and the slow tease of water drops plinking the virgin surface of a mill pond.

Soon he rose, feeling shame. Why did shame persist? How many times had he masturbated in his life, starting way back as a too-tall boy in junior high? Lots. His shame was no longer the dark shadow shame of a teenager caught red-handed in noon sunlight, but it was still there, still a shadow, perhaps the kind cast in a hazy sunset evening.

From the living room came a roar of surprise, which then broke apart into individual fits of laughter. Mary had told them some sort of joke, or someone had burped.

Shame. Del's big toe ached, right at the tip where a toenail should have been but where there was only a smooth bulb of scar skin, like a recent burn. The ache had begun that morning, and flamed sharply whenever he thought of last night. That word.

He could clearly picture them all there in the living room, sitting up straight, following Mary around with their eyes, eyes that suggested they came from a planet where everyone walked

slowly, carefully, and at an odd angle. Lulu, about sixteen, with a
short, misshapen body, the dark eye-bags of an insomniac, and
an acid hatred of everything alive. Lars, ageless, who never
talked unless asked a question. He simply stared with tin eyes out
of a metal-smooth face and did everything anyone told him, a
robot owned by all. Shelley, a shy teenager with buckteeth so
large she could not close her mouth. Speech-impaired and spas-
tic. But Shelley's eyes, when she shyly gave them to you, spoke
of a tender soul and a brain smarter than her body let it be. Fraser,
seventeen, smiling always (and Lulu's foil in so many ways).
Tall, with a high forehead, the bent shape of which reminded
Del of a crescent moon. He was bone weird. Wild-eyed and
manic, he talked nonstop about everything and nothing. These
four were Del's favorites, Fraser most of all.

Naked, he searched the closet for a pair of pants. He'd fan-
tasized today about pigeon necks. Lord. It was all Mary's fault.
Del couldn't recall exactly when it was she'd announced, "Our
sex life has to go the creative route if it's going to survive." A
couple of years ago it was, anyway, not so coincidentally occur-
ring around the time Mary started dance classes and then was
given a copy of the *Kama Sutra* by a classmate. Around this time
she'd taken to snuggling up to him after making love and cooing
in a child's whisper, "That was . . . so nice. I had . . . an orange
orgasm." Sometimes it was blue, sometimes it reminded her of
drunken horns or teasing electric guitars. "How was yours?"
she'd ask, and Del, strangely nervous beside a wife strangely
new, could only say, "Well . . . it was really, *really* nice."

Del sensed Mary's disappointment. Then came her creative
dictum. Soon Del learned to talk about blue orgasms too, and
pink ones and subtle beige ones, and he almost believed he felt
them. He found he could really please her when he got clever on
his own. She was especially pleased one night when with no
prodding at all he lay back and said that this time had been "hard
but sweet. Like little bullets of fire."

But metaphor was not enough. Next came her call for "more
space, so our encounters will be like a nice contrast," and soon
they were sleeping in twin beds. To gain visiting rights Del

found he had to court her, had to wink and plant suggestions from six feet away. There she lay on her side, her back to him, her shoulders bare above the blanket, her wonderful brown, faintly Asian skin, her rich black hair falling over everything like a languorous tropical weed. So tired from her dance class three nights a week that she often grunted "no" from this position. (And Del wished more than once for a tranquilizer gun.) Before long, Mary decided it would be easier if they simply kept to a schedule. To start, say, Sunday and Thursday?

"But what about desire? Who cares what a calendar says?" Del was horrified to hear his nasal whine. "What about Monday and Tuesday and Wednesday and— "

"Can't *you* take care of that, Del?"

"Take care of . . . ?"

"Haven't you heard that masturbation in marriage is considered healthy in the eighties?"

"Considered by who?"

"*Whom*. By me, for one."

So Del's fits of spontaneity had to be satisfied in solitude. It was his slightly sassy whim to satisfy them on Mary's bed.

"So. Did you masturbate today, darling?" she took to asking, chipper and businesslike as a nurse, untying her scarf as the winter air flooded in the door behind her.

"Um . . . well, yes. Yes, I did." Perhaps the truth would shame her in some vague way, though it never seemed to.

"And how was it?"

"Solitary."

But such snippy answers froze her further. She wanted a shared marriage no matter what form that marriage took. It bothered him that she still expected him to share, without resentment, stories of his involuntary exile. To share, as if nothing was wrong, his feelings from the shore of his sexual island.

"It was hard but sweet, bullets of fire, you should have been there."

This was as close to anger as Del ever got.

He joined Mary and the chimps in the living room. To an eruption of giggled hellos he smiled and nodded into the carpet, accepting a teacup from Peggy, an enormous mongoloid girl who poured with steady grace as she squinted through her dull Chinese eyes.

"Hello, darling," Mary said, rising. She kissed Del on the cheek in a way that told him he was half being greeted and half being used as a tool to demonstrate proper matrimonial behavior.

Fraser, good old Fraser, leapt to his feet and pointed at husband and wife. "Yes! That is our *future!*" he shouted from behind his bottle-bottom glasses. "That is *marriage!* And marriage is our *future!*"

The future had been Fraser's obsession for the past month. Any new car ad, any election campaign poster or *Time* magazine cover, would have Fraser waving his arms and proclaiming, "Our *future!* The future is *now* for the handicapped young adult!"

The debate had gone on for years as to whether Fraser was insane, retarded, or both. He often shouted Marxist or right-wing slogans (both with the same fanatical flair), getting all the words right. But he could not count. Nor could he tell time, and yet any clock he spotted gave rise to this: "Our future is *now* and *now* moves in the hands of all our clocks!" With his grin he showed the world his crooked horse's teeth. Wild hair and, when he shouted, clawed fingers. Eyes swimming big as plums behind his glasses. Del liked Fraser because it was impossible to tell whether he was ever serious about anything. If Del had read a little more into this he would have recognized he liked him because they were opposites. For Fraser embodied a retarded but nonetheless grand kind of staginess. No plain green pepper-head, he. Too bad Fraser couldn't take care of himself. If let loose from his group home Fraser would be perpetual street theater. But he'd die.

"Yeah, Fraser, that's your future. Marriage. Good luck," said Del.

The dig passed Mary by. To Fraser she said, "That's right, Fraser. Some day you might have a wife to kiss." The seven other tea drinkers howled at this outrageous thought. "But first you have to learn your skills."

Kissing skills, bedroom skills . . . . Del knew it was the perfect time for a joke. Nothing gave wild glee to these folks like a little naughtiness. His brother Frank wouldn't have wasted a second, would've delivered an in-and-out joke and then in the uproar turned to Mary and leered like Vincent Price.

Mary thought Frank was a show-off, among other things. Mary, loosen up. Del found himself hoping she'd get a bit drunk at Saturday's party. Drunk and laughing. Drunk and dark and seductive. "Mare," he'd whisper from the back of his throat when the guests were gone, "Mare, let's leave this mess till morning." He'd scoop her up John Wayne–style, growling. She would stare up at him horny-eyed, desperate for it, but playing coy and dark and dusky as a proud harlot. Prepare for the magic chopstick, he'd growl in her ear, an old joke.

"My future is future *skill*," Fraser yelled.

"Shut up! Shut up, *stupid*!" Lulu hissed from her corner. Her teacup clattered in its saucer. She'd had her eyes on Fraser through all this and was seething.

Mary sighed a tired mother's reproach as she rose to get cookies from the kitchen. Cookies were always the final treat. In fifteen minutes she'd board their bus with them to see them home.

Dammit, the party. He'd forgotten. This morning Mary had called wanting to know about the progress of Wally's damn party.

"I've done most of the phoning," Del announced when she returned with the cookie tray.

"You've done *most* of the phoning."

"I wanted to check with you about some people. I thought that, for example, if we ask Wally's friend Larry, then we'd have to ask Larry's friend Neil. And Neil isn't exactly Wally's favorite person anymore. I mean, these fags, you can never— "

"Del, it's Saturday *night*." And she whispered, "And don't say fags."

"Well I just wanted to check with you. I didn't know how many of Wally's . . . type you were expecting."

"*I'm* only expecting that since it's your best friend Wallace's party you would deal with the invitations on *his* terms. He still sees that same man friend?"

Deal with? Terms? Man friend? Del wondered whether, six years ago, he'd ever suspected that the hippyish girl he was marrying would one day be capable of using such words with a perfectly straight face.

"Well, that's just the problem. I mean . . ." Del smiled and thought, why not? "I mean, *Wallace*'s current *man friend* has been a *man friend* with half of Wallace's *old* men friends, and so we have to *deal with* the fact that they're not all on sparkling or even speaking— "

"You told them it's a surprise? Eight sharp?"

"—*terms*. Yes, I told them." Had he? "Yes, and . . . and Frank's coming to town in time for the party."

Poor timing. It was no secret his brother wasn't fond of fags. Wally he still loved, but he couldn't tolerate Wally's friends. Mincing meat pies, he called them, often to their faces. Mary would now think Del had neglected to phone Wally's friends on purpose—that is, because of Frank. And Mary, already stiffening into a mood, would see it all as part of an old battle: Frank and Mary, rivals for Del's best loyalty.

"But ol' Frankie's got a date," Del said quickly. Slapping a little drumroll on his knees, he smiled hopefully and raised his eyebrows. He saw Mary's mood ease off a bit. If the truth were told, the thought of Frank having a date settled Del's fears too. Laura, her name was. A Laura at the party would guarantee a more civilized Frank.

Lulu, who all this time had been growling at Fraser (who happily punched buttons on the stereo as though it were a typewriter, mumbling inanities about the future), suddenly began screaming at him.

"Stupid! Shut up, *ass*! *Ass*!" Just as Mary began to remind her again about manners day, she made as if to lunge at him. Fraser reared up stumbling and kicked over his teacup. But he gathered himself and stood facing her, owl-eyed, his smile gone, a rarity. Lulu, beet red, nostrils flaring, leaned at him from the edge of her chair.

Fraser's neck flipped in a spasm, and he threw up on the front of his shirt. The room snapped silent as Fraser looked down at the mess of milky tea, studied it, and grinned. He saw everyone staring at him. "Hi!" he said, delighted.

In a new rage Lulu bounced and howled in her chair, pointing at Fraser. Others shouted, and soft-hearted Shelley closed her eyes and began to quietly cry, dropping her chin and sticking her teeth out farther into the room.

Mary stood. "Lulu. You. Into the kitchen for a towel. You will help Fraser clean his shirt."

Lulu hesitated for only a moment before stomping away for the towel, her eyes wild, her breath coming in apoplectic snorts.

Del wasn't about to watch this. He for one wouldn't care to sponge up a friend's barf, let alone an enemy's. Sometimes he questioned his wife's strategy.

"I'm off to the den," he announced to the carpet, getting up, but Mary didn't answer.

Del closed the den door behind him. It closed with a solid thunk like the door of a good foreign car. Del was proud of that door. He'd ordered it extra tall and he'd cut away and modified the door frame himself.

Ah, he loved this room. He was so sad when he finished it. He should have been a carpenter for the earthy joy it gave him. Football reffing was getting . . . rough. Tilted. Too many stars in the game now, too many Americans, their big salaries. Refs were treated like necessary scum. Striped, whistling scum, marking off penalties to a roar of boos and a stadium full of hatred.

A horrid scratching at the door, his perfect door. Del grimaced and jumped to open it. North America padded in sloppily, stopping at Del's feet to look up with half-lidded eyes and lolling tongue, then carried on to the corner, turned a mindless circle, and flopped sighing on her spot between the wall and the easy chair. Even from six feet up, Del could smell her. Northam burped once and fell asleep.

Del closed the door. Some chimp in the living room was croaking hysterically, and it was hard, sadly, to tell if from fury or joy. Mary had a tough job. He shouldn't be so hard on her.

Del fell back into his La-Z-Boy, hit the lever. Up went his feet. Northam woke and thumped her tail on the wall. Del removed his left shoe and massaged the bone-sore toe. Rain coming. Laugh all they cared to, the toe stub never lied.

He surveyed the room. The oak luster, the shelves stocked with books and basketball trophies, the TV screen bulging out dark and smooth like a huge gray gem. Pleated curtains, tastefully dark. On one wall, Mary's degree, a wedding picture, his dead parents. On another wall, a photo of Del and Frank in uniform, each of them squeezing a basketball aloft with a single hand, two teenaged toothy smiles (Frank's slightly sinister even then). Another of an older Del alone, hair ebbed a touch, in ref's stripes, holding a football now. The youngest head ref in the CFL. In all pictures, the ageless Roman honker.

A faint piddling sound issued from the bathroom, then Fraser singing to himself. Del recognized "The Lemon Song" by Led Zeppelin and recalled that Zep was making a comeback with youngsters. Fraser would make a perfect punk singer. Del imagined Frank's bent lyrics coming out of Fraser's bent mouth. He heard the toilet flush. His door opened and Fraser's face poked in. He was shy and wouldn't look at Del directly.

"Our future is our future," he said quietly, "and our future is now."

"Right, Fraser. You go be nice to Lulu now."

Fraser withdrew. Del decided he would formally tour the party through his new den Saturday night. Wally had helped with the color scheme, so he'd be proud too. His nelly friends would get witty as hell as they stood in an honest-to-god jock's den. Del looked around some more and forced himself to smile.

But Fraser was right. He had here, staring him in the face, a vision of his future: this room was good for nothing but watching TV, escaping Mary, and breathing in the dead-meat odor of North America. His reflection in the TV screen gave him a neatly packaged display of his own life reclined at a very un-dramatic halfway point.

A clamor and roar, Lulu's, shook the house. Del could make out Fraser's wheedling, "It's NICE. Trying to be NICE. It's NICE."

He felt like crying, and he hadn't cried in ten years, not since his father followed his mother to the grave. He knew he was feeling sorry for himself, at the peak of a vague sorrow that had been building for weeks. Years? Who could say. But last night Mary's word had brought it to a head.

Why couldn't he have it out with her? For years a tension had been building. Invisible, creeping, hanging unspoken between the lines of their domestic chitchat. Why? It made Mary freeze up and Del get meek and polite. Sometimes he trembled. Sometimes he locked himself in the bathroom, or this den. Sometimes he fled and masturbated like an overwhelmed and bitter boy.

Where were his guts? He, who had only to blow his whistle for a field full of violent mesomorph heroes to halt and wait for his judgment, wait for him to tell them where to go and what to do, why couldn't he arbitrate with Mary? He was fair. He could ref their marriage. Why couldn't he tell her what he saw? He knew she would love him for it. Last night, pretending he hadn't heard. This morning, in the breakfast-nook tension, he had tried the warm and rosy tactic again, and this lie always forced her further from him. He couldn't blame her. She wouldn't talk either, but at least she didn't lie. Why were men the romantics these days, and women the cool watchers?

Del drove the chair to horizontal. He moaned at the ceiling. "The . . . marriage . . . cul-de-sac." He'd heard the phrase on "Family Ties" last night. But this was nothing like TV. He thought for a moment what "this was like." This was like . . . losing the biggest game in life.

Tenderly, Del put his shoe back on. He smiled at another thought. Frank, sneering, had called him the happiest man he knew. The fraternal optimist. Wouldn't it surprise his brother to see him now. Frank didn't know he could be so well rounded.

CHAPTER TWO

Frank

There is no limit to sanity. It has no top, bottom, or sides, and can grow profound to the extent of including God. Mental illness has no limit either. It has no top, bottom, or sides, and can grow profound to the extent of including sanity.

—Felix d'Amboise

"More bullshit."

Its pages flapping like the wings of a pulp dragonfly, the book flew through the narrow boat cabin and thocked the helm window, narrowly missing the compass, which always pointed due north no matter how mad Frank Baal got. Striding the seven and a half paces to the other end of *Tammy*'s cabin, Frank grabbed up the book and threw it in the other direction. Frank had become a calm, mean cat batting a mouse around. He was bored. He threw the book several times more until, bored of cruelty even, he stood and stared down at it, spine-buckled and pathetic on the floor, fanning its pages at him like a western whore her poor gray petticoats.

"Bullshit." He sighed the word this time. Stooping, he raised the forward bilge hatch and fired the book in there. Another one for the "black hole," the oily dank hell he reserved for the year's worst books. This latest dog of a book told the life story of a typical idiot savant hero who'd tattooed his forehead with an exclamation mark and then commenced to lead a tragic life.

Later on he found God. Something like that. One more stupid author, lecturing shamelessly, having no right. Frank pictured the other books (he'd gone through a dozen dogs this year, at least) floating in the perfect gloom of the bilge. A dozen printed bodies swelling into mush-flesh.

Before Frank knew it he found himself at the open cupboard, his hand tight around a bottle of sake. Hmmm, he thought. Habit? He hadn't had a bottle since . . . yesterday. Well then, a habit. Japanese water. A nice smooth drunk, and yet a habit easily broken (he reasoned as usual) because its hangovers were so godawful.

Frank cracked off the twist top, poured a full glass, picked up Malcolm the Uke by the neck, and sat on the bunk. He strummed twice, then flopped on his back to tune it. He smiled now, feeling the sake warming his middle, confident that he lay on the verge of a night where biting lyrics would rise out of nowhere. Bad books helped that way sometimes, especially big, earnest bad books. Something in the way they tossed their grand ideas around gave Frank his best cynicism, his clear midnight mood where lyrics rose—as they did now to his tuned, plinking uke— like unbidden neon flowers. He stopped plinking to scribble quick words on his notepad. He wrote all the lines without once pausing:

> I hafta paya man to kick my butt,
> I hafta paya man to stick my mutt,
> I hafta paya movie star to wet my lady,
> I hafta paya throb-head to teach my babies.
>
> They call me mister soul-gone croak,
> They call me mister go-for-broke,
> They call me mister no-cunt-poke,
> They call me mister modern.

Good enough. Enough, at least, for The Snuff, a know-nothing neo-punk outfit who wanted to see a batch of "original lyrics" by the weekend. That was five days away, and Frank had no time. Frank Baal, a man who had nothing but time, for once had on his hands a busy week. Besides the songs, tomorrow he had to dinker all day with *Tammy*'s engine, because Tuesday through Thursday he had charters. Three in a row. To make matters worse, the salmon were running well. Even tourists knew when salmon were running—they heard about it in every bar and gas station they stopped at. They'd arrive dockside at six a.m. with eager shy smiles and the kind of salmon-expectations a month of fishing wouldn't satisfy. Anyway, Frank would get *Tammy* purring, take his three boatloads of tourists out, and slaughter them a lot of salmon. Maybe he'd get the big tip. But the busy week didn't stop there: Friday he had to motor to town to Del's. Wally Kenny's fag party. He'd run in a load of cod to sell to the Chinamen Friday afternoon, and arrive at the party stinking of fish. Perfect. It would remind those city cream-rinse-heads that there was honest work to be had out of sight of skyscrapers.

But first, The Snuff. (Or were they The Bardo Liars now? Bands these days seemed to think that the group name was the only key to success, and they changed it constantly.) Frank poured more sake, then checked the cupboard to see how many bottles he had on hand. Four. Could he scare up five songs tonight? Even if they weren't great songs, a band like The Snuff would buy one or two just to keep him interested. Suburban brats with spending money, a better synthesizer every Christmas.

He turned to the napkin with scribbled music on it, another simplistic four-chord sequence one of the young cretins had no doubt "discovered" one night, thinking it hot damn. Frank strummed the chords impatiently, and soon more crippled neon flowers came. He wrote:

> You be so *craven*. You be damn *bogus*.
> Lookin' at her *glass* house,
> choosin' only *safe* rocks.

> She will find no *exit*, except when you are *sleeping*,
> steppin' in the *traps* you laid,
> in her pink *pyjamas*.

> Can you find a *synonym*

for a *cock with cancer?*
I think the only word that fits is
you, you, you, you.

The gist of two songs in under five minutes. Not bad.

The following morning, down in the gassy guts of *Tammy Wouldn't Die*, wrench in hand, his body twisted and nearly upside down, Frank coaxed a stuck spark plug and mulled over more lyrics. It was too hot a day, by far the hottest this spring. Amidst all this stubborn machinery, this smell of fuel and rust and neglect, nothing but the worst cynicism came, no humor to speak of. A half-empty sake bottle sat ready on the deck above, warming in the sun. Only one line had come to him, and he couldn't get past it. "The world turns on a spit. Daytime the sun burns us, nighttime the moon sucks our juice." The line depressed him; it depressed him further when he recalled that it was a line he'd read in that dog-bad book from last night.

The plug twisted free. He tossed it up past his head and heard it plop in the water beside the boat. He replaced it with a fresh one and unkinked himself to rise from *Tammy*'s bowels, done for the day.

Frank took up his sake with a flourish, twirled its top, and took a pull—the first deserving, guilt-free sip he'd had in several bottles' time. Footsteps on the dock and a curt "ahem" caught him in this embarrassing midmorning position. He hated being thought a lush.

"You mail." A sky blue envelope skimmed onto the boat deck. "I vould not haf brought it except I haf to check ze damn ties on ze tourist boats off you damn bow." Mr. Munich didn't look at Frank as he said this. He clomped off down the dock. His name was really Mr. München, or some such, but to all he was Mr. Munich, the sour-head German who owned Bob's Lowtide Motel and Resort and who did nice things for people a dozen times a day but spent twice the energy denying that he ever did nice things. Frank and *Tammy Wouldn't Die* had tied here for two years now, and it was the truth that Frank had never seen Mr. Munich smile. Frank liked the man more for this, as he liked all caricatures, especially those who lived an exaggerated hell, as if plucked from a painting by Heironymus Bosch.

He toed the letter up to his chair and read the return address. Laura. He took another long pull of sake. Not good, he knew, to get drunk so early in the day. But not exactly bad either. What would it change? Today he had only to finish the damn songs and tie a bunch of hooks for tomorrow's charter. He could do both (and do both better) drunk as a monkey.

He let his head loll back to catch the spring sun on his face and closed his eyes. Gulls screeched and mewed in the distance, hungry or sex-starved. Somewhere out on the bay children in a rowboat squealed, splashing water with their oars. Frank recalled there hadn't been a drowning around here in over a year.

The skin on his huge Baal nose felt tight, ready for its annual burn and peel. He lifted his head and scanned the treed shoreline. As usual, he'd forgotten to witness the spring. He'd missed it, the leafing and blooming. Frank closed his eyes now, and took himself back to a landscape of trees which looked weak but hopeful, waiting for a chink in the bad weather to shyly present their sickly green buds. Frank concentrated hard on these trees and on Laura's unopened letter in his hand. *Go on, do it*, he hissed, and in the periphery of his wilful vision, he saw each tree in turn jump awake at his command and blast loudly into leaf, *bang, pop, bang, bang,* a string of green firecrackers going on and on for miles.

Frank opened his eyes and looked. There, summer.

Staggering just a bit, Frank hiked along the shoreline path to the shack of fat Felix d'Amboise. The double whammy of the Laura letter and two bottles of sake blinded him to the beauty this hike more or less threw in his face. He stepped past huge ferns that steamed, junglelike, in the noon spring sun. Within spitting distance were arbutus trees, their nude red skin as sensual to the hand as a woman's muscle. Within rock-throwing distance

Pender Harbour lay darkly crystal on this windless day; a school of herring sculled just under the surface, frantic and big-eyed over two things only—danger and food—and their darting in unison showed a shared, simple mind. Lastly, within seeing distance were the bald harbor islands, the small mountains beyond them, the snow-capped peaks beyond that, and beyond all and everything a solar purple sky.

"*I wanna beer, Felix!*" Frank screamed in mock anguish, fifty yards from a bare wood cabin. This was Frank's usual greeting call, and also his ongoing joke. For Felix despised alcohol, and lectured all who used it. Frank, loving it, lectured all who didn't. In any case, he yelled not so much out of an actual barley thirst as out of respect. Frank was hermit enough himself to know that true hermits needed a moment or two to compose themselves for a visit. God knows what Felix d'Amboise did in solitude. And Frank suspected Felix liked to be caught at his writing table. (Once when Frank was having coffee with Felix and more visitors came, the fat hermit seemed to forget Frank's presence as he humped himself over to his table and arranged a few papers before calling a gruff "Come in.")

Felix was so fat he looked out of place in a part of the world where men chopped gigantic trees and loaded salmon by the ton; even in a city he would have been freakish, falling into that category of fat man at whom tots, tugging their mums' skirts, shout and point as he waddles by. Maybe that was why Felix lived in the country, in a shack inaccessible to mums and tots.

All who knew them were surprised that Frank Baal liked Felix d'Amboise, the snide fat man from Quebec. It was uncharacteristic of Frank not to hate people who thought they *had* something (rock stars, Latin lovers, gurus, witty homosexuals, and writers were the worst), and Felix had the most massive ego on the coast, holding his own intelligence in the highest esteem. So sure of his brains was Felix that he'd let everthing else go: his body, his hygiene, his future, his sex life, even his personality. He lived on welfare (a cheap diet of potatoes fried in lard kept his bulk up and his skin the color of chalk and bruises) and spent all his time writing a multivolume encyclopedia of his own insights called *Truth on the Living Globe*.

"*I wanna beer, monsieur*," Frank called again from just outside the door. Felix's shack, standing alone on the seashore tree line, was devoid of any distinguishing marks. No woodsy deer antlers over the door, no driftwood or shells, no back-to-the-land displays of macramé, potted herbs, or stained glass.

"No beer here, Mr. Baal," came the honking voice.

Frank entered to find Felix spread out behind his writing table, lips pursed, studious. His eyes were small and piggish but sparkled midnight black with Gallic pride; his head rose bulletlike out of the folds of his neck; his short hair appeared coiffed by a knife. In front of him were papers stacked in various piles, along with a dozen pencils lined up like privates willing to die for their general. Otherwise, the cabin revealed an overstated poverty: swaybacked cot, three lone books, a woodstove, and a corner that harbored a sack of potatoes, a lard pail, and a case of canned beets. There were, however, an extra chair and coffee cup—Felix's one concession to company. He rose, looking pained, to make tea.

"Feel," Frank said, falling drunkenly, comfortably, into the extra chair, "I've come to talk to you about women."

"Ah. Laura. Frank and Laura. Laura and Frank," Felix said, his back to Frank, his bulk hiding the sink and kettle and tea fixings completely. A bulbous elbow shot out now and then to indicate that he was in fact working at something.

"Yeah. Laura." Frank could see that Felix was pleased at being an accurate seer. For his part Frank was peeved at being so predictable. "You're the only man in the world I can talk to about women because you are the only man in the world who doesn't threaten me." Frank hesitated cruelly. "Because you are so fat."

"Yes. Of course." Felix had set himself up in public such that his rationality was all, his person nothing, and thus he could not be insulted. Frank could say anything, and often did.

"Let me read you this. Tell me what you think." Frank stood up, pulled the letter from his pocket, struck a formal pose, and flicked the pages. Felix sat, his sly eyes watching the kettle, feigning boredom. Frank began to read.

It was through Felix that Frank had met Laura.

"Once a year," Felix had told Frank several years back, "I celebrate my existence. Once a year, I *fête* myself."

In his cabin Felix kept an old tobacco tin, into which, each month after cashing his welfare cheque, he would deposit a one hundred and a fifty. Every summer, on his birthday, he would empty the tin, go to Vancouver, and settle into a luxurious suite for three nights. He had made meticulous arrangements.

The first evening Felix would take his yearly bath (unless one counted sponging off at the sink) and then rise, dripping, to usher in one or more ladies of the night. His contact was impeccable, knew Felix's taste in womanflesh, and the girls were invariably friendly (that is, good actresses), tall and lean, smart but silent, and extremely creative and forceful in bed. For Felix's one modest psychosexual kink was the need to feel he was being seduced, corrupted, and impinged upon. His ladies always arrived bearing satchels full of feathery prods, oils, and rubber things resembling giant mollusks. The nature of the business contract was that every inch of his immense gray body was to be corrupted and impinged upon until he fell into the satiated, skin-irritated sleep of a fawned-over sultan.

After sleeping all day, on his second night Felix would proceed to his favorite five-star restaurant. There he would gorge on lobster in Devon butter, Montreal spareribs, lemon prawns flambé, and roasted whole garlic cloves. For a main course he had Greek spiced game hens, which he popped into his mouth like meatballs, and veal so pale it fainted in ecstasy when his fork parted it. Felix's stomach, so stretched from eating so many potatoes, could surround a huge displacement of solids. The first year he had repelled and amazed the restaurant staff, but now he was something of a celebrity: desserts were free, so of course he had several, each one richer than a blend of rubies, butter, and gold. After noshing so, Felix would rest a minute, take a brisk walk through the premises, perhaps eyeing and taking note of other patrons' choices, and then reseat himself and dine anew.

Felix would arise the third day feeling sick, bloated, and ill-of-soul. He made his last important phone call, one that would bring him his ease. Sometime that afternoon a man calling himself Mr. Fixit would arrive. Mr. Fixit had the look and bearing of a sideshow hawker and wore cowboy boots, hat, and shirt. He would spend the next twenty or so hours with Felix without saying a word, his one function being to inject Felix with either heroin, cocaine, or a combination of the two, in prearranged doses at predetermined intervals. Felix would position himself in front of the TV in a huge, billowing chair he'd had specially ordered through the hotel. After heroin he'd nod and dream; on cocaine he'd watch the TV and "tsk" at it disgustedly and perhaps jot something in his notebook; on coke and smack together he gurgled at the back of his hammy throat and laughed loudly at his own labyrinthine thoughts, on occasion turning to Mr. Fixit to gaze at him with profound liquid eyes, as if he and Mr. Fixit were suddenly pure friends engaged in sharing the painful truths of the universe.

When he checked out of the hotel the next day, if anything remained of the eighteen hundred dollars Felix would give it to the first bum he met on the street. The sum usually wasn't large.

"Though my public bearing is that of the perfect spartan," Felix told Frank when describing his last *fête*, "in fact I am none other than a satyr of the senses. A gourmand—yes, I admit it, *gourmand*—of tactile explosions."

In any case, a year ago, after much nagging from Frank, Felix had revealed his call-girl contact. It was reputedly the best stable in the city, supplier to the rich and famous, and the girls were beautiful, elegant, and expensive. Frank, deciding that he too deserved a treat, made a call during a visit to town. An hour later he opened the door to Laura.

She was what he'd ordered: medium height, medium chest, long brown hair, smoothly but amply muscled. Her face, though, was surprisingly fresh and pretty—she could have modeled a teen magazine cover. Perhaps this was the result of his asking for "something wholesome." He *had* said some*thing*. On the phone the entire enterprise had kept to the realm of fantasy, but now some*one* was here before him, very real, saying nothing very prettily, staring at him in a most unreadable way. The girl had the eyes of a telepathic cat.

Frank was surprised at how nervous he was. Aside from his graduation night, when in a bitter mood he'd scorned all ceremony, taken Del's car, and driven to town to buy a cheap hooker (Frank was drunk and disgusted; nothing happened), this was his first time with a pro. And though he had all the power, all the advantage in this game—he had paid a lot for it—he felt no power at all as he stood and looked at her. In normal sexual affairs he fell easily into the bully's role. Why not now? Perhaps because she was, after all, professional.

"We *do* have all night," Laura said.

"Never paid for it before," Frank mumbled sheepishly, honestly. At least he didn't have to impress her. He had paid for that freedom as well.

"It?" She lit up the hotel room with a charming ironic smile.

They both laughed, and now Frank felt okay with her. In the end they had a genuine good time, sharing cynicism and jokes, partaking of "it" several times, lying in bed smoking cigarets like in the movies and, like in the movies, telling each other their life stories, their reasons for being who they were and doing what they did. Laura said she was new at this, and Frank believed her. She had had a failed dance career, had turned to stripping, and now to hooking because the money was so, as she said, "queenly." She had a two-year plan: make a lot of money, quit, move, and set up a dance studio to teach choreography.

Frank looked at her. The innocent, good-hearted hooker. Like a twin, she too was a cliché from the cinema. He shook his head at this. And found he wanted to impress her after all. He watched her as he described his life aboard a boat moored up the coast, how she closed her eyes and breathed deeply at the salt-air thought of it. They found they hated most of life for much the same reasons. When she left the next morning, Frank felt a tad jealous of her ensuing nights, a little in love.

He'd seen her four times since. The last two times she hadn't charged him for "it." She spent a weekend with him aboard *Tammy*, where Frank became the moody bully with her.

But then she called it off. For Frank had demanded that she keep herself to stripping only, and not see other men.

"When you're a hooker," was how he put it, "you're no better than me."

And now, her letter. Reading it to Felix, Frank struck a dramatic pose and put on a sweet, mock-Laura voice.

" 'Franko'—that's what she calls me, Felix—'Thanks for your last letter. Loved the filthy parts but I don't believe you. I still wish you had a phone. Anyway, I haven't written you for a while, I think you know why. I've been trying to sort things out, and, God, I guess I have'—I'll skip the bullshit stuff. Sure you don't have a beer stashed somewhere here? No? Okay—'Frank. I've decided to give it a try. If you still want to. That is, I'll quit my main job. On the one hand I've had a bit of a morality attack lately, and all men are starting to look like pigs, and I don't want that. On the other hand I realize I feel good around you, stupid as that may be. You and your black heart. I've hesitated over this— seeing only you—because I have to admit I'm scared. Frank, you're such an asshole. (She says lovingly.) But it's true. You don't seem to care about *any*thing (is this an act?) and this means you might never care about me. Ever. I've hesitated, because it's safer to fuck ten men than to make love to one. It's pathetic, but all this tantalizes me. It's pathetic, but it all makes me soft as butter for you. So anyway, that's it.' " Frank grinned down at Felix. Actually it was more of a leer. "Soft as butter, you heard her."

"So. A pretty, honest, romantic prostitute. I don't blame you for being in love. Have you ever seen the movie called *The Blue Angel?*"

Frank didn't answer.

"It's about a man, a lonely man, older than you but still a lonely man, who falls for—'falls' is a grand word, no?—for this dance-hall girl. The moral equivalent of today's prostitute. His soul gets dragged through— "

"Is that that French or German thing?"

"Yes. His soul is dragged by its soul-testicles until— "

"I've seen it." Frank waved a hand in Felix's face. "And you're way off base."

"Perhaps." Felix paused in the most pompous way. "But does it not burn your mind to imagine that she has pleased so many men, doing everything they wanted? Men like me?"

"You trying to speed up my hangover or something, Felix?"

"I'm forcing you to admit reality to yourself. It helps to say it out loud."

Frank decided to sit down for this particular exercise. He took a breath. "No, Felix. No, you French softball. It used to bother me, but it doesn't now. It used to bother me to think of her thighs sticking up in the night, green with the glow of neon on them. But it doesn't now. How's that, Felix? Am I a man facing reality, or am I a mouse?"

"A man, it appears. But still a dreamer, no?"

"No. She's come round. You heard her."

"You mean to say she has kept you dangling. You mean to say you accept not only a harlot's past but the harlot herself . . ."

"I mean to say I'm fucking irresistible, Felix. She's been a slow learner." Frank settled back back in his chair, smirking, his nose high up in the air.

"Well said," Felix answered, a chessboard king praising a pawn for its puny move. "You are irresistible as a friend: beautiful women adore men who stand waiting in the wings, too timid to demand honesty from them. She feeds you enough to keep you in place there with—pardon me—your zipper precisely one-third of the way down. My friend."

Frank snorted. "Well, my *friend*, regardez the large expert on women and— "

"I observe relationships from a distance. As a consequence my eyes are clear. That's all."

"Bullshit, monsieur." Frank eyed him hard but, busy now at the sink, Felix didn't respond. The conversation had come to a close, and in any case it had gone nowhere. He *had* come with a problem about women, but as usual he hadn't explained himself and as usual Felix had twisted things around. His problem lay in the type of woman he loved, for it seemed he could love no other. All his life he'd been pulled to the typical stand-offish bitch, the coy, stiff, game-playing femme who provoked in his heart both a sneer and a delicious craving. Frank, though he hated seeing himself in such a juvenile, simplistic light, knew he was a hunter who needed a constant challenge. And here it was again, a girl come round, a challenge met, and now the affair would grow boring. Laura had accepted, and therefore she had paled. Watching an inaccessible tart come round and turn kind was like watching a gazelle turn into a milk cow.

That was his problem, and it always had been. Not that he was too much in love with a Blue Angel but that he could no longer love. How to explain this to Felix, a grotesque who paid other grotesques to relieve him, like robots flipping a greasy pleasure switch?

"You ever had a long-term thing, Felix?"

Felix's eyebrows rose slowly to their supercilious peak. "A . . . long . . . term . . . *thing*?"

"Married? A real girlfriend? Engaged? One of those."

"*Sacrement*, no."

Frank went silent and studied Laura's letter. He had something more to ask, which was the real reason he was here. Since Felix wasn't watching, he allowed the honest concern to show on his face. Then he rose from his chair, but in doing so stumbled back and had to grab the arm.

"You're drunk, huh?" Felix said under his breath, not looking at him.

"Yeah, a bit," Frank laughed. "I'm a man with a question. I haven't finished reading you this letter. There's something weird in it."

Frank waited for Felix to take his own chair, looking away in disgust and pity from the sight of the fat man's veins bulging with the strain of simply lowering himself. Frank waited for him to settle, and then read in a softer voice:

" 'And Franko, sure I'd love to come to your friend's surprise party with you. I haven't been to the 'burbs in years and I'd like to meet your brother Del. You make him sound like a librarian saint, but I'm sure he's as bad as you. But about the party—Felix has something to tell you. He knows what it is. I won't go to the party unless he tells you first. Soft as butter, Laura.' "

When Frank looked up, he saw that sometime during the past minute Felix had turned from sickly gray to ghostly white.

"So what's this thing, Felix?"

Felix lurched like a speared pig from his chair. "Some tea, Frank?"

"You slept with Laura! Is that it? Well I'll sure as hell have to punch— "

"No."

"—you in the face, but I can forgive a friend. Better you than someone remotely attractive."

"No. That's not it. If only it was. It concerns your brother and his wife. Mary." Felix stared at the floor, stricken.

"What do *they* have to do with Laura?"

"I didn't want to tell you this. But this coincidence has begun to bark at my heels like a dog. Remember my one meeting with Laura, a year ago, before you met? When I deemed her not up to my standards and rejected her?"

"*Rejected* her." Frank could not bear this thought. "She wasn't one of your Dracula junkie slut-heads who will stick goldfish up your fat ass. She was too decent for you. Is that what you mean, you French push-wad?"

"Settle down. We did not take to one another, no."

Felix went on to explain that after her rejection, Laura had offered to introduce him to other of her colleagues, who were that night stripping at a club. At the club Felix took a liking to one of them. He was waiting for her outside the dressing room when another dancer took the stage. Felix had nearly choked on his Perrier. He wasn't certain at first, because Del had brought his wife up to Pender Harbour no more than a handful of times. But there were the gestures, the grin, the idiosyncrasies of stride and shoulder. It was Mary.

"My mistake was to tell Laura," Felix said now. "That we were watching none other than a scandal involving my best friend's brother's— " here Felix hesitated, and blushed at his slip, "wife. Now Laura knows you, it appears she will meet the happy couple, and it is all very complicated."

"You're sure."

"I possess the eyes of a falcon and the memory of a whale, my friend."

"Well this is just *great*. *Fat* man."

Frank leapt from his chair, crossed the cabin floor in two tall strides, and slammed the door behind him. His hooked face had the intent of a hatchet, and its color had turned to that of an approaching storm cloud.

Felix smiled sadly. He whispered to himself: "A one-man . . . mob . . . of ill will."

Frank usually had this effect on him, that of making him smile sadly. For it was a comfortable enough game they played, and sometimes through the wall of postured words they touched. But this time the smile lasted only seconds. It was indeed *vachement merde*, this affair of his brother and the wife, Mary. But in the next instant Felix was doubled up over his papers, scribbling, his nose beaded in sweat. He was on volume thirteen on his encyclopedia, and what he wrote now was this:

I am not my body. Just as my eyes are a lens through which my body sees, so my fat body is the lens through which *I* see. The experience of my body is *my* perfect window. Through *my* fat, truth enters an immense channel. Truth loses its edge when pushed through the quilt of alcohol. *My* lens is clear and huge.

CHAPTER THREE

North America

Having eschewed Family, I watch over the blind chess match of relationships. Man and woman are Alphonse and Gaston in an oven. Children are agents provocateurs. *My limbs are my family, my Self the patriarch. Well fed, we cohabit in luxury and understanding. With my limbs, I am* gai.

—Felix d'Amboise

Reclined in his den, as chimp noises rose and bubbled and at times roared in from down the hall, Del watched the Muppets on TV. He had decided that Kermit was an emcee—a ref, in effect—who kept control through a ploy of affable ignorance.

He dropped his gaze to the side table and then, for some reason, reached out and rapped the top of the phone. Exactly a second later it rang, making him jump. He stared at it, amazed. It rang several times more before he picked it up. Del now knew who it would be.

"Hi," Del said.

"Hey Beak, need a hand here."

Beak was Frank's boyhood name for his brother. Once at recess some friends had voted on which of the two Baal noses was largest, and Del's won by a vote. Perhaps his had been greasier, more glaring that day, for Del had no doubts they were identical.

"Need cash, Beaker," Frank shouted into the phone.

Frank was drunk. This always made Del instantly sober.

"Sure," Del said quietly. "How much do— "

"If I'm gonna sail to town for Wall's poo-push party, gonna need some travel scratch. Pay you Monday the latest. So how's it going? You wouldn't believe the action here, salmon galore and . . ."

Del's toe suffered a familiar blip of pain. It was early afternoon, his brother was falling-down drunk, not listening. It wasn't the asking for money so much as Frank's con artistry that got to him, that fake chattiness his brother used to squeeze money, or to talk to women and cops. It depressed Del profoundly that Frank saw fit to use this tone on him.

"Okay, Frank. I'll wire some money to your bank there. Pay me whenever. And don't tell Mary, right?"

Frank caught his breath. He went silent a moment.

"Nope. Better not tell good ol' Mary."

Another silence, and a tension so loaded Del could feel it in his ear.

"Well, great . . . . Hey, when you comin' up? We'll do a double salmon-ski, eh Beaker?"

Salmon-ski. Del had seen it once. They had been anchored in a pack of boats, nobody catching much, when Frank hooked into a big one. He got Del to hold the rod while the salmon peeled off line. Frank stripped to his shorts, donned a life jacket, grabbed back the rod and jumped howling into the water. Frank screamed and hooted as the fish towed him slowly around. Some of the other fishermen laughed, at least at first, but others didn't take to the idea of a drunkard mocking what they took so seriously. When the salmon tired, Frank jerked hard on the line, breaking it on purpose. Back on board, in sopping undershorts that bulged and showed some pubic black, he bowed to his audience. Del was thrilled and humiliated.

"Right, a double salmon-ski. That'll be great, Frank."

His brother kept rambling. But he'd heard what he'd wanted to hear about the money, and his tone was calmer now. He talked for two minutes about nothing. Since he hadn't called collect this time, Del knew he must have gotten someone's credit-card number again. More trouble down the line.

When their father died they'd both been left equal sums of
money. Del had invested his, and now years later he reaped over
a thousand a month in dividend cheques. That plus his ref's
salary, the beer commercial he'd done, and Mary's own job
meant a fairly worry-free wallet if they didn't splurge. Mary
went rigid whenever Del lent (she used the word "gave," which
was indeed more accurate) Frank money.

Frank's inheritance was gone in three years. He still had his
boat to show for it, but the rest he'd squandered or used to pay
fines for income tax fraud, drunk driving charges, and the like.
Halfway into a night at the bar Frank would buy rounds and try
to play the sheik with women. Once he gave away his car. He
sometimes gave Del and Mary gifts even now: radios, clocks,
jewelery, liquor. On her last birthday he'd given Mary the TV
set that sat in Del's den. She didn't like the TV, not a bit,
suspecting that it and the other stuff had been stolen. But Frank
had set it in the living room, draped it with a bedsheet, yelled
"Happy Birthday," and unveiled it like a work of art. He wore a
grand grin while watching Mary out the corner of his eye as she
checked for a serial number.

"Look, Frankie," Del interrupted. "You bringing someone to
the party? Mary needs to know. Has to buy the right amount of
cheese and that. And she knows— " Del forced a laugh—"you'll
behave yourself if you figure on getting laid later on."

Again a silence.

"Right, Beak. Mary wants a proper party. All coupled off.
That Mary."

Another awkward pause. Frank seemed on the edge of saying
something. When would Frank and Mary make friends with
each other?

"But right she is! Getting laid!" Frank's laugh was as insincere
as Del's. "And, yes, I have managed to scoop a frail. A deluxe
waif. One look at her and Wally will regret going the poo-push
route. We're practically engaged."

Del hoped to God he wouldn't be so . . . *Frank* . . . at the party.
Poo-push. God.

"Laura? That one? The dancer?"

"The *stripper*. The *teaser*. That's her. We're in love."

Del guessed his brother was lying about a date, but he would hope for the best. The brothers settled on a loan of five hundred dollars (on hearing Frank's instant calm, Del realized he could have offered two hundred) and hung up.

Del's toe had settled now to an earnest long-term ache, and with a curse he ripped off his shoe again to rub it. North America lurched up and waddled over, wagging, to plop her head on Del's lap. The dog peered up with a knowing look. Though her eyes were full of simple, stupid love, she also seemed to know she was giving Del some kind of medicine. Ah, Northam, Del thought, you smelly joy. Wally Kenny's gift, six years ago.

It had been odd, and yet at the same time so typical of Wally. Odd the gift of a dog, but typical in the way he gave it.

The evening too had been odd from the start. A dreary Vancouver winter light fell from ashy oyster to a darker dullness and finally to a clogged black night. Del and Mary sat propped on bar stools in the rec room of a football friend with eight or so others, celebrating their second anniversary. It was a case of a few friends sitting around drinking, spewing corny talk of marriage and good luck and here's to two more years of wedded bliss. Del spent the rest of the evening feeling uneasy. Not that he wouldn't have gone back and married Mary all over again. But there was just no doubting now that the love spiral had begun to wobble and fall. Marriage had become simply marriage, and he felt a bit hypocritical as he smiled politely as his friends toasted them, making a matrimonial mountain out of a pleasant enough domestic molehill. Several times he looked over and tried to catch Mary's eye. Perched on her stool in a corner, she sat up straight but looked owl-eyed and distracted. Cut short, her black hair hung too perfectly, a kind of helmet.

Then Wally Kenny arrived. In he strode, talking loudly, dressed in rose and pink, holding brash hands with his current friend, a large bland man named Tom. From Wally's other hand

dangled a rhinestone leash, at the end of which huddled a panic-
striken yellow dog.

"Heard about some big *party* here," Wally Kenny over-
vamped, his hip cocked, "to congratulate our *love* birds."

Del could feel the room's collective cringe. There stood his
high-school buddy Wally, small, wiry, with an overlarge head,
looking like some Howdy Doody puppet. Since coming out of
the closet, Wally seemed to grow daily more doll-like, as though
his face were etched with cartoon lines. And there stood his
Tom, shy but drunk enough to grin defiantly, looking all the
more a sissy for being so big and so soft. Del nodded slowly and
gave Wally the brief sort of smile that said he saw through his
ploy, which was to flaunt himself yet again in front of Del's
straight friends. One thing about Wally, real estate lawyer by
day, West End flamer by night—he had guts.

Mary bounced up too eagerly to thank and kiss him. She
always acted up around Wally, and Del was certain everyone
could see it, yet, fearing her wrath, he could not bring himself to
accuse her of reverse prejudice. But she was guilty, and had been
for two years—Wally had come out about the time Mary and Del
were married. He had heard about it this way: in answer to Del's
request that he be best man, Wally had said, "Sure. Thanks, Del.
I love the irony. I'm gay."

The news shocked Del and threatened a long depression. But
Mary rallied around Wally and his cause, defending him in front
of small-minded friends, inviting him and his latest beau over for
tea. So Del began to see more of Wally now than he had when
they were normal buddies. It pained him to sip tea and watch
while month by month his friend took on one gay affectation
after another. God, the clichés were real! The extended pinky,
the sashays, the touchy-touchies and general naughtiness. By
staring at him darkly and lifting an eyebrow, Del could sometimes shame Wally into switching from Wally the fairy back to
Wally the star guard and dressing-room joker of Fraser Valley
High. But, seconds later, someone would tell a story about
somebody's wardrobe and there he'd be again, screeching like
Carol Channing. Few of his friends were so outlandish. It was as

if, in trying to catch up, he had surpassed them. Del even began to doubt the quality of their past bond one night when Wally mocked Del's ambition to become a professional football referee. And then, when Wally left and Del mimicked him, Mary said, "Del, Wallace is more macho than *you* are sometimes."

And now, two years later at an empty-hearted party, Wally was giving them a dog on a rhinestone leash.

"Happy anniversary," he said, lisping on purpose to get a further rise out of Del. "This is North America." He gestured flamboyantly down to the cowering dog. All eyes on it now, the dog wagged its tail a bit, squirmed, whimpered, then squatted and peed in quivering hope. It whimpered again and looked about quickly when some of the people laughed.

"You can get these kind real cheap at the pound," said Wally's Tom, still drunk and defiant, and the look Wally gave this stupid try at small talk told Del they wouldn't be lovers for long.

On the drive home from the party, Mary and Del noticed North America's smell wafting from the back seat.

"Should we visit the pound tonight or tomorrow?" Mary asked tiredly. It was after midnight and Del was a little drunk.

"Well . . ."

"If we keep it overnight it'll shit."

"Our carpets are shitty already," Del joked, but Mary didn't respond. "Fact is, Mare, I've been kind of thinking about a dog. *Having* a dog."

The yellow mutt thumped its tail and whined as Mary turned to study it with disbelief.

"You can't be serious."

"North America can be shortened to Northam."

"It's barely grown and already it stinks. God, it's already rotting."

"Let's give it a chance at least."

"I'll give it tonight, and that's that."

"Wally will be disappointed."

"Wally got drunk and bought us a joke at the pound. Screw Wally."

Mary looked headachy, and Del knew more talk would be fruitless. Screw Wally? Little did Mary know that Wally would feel snubbed, deeply hurt in fact, if they returned North America. Little did she know—Del burped and swerved as he thought of this—that Wally's dog was not exactly a dog but a baby. Not exactly a baby, but an amulet.

Wally Kenny had acted strange all night. He'd danced once with each woman, made a show of ignoring his Tom, and tried to embarrass Del with one of his referee jokes, in which he pretended to be a histrionic, high-voiced black arguing a penalty call, standing toe to toe with Del: " 'Fensive innerference? Ow, *man*, you *mama*, you be tall an' *dim*." But he soon lapsed into the sullen fatigue shared by Del. He walked over finally, sighing, his every movement advertising this new mood, and sat beside him on the couch. Though the party was almost over they hadn't yet talked. Now Wally leaned in close and said, "I'm serious about the dog."

"What's that?" Del said cautiously, not knowing if his friend was just sliding into a subtler, more perverse phase of humor.

"I mean the dog really *is* something for you and Mary," he said in a fierce whisper now, leaning closer and widening his eyes, which remained small in that big head of his. Del decided he was sincere.

"Well thanks, Wall. Thanks again. I think I like her."

"No. Mary has to like her too."

"I'm sure she— "

"You don't have kids. You don't look at each other much. Pardon me for saying this, but I think you two are on rocky ground."

"Hmmm." Del didn't know where this was going. "Well, I wouldn't put it quite that way, but . . . No. No, I think you're wrong." Gays had the weirdest interest in straight relationships. Observing from a safe perch, they clucked like hens and presumed all man-woman bonds doomed to a slow, unavoidable death. But my God, Del thought, taking his eyes off his friend, look at *their* unions. Fast bumhole in a slick anonymous night.

"I just think you and Mary need something to bring you closer together. Dogs do that. Am I not right?"

Del shrugged. It isn't that simple, Wally.

"And you know, Del, through you and Mary I come as close as I ever will to the marriage me poor ol' mum always dreamed of for me."

Wally was grinning again, the muscles of his face rising easily back to the pose of coy irreverence.

Before Wally could stand up, Del put a hand on his arm. They caught each other in a momentary stare. Del was trying to show proper thanks on his face, and Wally, for his part, delayed for a while his return to poses.

They were, at bottom, the same friends they had always been, despite no longer being back-slapping teammates, despite their divergent worlds, despite Del's referee job and utterly straight ways, despite Wally's look-at-me clothes and studied Mae West moves. Despite all this, something warm and sober could still pass between them eye to eye, unrefracted by the off-angles of recent years. In one second, Wally's eyes had become those of the fifteen-year-old Del knew so well, and these eyes said: Look at us sitting here! You're married. I'm wearing pink. It doesn't matter. Our lives are costumes. I'll take mine off for a moment here. Haven't things gotten strange since we left the valley? I've just given you a dog. Can things get any stranger? I hope so. Now watch me slip back into my clothes.

Wally stood up. He looked suddenly, willfully, drunk. Costumed.

When Mary and Del returned to their apartment later that night, North America went into her cower again just inside their door, jerking a head up at every movement they made. Del felt a bit frantic. He began to pace, counting items off on his fingers.

"Water dish. Food dish. I'll get big ones. Northam could get bigger. And milk bones. But let's stash the slippers just in case, eh Mare?" Mary still wasn't responding to his little jokes, a bad sign. "New leash. And dog toys! Do they still have dog toys? Do

you know? Mary?" His wife stood at the kitchen counter pour-
ing herself some wine. Del kept on. "The dishes can go over
there by the fridge. On some paper. And we should fold her up
an old blanket. A bed. Hey, don't we have one of those wicker
laundry things somewhere? Would she fit in one of those?"

"Del. We don't even know if it's housebroken."

At least she was talking again.

"Well I know how to do that. Anyway, she'll be outside a lot.
Hunting."

"Del." Mary met Del's eyes for the first time in hours. "Look.
We both work. We live in a goddamn small apartment. It'll
either be in here, shitting, or out there all day in a parking lot.
Nice."

Mary was getting mad, and stern. This usually worked to
make Del as gun-shy as on the day they met. But what he said
next slid out so smoothly it surprised even him.

"We'll move. We'll get a house. We'll *buy* a frigging *house*."

Mary peered at Del closely, as though trying to see through a
two-year-old growth of opaque skin. What she saw sobered her
a bit. She mocked more softly.

"Right. Good thinking. We'll go out tomorrow and buy a
house for a smelly dog we had given to us an hour ago."

"No. Let's just get a *house*," Del almost shouted, and then
stopped in his tracks, looking confused. He tried for words.
"Mary," he started. Then he brought his hand up and pointed
into her face. They both realized that he had never done that
before.

"*Mary you know we should.*"

"I think you're pissed out of your head." She set her glass
down and turned for the bathroom.

Del poured some wine of his own into a beer mug. He was
breathing hard, and when he closed the fridge door too roughly
several magnetic apples and oranges and then sheets of paper fell
to the floor. Dutifully he stooped and gathered, and stuck everything back in its place. A nature sketch of Mary's that had turned
out well. A diet clipped from a magazine. A picture of a pig,

under which she'd written, "Mary, settle for the apple." In the pig's mouth she'd drawn a crude apple.

Ah, women. Ironic. Mary's fear of change wouldn't let her move from the impermanence of an apartment to the security of a house. Women: they would one day rule the continent in an outward as well as in the already hidden way, but they would make edgy, self-doubting lords. At least when men ran things they learned to believe in their show of confidence. Mary, your fear makes you stiff in the heart.

At that moment Del's eyes widened and he stood back on his heels drunkenly. He'd had a new and awful thought: it was very possible he would never come to understand his life's mate.

A great long fart, then a shorter one, echoed from the bathroom. Del walked from the kitchen shaking his head. Northam had hidden in a tight ball under the glass entranceway table but stared curiously in the direction of Mary's noises.

Ah, Mary. Even her bathroom sounds had strange allure. They were self-conscious, not unsexy, almost cute. To Del they weren't shit sounds, they were poop sounds. Was that, odd as it seemed, love? Mary. Why couldn't they just relax and forget the small things and see how deep they could go into one another? Even her farting was not quite relaxed, not quite right. Del saw this as symbolic. She had begun two years ago, shyly, at Del's insistence that a husband and wife can, should, be able to do such things in front of each other. Her farting had continued, but lately from a straight-backed, vaguely feminist pose of self-assertion.

Del's beer mug was somehow already empty. He turned his doubling gaze to North America, who looked up and pathetically nipped the air.

"Hi, Northam," he said.

"What?" came Mary's call from the bathroom.

"Hi *Northam*," Del said again, approaching the glass table. The dog was shaking with scared excitement, and as Del drew closer he hunched down and screwed up his face to make it look as excited as the dog's.

"*Hi* Northam. *Hi* girl." Del was now three feet away. The dog clambered up and edged out, eyes immense, tail wagging furiously. At each wag her body twisted like a sausage.

"Northam," Del whispered, extending his hand. Northam stretched her neck forward, her nostrils wide. Relaxed, Del's hand drooped like that of Michelangelo's God, and the limp yet charged forefinger touched her wet nose.

The dog gently sniffed. Then looked up.

"*Hi Northam!*"

Whatever it was she saw in Del's face or heard in his voice made her grin so widely and strained that her head looked about to burst. Then she barked, from the guts, a pure sloppy sound. Del barked back, trying to copy it. Northam began to wag and wriggle yet harder, as though trying to fling her flesh through her robe of skin. Whacking the sharp metal edge of the table leg with her tail, cutting the tip, she yelped once but didn't pause in her grinning and wagging, so full was she of a sense of escape— the cages, the leash, the many faces; she had escaped to a dog's heaven: trust.

Del was kneeling now, rubbing the skin and skull and eyes of his dog. It was his anniversary. He was crying. He didn't give a damn about the blood flicking in crimson streaks across the door and wall of his apartment.

"Northam. Sit."

Six years ago that was. They had gone out and bought this house, the one Del liked because of the unfinished room he pictured himself one day transforming into a den. Mary loved the house from the start too, and after Del had carried her across the threshold, and after they made love on their new bed, Mary baked her first-ever loaf of homemade bread. So corniness was allowed for a time, as was lust: during the first week they made love in every room of the house, checking, they joked, for the building's erogenous zones.

Maybe—Del sat thinking, watching his dog watch him—despite or perhaps because of their transient affairs, fags did know about love. What, Wally, is wrong with him and Mary now? Should they buy another house? A new dog?

His toe ached so. He couldn't go on like this. He would confront her now. Damn the chimps, they could free-for-all today. He would have it out with Mary now, even if it finished them. Let's move again, let's divorce, *anything*.

Northam backed off and barked as Del rammed the chair lever down and jumped up. As he did so he heard the kitchen door slam. He stood still for a moment while Mary passed the window. Then he crept over to peek past the curtain edge to watch his wife, his erect, stern, social worker wife, usher her chimps down the walk. From the looks of it, Lars had been ordered to keep Fraser moving by walking behind him and poking his back whenever he stopped to rave at something. Lars would keep his finger up all day long until Mary told him to stop.

"There she goes, girl," Del told his dog.

Northam's last inch of tail still poked off at an angle. She had grown fat, with matted fur and a smell that was not at all cute. Del pictured Mary sitting straight-backed on a bus that roared somewhere. She would be harder than usual on her charges to make sure they behaved well in public, glaring normalcy at them; yet as each one rose to get off at their stop she would wear a look of such sadness and a smile that came from the heart. But she would be stern again when she came home to Del.

Maybe they should just move again, he thought, more serious than not, and then he recalled a line from one of Frank's sillier songs: "Oh, time she is a puppy that dogs then dies."

Del's toe had finally stopped aching. He sat up on the edge of his chair and once more scanned his den. Then he decided to forget everything: his past, his wife, his brother, the looming fact of death itself. And, as was his habit, he punctuated his solitude by promising he'd begin tomorrow by practicing goodwill.

Alone in his den. So quiet. He felt like a boy who had happened upon a secret cave. A kind of dankness here, and a lusty, throat-swelling privacy. He pretended away thoughts of the real Mary—her cool voice, her moods of late. He pretended himself courageous, her adoring. He pictured her reclining body, and her tawny skin, which soon took on the wondrous sheen of pigeon necks. This vision did little for him twice in one day, so the skin was hungrily transformed into the creamy pastel fizz on a daiquiri.

CHAPTER FOUR

Shiva's Dance

You have to watch after each other in the years to come. Okay? Jeez, boys, I guess I don't have to even say that. You'll do it anyway. But you gotta do it right. Do it by always telling each other the truth.
    —Dr. A.A. Baal to ten-year-old Frank and Del

Little did Felix d'Amboise know how soon Frank's black mood vanished after he'd stomped out of the cabin. Nor did he know that Frank was in fact thrilled by what he'd learned. Frank did not dislike Mary. In truth he admired her, always had. It was that he did not like her being with his brother. He hated seeing his brother ruled. And now tricked. Cheated.

Frank's thrill turned into an afternoon plan. After an hour's walk through a bird-loud but otherwise peaceful forest he reached his destination, a sprawling cedar-and-glass bungalow set back in the trees bordering a secluded cove. Frank visited such places only on certain thrilling days, as now.

He stood in the driveway. The Morgans, the sign said. Such a sturdy Yankee name. Californian. He'd seen them in the pub a few times: Mr. was portly, sporting that confidence of corporate victories and wealth under the belt. Mrs. was a loud laugher. Horse teeth, painted wrinkles, and jewelry. Frank had studied her jewelry closely.

He rang the doorbell. He waited one minute. He rang it ten times more in quick succession and then waited another minute,

just in case. But no noise from within. Even the local birds had
shut up. Perhaps they watched. Frank knelt and laced his right
work boot extra tight. He stood up, took a deep breath, held it,
and with a scream kicked in the door.

Inside it was dark and cool. With the nuts and bolts of daily
living stashed away for the off-season, the house looked unlived
in, as though even the ashtrays and food smells had migrated
south with the Morgans. Frank would have to do some searching. He withdrew two garbage bags from his back pocket and
worked one inside the other, doubling them. Then with tall
frame bent with purpose, angled like a spider, Frank began his
rounds.

In the dining room he broke open a locked cabinet and found a
silver tea service and two candlesticks made from what looked
like soapstone. If he was lucky, jade. The bedroom produced a
clock-radio: compact, solid, Swiss. A mudroom off the kitchen
offered a Hardy trout reel, a Craftsman socket set, and a varia-
ble-speed drill, all brand new. Mr. Morgan fancied himself a
handyman, hmm? The liquor cabinet served up a half bottle of
Tia Maria, which he drank as he stood, silly milkshake that it
was, and an untouched Jim Beam, perfect for Saturday's party.
Into the bag it went. Other than that, Frank deemed baggable
only a Braun shaver and the needle off the stereo. Mrs. had
indeed flown south with every jewel around her neck.

Everything else was too large. Normally the TV would have
been snatched as well, to be bagged and stashed in the woods for
future pickup, but the Morgans spent their summers in front of a
huge console. Fake carved oak. So typical, Frank confirmed yet
again, of the tasteless nouveau riche.

He worked quietly, unthinking, as though picking berries or
mushrooms, his arms guided by an efficient grace. His heart
raced, but otherwise he was calm, his senses precise. The Tia
Maria had him on the brink of a smile.

He knotted his bag, deposited it by the front door, and walked
back, humming, to stand in front of the TV. Now he was smiling
for real.

"Soft as butter," he whispered, and then kicked in the tube. The loud vacuum *pop* and shattering glass shocked the house's calm utterly, and Frank laughed. He picked up the fireplace poker and tested it in his hand. So, these Morgans. So Canada was a safe place, was it? Quaint, maybe? Lots of salmon and deer? A haven for holidays, a country nest for the dishwasher, Yank kiddies, fake-oak TV, corporate and jewelified smugness? No pimply roving Chicanos here. No, just pale Canucks who palm your tourist money and nod out of polite habit.

"Soft as butter." From a Babe Ruth stance Frank swung the poker and a smoked glass lamp beside the couch disintegrated. He ran over to the fireplace, beaming at the row of treasures on the mantel.

He gazed like a spiteful baby at the knick-knacks. About to say "soft as butter," he whispered instead "Shiva's dance," surprising himself with something he'd forgotten. He'd learned about Shiva in one of the hippy religious books Del had forced on him years ago. *Shiva*, the chapter title read, *The God of Destruction*. It was the only section he'd read. These Hindus were okay, he'd thought, reading. They saw the whole picture. They worshipped both ends of the cycle. Frank was struck with the delightful image of Shiva, a buxom blue giantess, dancing into sickrooms and kicking the afflicted in the jaw, delivering the final death stroke. Her face would be that of a Jewish princess, but one wise beyond question. He pictured her pirouetting at the seashore, causing typhoons and pestilence; he saw her whirling *en pointe* through battlefields and trenches, clanging her thumb-cymbals at selected soldiers, who fell sighing in sequence as she passed. Shiva danced in the bacteria that decomposed fruit rinds in the ditch. She worked her magic in stomachs digesting the night's pot roast. She swayed through rotting barns, lavatories. Frank was glad to see that one race, at least, saw that disintegration was as necessary as it was inevitable.

Shiva danced through marriages.

Frank stood at one end of the mantel, his poker raised ceremoniously. "Mary, Mary, Mary, Mary, Mary," he sang in falsetto as he took down on the run a porcelain mallard, several

china beer mugs, and a nauseating schooner-in-a-bottle. It was
wonderful, the ease, the gratitude almost, of things breaking up
into smaller units. Soft as butter. He was just speeding things
along a bit, encouraging a sharper, faster sort of melting. Dust to
dust, Mr. and Mrs. Morgan.

Thrusting and parrying, playing the tallest musketeer with his
poker, Shiva-dancing from room to room, Frank found many
more household items that seemed to burst apart happily and
enjoy their new freedom as particles.

He set sail for Vancouver, the party, his confrontation with
Mary. Frank liked storms, in that food-for-the-character English sort of way, but he preferred these perfect days for a cruise
into town.

Standing with feet spread at the helm of *Tammy Wouldn't
Die*'s upper deck, hands comfy as doves on the old wooden
wheel, Frank surveyed the waters of Georgia Strait. Calm, blue,
perfect. *Tammy* droned effortlessly on, slicing her perfect line.
Three gulls soared behind, mewing for food. A larger gull arced
overhead, then dive-bombed to chase the others. In its attack it
screamed and shat, and Frank watched the white gob spatter on
the water and disperse into a milky cloud lit with sequins.
Herring scales. He recalled the time when, having just moved to
the coast with Del and Dad, and taking a first ferry ride on these
same waters, he'd looked up to watch the gulls and, mouth agape,
he'd caught a small gob full on the tongue. A mad spitting dash to
the water fountain. It was oily and fishy and so so salty, not at all
shitlike. Years later, eating pizza, he discovered that seagull shit
tasted exactly like anchovies.

A perfect day, and life was good. Grilse leapt at *Tammy*'s putt-
putt approach. The sun was almost hot, so Frank removed his
shirt. In the breeze his skin tightened with goosepimples and his
nipples shrank up hard, but Frank's credo was that a very tall,
very gawky, and very white man was just asking for bad luck
with the girls. One had to stay as brown as one could to keep the
body on the right side of grotesque.

In *Tammy*'s hold was a load of cod in garbage bags. He'd
bought them from local kids the day before, and tomorrow
they'd be rank. Frank swore yet again that the day was near when
he'd get himself a proper ice-hold. He was quickly running out
of Chinese merchants dim enough to buy half-turned fish. Frank
sold at bargain prices (to make a good show of it he bought ice on
the dock to pack the cod in before displaying it) but still, the last
time he was in town an old opium-head he'd sold to had accosted
him in the middle of Chinatown, yelling in pidgin English,
threatening him with the law, demanding to know how it was
possible for fresh-caught fish to go rotten only one hour after
he'd opened the shop. Frank had had to accompany him to his
store to settle up, and when the old fart wasn't looking he kicked
loose a valve on his refrigeration pipe, called the guy over and
yelled, "*There's* your problem. Do your homework before you
go callin' names, pigtail." He put on a good show of stomping
out.

Today's cod—if he could shark up a buyer—would fetch a few
hundred dollars. Added to that was Del's cheque, plus this
week's charter money he had wadded in his jean's pocket, about
a grand. He had money to burn. Laura: pick your restaurant. Like
those shoes in the window? Shall we sip this cognac in the park
like poets or move on up to this little penthouse suite I just
happened to rent for the weekend? Or how about—can't resist
that smile, you charm-head, never could—how about a tiny
diamond for that wanton ring finger of yours?

Could he still love her? Had she danced so close she'd snuffed
his fire? He would see. He could try. At least he could pretend.

Summertime and the dollars were blooming. God only knew
how much of it he could fence, but double-bagged under the pile
of cod were various clocks, radios, pieces of silverware, crystal,
tools, a suede coat, two shotguns, a Sony TV and VCR.

Better to bank some of it. Laura might prove expensive. If it
was her whim she could very easily, meeting no resistance at all,
suck his wallet out through the openness of his big ol' heart.

Still, he'd never be poor, not him, a man with infinite devices.
He was a goddamned Renaissance man, and the means to money

never stopped. For pocket change, he had his songs to sell. At least two were good. He had his notepad propped and ready beside the compass, waiting for a final song. The Snuff had also requested a kind of love song, a "semi-syrupy ballad or anthem." So far Frank had managed only four lines:

> I hate to love you playing it cool,
> I hate to love what isn't mine.
> I hate loving your dying baby body,
> but I love, oh I love, hating time.

Not exactly syrupy but, Frank reasoned, The Snuff were snuffing up the wrong pantleg, thinking they could squeeze sentimental syrup from an honest man.

Hands on the wheel, standing tall and firm in the sunshine, Frank admired the openness of his heart. His whole body felt like a hollow flute. The lone note it played was low and wistful, a tune of spring blossoms falling and fluttering to earth in the warm breeze of melancholy. But, Frank considered, wait. Something was off. Why melancholy? Why wistful? Shouldn't it be a bouncy sort of piccolo? A light skip, a squeeze-her-hand, twirl-your-gal kind of jig in the gut? He was getting damned sentimental, was the problem. Even now in the midst of a sunny day, in the midst of love itself, his toe hurt. God. Sentimentality had wormed its way physical, had soaked right in, had taken root in the marrow of his goddamned digits. Poor Del.

Damn Felix. He'd been listening to the fat man too much. Him and his encyclopedia of vanity. Words, words, words. He'd show Felix and he'd show his own dusty heart: he'd scoop Laura and split her like the young oyster she was, he'd woo her and love her, and sit down in the end with purple pen and write Felix an encyc*lolita*, a treatise on hearts that know how to bubble like champagne.

Odd how people were convinced by words, by the Felixes of the world. Del for one. During his visits to Pender Harbour, Del had met the fat Quebecker. He'd spent an afternoon reading Felix's writing and letting the throb-head lecture him mercilessly, and came away with something looking hideously like awe. Frank wouldn't admit to feeling jealous, but felt hostile when Del cornered him and said, "You really should read what Felix has written about human suffering. He calls it the Trap of Desire. He says ..." Or, another time, "In one page, Felix taught me more about the job of refereeing than five years on the circuit. He says a ref is in fact a Solomon who *must* bring down the sword and divide up the baby. He says that by combining perfect discipline with perfect justice, you can ..." Blah-blah-blah with echoes of a superior frog accent. Frank could listen no further, preferring instead his image of Felix alone in a forest squatting on a stump like the bulbous toad he was, a whistle in his wet lips, waiting for some unlucky sucker like Del to walk by and be refereed at.

Poor naive Del. Poor top-lofty Felix. Lucky Laura and himself. Frank tried for the piccolo mood again and failed, as he knew he would. The toe. Selfish Mary. Poor damn Del.

Frank hated feeling it sometimes. This bond unasked for. Forced on him in the womb like a blind Hindu marriage. He had thought long on this. The one love he was capable of was a burden and a bore.

In any case, it appeared he was being forced to break up Del's marriage. Again, this thrilled more than depressed him. In the long run he'd be doing his brother a kindness, the compassion of Shiva. He'd be helping free Del from his trap of idiot goodwill, of dumb patience. Frank had no choice and he knew it. He couldn't keep mum, couldn't let Mary get away with doing such a dirty. He could abide Del being a fool, but not such a fool.

The task at hand would be easier if he could bring himself to simply hate Mary. But he couldn't. In the past, even while they clashed, they often saw eye to eye. And he found he sympathized with her now, just a bit, in what he guessed to be her flight from awful domesticity. Del was no Latin lover. Del was the sugar-head sort who thanks an elevator for opening its doors.

Yesterday Frank had seen Felix again, and Felix had summed up Mary well. Frank was trying to enlist his services, asking him to come to the party to lend support (since Del respect him so much) while he did the deed. Felix of course refused.

"Already I have been the bearer of foul tidings. To pursue further the role as agent in a family crisis would not befit my position as pure Observer."

Frank, knowing a prepared speech when he heard one, was about to counter with an obscenity when he had a sudden thought.

"What was Mary like, up there on stage?" he asked. "What was her face like? Was she sad, or drugged, or forced, or what?"

"She was positively rosy, my friend," Felix said. "She loved teasing the hungry dogs in the front row. She was, several times, licking her lips. But at the same time she stood apart. She had the clear arrogance of a feminist."

"My sister-in-law is a bitch."

"It seems Del is married to a feminist who is also a sensualist and adventurist. I propose that your brother is wed to a creature who writhes in hell."

Life, Frank thought now, on this pure blue day, is indeed rich.

He took a deep breath of salt air and slapped his pocketful of dollars. Without looking down he took his coffee mug of sake off the seat and gulped it sloppily through a wide smile. A true Renaissance man, the last possible version of Renaissance man, he would do well in this soon-to-be-bombed-out-world.

He came upon a fifth line to his ballad, and jotted it down:

And I love hating love go slow.

Feeling the sun hot on his jeans, he pulled them off and stood naked. As often happened when he was alone on *Tammy* and out in the middle of nowhere, he had an attack of utter boyishness. He found himself grinning like a fool and wiggling his pelvis back and forth, which made his penis whip and slap against his thighs. Standing tall at the wheel, feet apart, his body so gangling and white, and gyrating like a flasher whose only intent is to shock, Frank peered down his formidable length of nose at the city that approached him across the waters of Georgia Strait.

CHAPTER FIVE

Case Study

*It has been discovered that at least eighty per cent of
pregnancies, if not all pregnancies, begin with
monozygotic twins. In all but two per cent of cases,
however, one twin dies during the first month of
gestation and is absorbed into the placenta wall. Two
notions arise from this. One, it seems that the
haunting thought of having a "ghost twin" we've
never met has some basis in fact. Two, it appears that
some law of nature has decreed that twins should not
be.*

—from *Twins*, by Edythe Crane, Ph.D.

D r. Baal began drinking scotch the moment his wife went
into labor. Though he knew that the longer Muriel took to
expel his progeny the drunker he would be, he enjoyed such
irony. Besides, he needed scotch to dull the sound of his wife's
groans and shrieks—the sound of a soul being wrung out like a
terry towel soaked in blood. Pain (a dog's pain, a goat's pain, a
wife's pain) was what he hated most about medicine. Pain affected him so much it had driven him to medicine in the first
place. And that fact, he knew, was the major irony of his life.

Allen Aaron Baal, who had long ago given up on the greatest
irony—life and death and the hooded purpose of both—as unthinkable, had decided that life was indeed bleak unless one
created for oneself a bright stage upon it. Which was why he

dressed the way he did. In an era in which everyone else was embracing modernism in all its linoleum and polyester guises, Dr. Baal lived in a log house with plank floors and dressed like a gentleman veterinarian from another century. His work clothes included pince-nez, gold watch and fob, suspendered tweed trousers tucked into high boots, and starched white shirt with arm bands. He loved those white shirts with arm bands. Because while spaying a young bitch, or checking a cow's teeth, he always managed to get blood or urine or cud on his sleeves. It didn't escape him that the sight of a vet's ruined shirt lent an air of dedication, of emergency even, to routine performances. Dr. Baal got handsome tips—a dressed turkey here, a bushel of corn there—and kept plenty of white shirts on hand.

It was this same quest for theater that, when his wife first whispered the news of her pregnancy, made him announce, "We will need no doctor."

So here he sat, drinking scotch, listening to his wife's gasps, timing them, surprised at his now overwhelming nervousness. Not only did he feel unlucky tonight, he felt also a solid sense of having done something wrong. Had he endangered wife and child through his little bout of braggadocio? Dr. Baal believed in hubris—maybe this time he'd taken pride too far. Certainly he could snip an umbilicus, he could keep the instruments sterile and his movements precise, he could arrest those hemorrhages that could be arrested, he could slap the bloody bottom of his child. But what if something went *wrong* wrong?

Nothing would go wrong. In any case, although Muriel's belief in his ability was wide-eyed and unshakable, she lay at this moment on a bed of such pain that even unshakable trust can be shaken; therefore he must show no worry on his face. Scotch would smooth his worry lines.

Dr. Baal was quite drunk when his wife screamed the imminent arrival of his child. He stubbed out his cigar, washed methodically, and teetered hardly at all. The beaming smile he shot his wife on entering the bedroom was the smile of a bad actor—insincere, aimed at the headboard above her purple face. When his smile was met by nothing but screams, Dr. Baal lurched awake and tripped quickly into position at the vee of his wife's legs. The baby's head came fast. His surgeon's hands had a good brain of their own, and they slid in to cradle the head, find the jaw, and pull ever so gently. Muriel's next scream and contraction brought the child out smoothly, a boy, and Dr. Baal guffawed in relief and glee. He'd done it.

He snipped the cord, tied and taped it. Deft, sure movements. The boy's left foot still hidden in the vagina, Dr. Baal made to pick up his child. And up he came. But only so far. His foot seemed stuck on something. And, even more curious, Muriel began to shriek and convulse anew.

The vet's joy became horror. He broke into icy sweat. This was it. His pride had taken them all to hell. The unthinkable had happened. Trying to stay cool to Muriel's cries, trying to brace himself with years of medical lore, he could envision only medical impossibilities: a gigantic and gnarled clubfoot, a cloven hoof caught up in Muriel's guts. He envisioned the time once when during a goat birth the kid's forelimb had buckled and broken at the shoulder and become lodged in the birth canal. The mother goat bleated its agony, and twisted around grotesquely to try to butt its baby back inside. Both goat and kid had died.

And this was his son! His son! Frantic, Dr. Baal closed his eyes, leaned back, and pulled.

Muriel screamed again, and Dr. Baal almost fell as the baby in his hands came violently his way. He opened his eyes and his hubris was answered: a second boy, a breech birth, joined to his son at the left big toe.

Dr. Baal didn't hesitate. He cut and tied a second umbilical cord with a severity that looked like anger and then, bloodying his white shirt, propped a baby in the crook of each arm and bore them away, ignoring Muriel's questioning whimpers. Out of the room he raced, out of the house to his operating room in the barn. He ran blindly, guided by habit, able to stare only at the spot just in front of his navel where two toes shared a common knuckle, and he could only murmur, "I'm sorry, I'm sorry."

He wasted no time. Poised over them with the rib saw, he decided within seconds that his first son, Delaware, would have the proper-lengthed toe. He would be normal. Taller, in effect. The other, the intruder—for that's what he saw him to be, if for these first minutes only—might have to learn not to limp. For there was no choice. It must be done quickly, it must be done now, for no doctor must know this secret. Or his shame. He would not be lectured to.

And so Dr. Baal sawed his boys apart, and in so doing launched the twins into a wailing that rendered merely human those screams of Muriel Baal's, which were only now echoing and fading into wooden walls.

The secret did get out, of course. Muriel couldn't help herself, and it was only the neighbor ladies, you understand. But soon the doctors came, then reporters, and headlines appeared in the Brampton and then the Toronto papers. And it wasn't half bad, Dr. Baal decided after some weeks, to be the father of famous twin boys. His "agonizing decision" was a marvel to all, and there was more than one reference to King Solomon.

The second word Del said was "papa." The second word Frank said was "mama." This became a touching little joke between Dr. and Mrs. Baal, but they didn't ponder its significance. Because more significant were the brothers' very first words. Their first words were each other's names. What Del said sounded like "Fwang." What Frank said sounded like "Dayo."

At age ten the boys began to read books about twins. Some they got at local libraries, others had been left by the doctors and psychologists. Books of mythology, fiction, and fact. Some, like *East of Eden*, were about brothers who were close, and in this case about a white sheep and a black sheep, so to speak, who fought over a lover.

In these books patterns emerged, and the boys would compare themselves, sometimes laughing and mocking the book, other times swollen silent with recognition. The patterns, the clichés, were often true, as clichés often are. They read about Leda's sons, Castor and Pollux, and excerpts from Dumas, Shakespeare, and Mann. Some of it they understood. They read about dizygotics and monozygotics. They read that the racial rates of twin births were 0.5 percent for Orientals, 1 percent for whites, 2 percent for blacks but 7 percent for Nigerians.

They read that Plato believed sexual love to be an attempt to rebuild a broken, mystical twinship. In the same book they read about the twins of Athens, how it was discovered by a brilliant politician that the reason Sparta continued to best them in war was because Athens, unlike Sparta, allowed its twins to live. So a law was enacted: all twins (like lots of female babies) were left on the mountainside to be pecked to death by eagles or to die of dehydration, and sure enough Athens nevermore fell to the Spartan sword.

Del looked up at Frank, nervously. Frank giggled.

They read about the life of the amazing Colombian Siamese-twin sisters, Maria and Roberta Mercedes. Sharing a common lower spine, they were otherwise completely different. Maria was saintly, patient, and a teetotaler, while Roberta liked her wine (Maria was not affected) and had a blistering temper. Del and Frank read in awe of Maria's marriage and her subsequent bearing of a normal child. Bitter Roberta remained a virgin for life. What, Del and Frank asked each other, did blistering-mad Roberta do on her sister's wedding night? What did she *do*? And what sort of man was Maria's husband? But the book didn't go into such detail. The sisters died at seventy-two, Maria going first, followed an hour later by Roberta. It was said that Roberta, feeling herself fading too, blamed it all on her sister and died cursing the dead woman at her side.

Their toes often hurt with rashes and unexplained bleeding. Frank's especially. When he was overtired he did indeed limp, as his father had predicted. But both toe stubs bled. No doctor (their father contacted specialists this time) could explain why. One warned that the toes might become cancerous. They suffered through two years of a rampant, itchy rash, then a year of

swelling. Even when the toes healed for long periods, the skin on
the end remained tender, more tender than a baby's fingers,
more ripe with nerves than the end of a penis.

Del and Frank read that the Iroquois regarded one twin to be
good, the other evil. " 'The younger one,' " Del read aloud,
" 'was seen to be a devil and was spirited away at birth to be eaten
by animals, whose spoor'—that's shit, I think—'would render
it harmlessly through the earth to the underworld.' " Frank
grinned wickedly hearing this, but Del felt uneasy for him. He
scanned the section and skipped over parts that said the Sioux,
the Algonquins, and some tribes in Africa all had a special, fatal
surprise in store for one twin, always the younger.
    They read about twins who were separated by adoption, who
led separate lives in distant cities, but were contacted in
adulthood by scientists. The findings gave evidence of a bond
bordering on the supernatural. Two brothers, for instance (and
there were many such cases), one from Seattle and the other
from Chicago, were found to have been married on the same day,
both to a woman named Joan. Both had two sons, named Robert
and Allen in one case and Bob and Alan in the other. Both had
been accountants, and both had been fired for embezzlement.
One was now a pipe fitter and the other a welder.
    "Close enough," Del and Frank agreed.
    Reading such accounts had an odd effect on Frank and Del.
On the one hand it made them feel quite proud and special. On
the other hand it often made it difficult, for a day or two, to look
each other in the eye.

In adolescence they grew quickly, and very tall. Until that time it
had been hard to tell them apart, though they themselves knew
how very different they were. But now these differences became
public.
    In junior high they excelled in basketball. Unlike Del, Frank
could never quite handle with grace his status of local sports star.

Del accepted accolades with that proper blend of humility and humor. His smile and shrug instructed friends and fans to keep things in perspective: after all, it was only a game. Frank, though, when not sauntering through school halls with what looked like sneering conceit, would skip practices, steal his father's scotch, brood, and declare to his brother when he got home, "I hate that fuckin' game."

Frank enjoyed playing jokes on Del. He often used girls as his tool, for whereas Frank had a way with them—aloof, sarcastically witty, acidly attractive—Del did not. Once, when they were sixteen, he discovered Del had a crush on a classroom beauty, Robin Underwood, typically cute and unattainable, and Frank knew Del would never call her on his own. Frank called Robin one night, unbeknownst to his brother. Imitating Del's voice was a cinch, and using his brother's earnest and desperate tone, Frank confessed a hopeless love and arranged a date for that Friday night.

Del was of course outraged, and petrified at the prospect of actually spending an evening with Robin Underwood. It didn't take Frank long to convince him he'd been done a huge favor, and in the end he even coughed up the five bucks Frank demanded.

Frank's joke didn't stop there. The night of the big date, saying he was off to the gym to shoot baskets, he contrived to walk the mile with Del to Robin's house. Frank gave petting tips and was properly brotherly the whole way. Just as Del took a deep breath and made ready to stride up the Underwood walk, Frank doused him with a palmed vial of their father's whiskey, then ran. Del's romance with Robin Underwood had its moments, but never really got off the ground.

Indicative of a huge but nameless difference in their character, or perhaps in their soul, Del never won any of his high-school fights. Frank never lost. Frank could kick a guy in the face from seven feet away.

They were six foot five and basketball stars. With the Baal brothers at the helm, Fraser Valley High won two successive provincial championships. College scouts salivated; several offers even came from south of the border, that fearsome aerie of basketball.

Del had had one more offer than Frank. Though they were always one-two in the scoring race, easily outdistancing their nearest rivals, Frank scored slightly fewer points. One perceptive scout wrote in his report: "One is cool as in cucumber. Also his name is a great one for fans. Delaware Baal. Sounds like a colored boy's name." Of Frank he said, "This one takes too many fouls too soon. There [sic] about the same ability but I think they try to look after each other and would perform better if they wernt [sic] on the court at the same time. Also this one sort of limps when he hauls ass." This scout was from Ohio State, the college Frank didn't get invited to.

The Fraser Valley nudges Vancouver, a spanking new city of two million. The valley is a farming district loomed over by mountains on two sides, by the U.S. border on another, and by Vancouver to the west, where the valley flattens out into a river delta. In the valley a boy could pick up a gun and have an awesome variety of targets: if he shot north or east, the bullet would land on a virgin mountainside trod on not even by Indians; if he shot it south, the bullet would land in America; to the west, the bullet might land on a movie star, banker, or condo roof. If he pointed his rifle straight up and the bullet came down on his head, he would have to identify himself. More likely than not he would see himself to be a kind of half-breed: not the old-fashioned country boy with naive city dreams, but rather a country boy who knows the city well enough to see both its good parts and its bad, both its treasure-smile and its hooker's sneer. So the choice facing a boy from the valley was no easy one. He had no illusions about the city, and yet his beautiful valley was so boring.

The Baal brothers had lots of friends in the Fraser Valley and went to many parties. These friends were a loose gang, perhaps even a clique, though a large one, of athletes, beer drinkers, and those who could tell a joke or slap a shoulder. They called themselves the Hodads, a name that poked fun at their own countryness while declaring how little they cared if their hairstyles were a year out of date, or that those in the city had of late grown gentle, to a man smoked pot, bought Donovan records, drove old VW vans, and laughed at the shiny jacked Chevys the valley boys still cherished more than a pretty girlfriend.

The Hodads noted the Baal brothers' differences from one another. One was that Frank could sneer just like Elvis when he wanted and somehow look just like him, even though his nose was so goddamn big. Another was that Frank always got a tad drunker than Del and was more eager to dally with any new narcotic that had made its way back country. And Frankie could sure hustle the girls, while Del was as bumbling as the rest of them. Frank had indeed sowed his countryside oats (he didn't brag much, but he'd made the rounds and there was no doubt), and at any given party he might have half the girls flirting with him and the other half staring pitchforks and thinking maybe to seduce a football player so as later to persuade him to go beat Frank Baal up.

One thing that struck the Hodads as odd was that, though the Baal brothers always arrived together and left together (unless Frankie scooped a girl), once at a party they hardly spoke to one another at all. All twins were of course close as close could get, but the Hodads wondered if these two were even friendly. For instance, in the dressing room the brothers would slap everyone's ass but each other's, and on the bench they never sat side by side.

Dr. and Mrs. Baal knew that twins were mysterious and that there were theories about how to raise them. One, you could ignore their idiosyncrasies and dress them up in the same outfits, feed them the same food, deliver the same punishments and the same birthday presents. This tactic Dr. Baal saw to be a selfish and simple-minded time-saving device on the part of parents, and thereafter decided that his twins would have a choice. If it was Christmas, and a present was to be pyjamas, he would buy a canary yellow pair and a bright blue pair, wrap them up together in a package saying "To Del and Frank," and let the twins do the rest.

So they were not only sawed apart but also pushed, and it is anyone's guess as to the wisdom in that. Later, when they were young teenagers, they agreed to quit finishing each other's sentences, which they could do as easily as anyone else could finish his own. They could also supply the middle or the beginning, and performed this little trick in front of schoolmates or company, though they sensed correctly that this game displeased their father. Their own conversations often sounded like this:

"So do you feel like—"

"No."

"Okay, we'll do *that* then. But tomorrow—"

"Okay."

It was Frank who suggested one day that they not speak to one another at all unless they could speak in an ordinary way. Frank looked troubled and nervous saying this, and mumbled, "You don't wanna end up like Maria and Roberta, right?" Del wasn't sure what he meant by this, and it's possible Frank wasn't too clear on it either.

But the Baal twins launched themselves into the adventure of thinking and speaking for themselves. In any case, when they were together nothing much needed saying, at least not out loud. So what the Hodads didn't see was that the Baal brothers, friendly to each other or not, simply didn't need to talk, and that if any exchange was necessary it was done with a boot tapping to the music, a knuckle nudging an empty beer bottle, an eyebrow, a change in breathing, or even less than that.

And, of course, in moments of adolescent crisis, there was always the toe.

Dr. and Mrs. Baal had raised their boys lovingly and, it can be argued, well. Neither husband nor wife romanticized parenthood, and so they were not distressed to see that the boys were something of an island unto themselves. Seeing that, by age twelve, neither boy had taken more than casual interest in his animals or medical instruments, Dr. Baal resigned himself. Similarly, though Mrs. Baal would have dearly loved a companion in her kitchen, a sewing partner, or someone to discuss her novels with her, she would have been horrified had any of her three men showed such an inkling.

But sometimes, when necessary, their parents did take it upon themselves to direct the twins' development, and sometimes their methods were colorful.

Once, during a phase when the boys had taken to fighting each other, Dr. Baal interrupted a fight and proceeded to beat them both up simultaneously, his idea being to show them that since they were so puny in the face of the real world, why fight each other at all? The tactic sort of worked and sort of didn't. Another time when, at six, Del asked for a "dolly" for Christmas, mom and dad worked in collusion and presented the boy with a doll that had a slow leak. The doll had been filled with cow's urine, and though Del washed it and washed it he couldn't get it clean. The smell grew worse, and soon the doll was a terrible thing that Del abandoned out by the barn, where even the scariest cats were afraid of it. And then there was the time Frank was caught dripping candle wax on the lame calf's rump. Pain-shy Dr. Baal was so appalled at the sight of the tethered calf's bawling and lame bucking that he immediately dragged Frank out of the barn, found the boy's pet duckling, and chopped its head off. To the crying Frank he shouted, "All animals are the same. When you hurt that calf, you killed this duck." No ogre, Dr. Baal helped preside over a good funeral for the duck, and Frank was not overly confused that day.

Up until Muriel Baal died, the family lived a disaster-free life. It took her about four seconds to die, and sudden deaths carry an

extra horror. She was a good woman, wife, and mother, and so all
her life Muriel Baal had been taken for granted: it was horrible
that two sons and a husband were so suddenly made to see this
and yet given no time to apologize.

It was June and the twins had just graduated from high school.
Del was cutting the backyard grass. Frank, who had been told for
the fourth day in a row to fix the loose sundeck railing, was in the
house sneering at cartoons on TV. Dr. Baal was in the barn
clinic, an Irish setter anesthetized upon a table. Muriel stood on
the sundeck, her hands cupped at her mouth, shouting at Del
over the lawnmower noise that lunch was ready.

Del had heard his mom, hadn't yet looked up, but was shutting
off the mower. Mrs. Baal was pressing into her second shout
when the sundeck railing gave way. On her way down, her shout
became a scream. Del screamed at the same time, and this two-
throated voice of panic had Dr. Baal running from the barn
before Muriel had hit the ground. What he'd heard was two
screams and a mower shutting off, and he pictured Del, basket-
ball-scholarship-bound, with a mangled foot. The screams took
a little longer to penetrate Frank's cartoon world, where Tom
and Jerry were taking turns dynamiting each other.

The sound of her neck breaking had been that of an ax blow
muffled by pillows. When Del reached her she was lying on her
front, her head folded underneath her. By the time his father
arrived, Del had turned her onto her back.

Dr. Baal knew his wife was dead. Yet a medical voice took
over nonetheless and shouted within, "Look. She cannot breathe
due to the angle of breakage. If you cut to her trachea she may
breathe." He wore his carpenter's belt modified for surgical
tools and he drew from it now, like a pistol, his pearl-handled
antique scalpel. He began to cut his wife's throat. She had a fat
throat, and it seemed an age before he reached the cartilage of her
windpipe. Then came her glorious rush of breath! But it was
only a trapped exhalation, and it was her last.

Frank came upon the scene just as Dr. Baal began to cut into
his mom's throat. He saw his mother. He saw Del to one side
gawking, his face a smear of nightmare. Thinking his dad was

killing his mom, Frank jumped on Dr. Baal's back and started to punch. Del, seeing slightly more clearly, jumped on his brother's back to wrestle him away. Thus the family—one dead, one cutting, one punching, one pulling—formed a terrible sort of four-bodied creature, at that instant the combined pain and love of which, had it been communicated in a poem, would have ended forever the world's need for poetry.

Sudden death in a family can be likened to a terrorist explosion. The outer circle of witnesses merely hear the bomb, then rush in to stare at the mess and to see if they can be of help. The victims themselves, the family, have been caught by the explosion each in their own way. One is killed, perhaps, one is deafened, another blinded, and one has lost a leg. The effects of Muriel Baal's death were equally stark and simple.

The shock Dr. Baal received eventually caused him to quit medicine. For he'd learned something about himself. He'd seen himself too clearly as he was slicing into the fat of his Muriel's neck. The fat was endless and yellow and tired, and it disgusted him. He caught himself musing, even as he cut, that no animal worth its keep would have such fat; the only other animals he'd encountered like this were spoiled, whiny, fat old dogs, kept by widows. And his wife's flesh exuded an odd grease, which at certain angles flashed a gasoline rainbow. How—Dr. Baal asked himself, even while cutting—was it possible that he could be thinking these things about Muriel? Such was the view of himself he received, and he never felt worthy of the title "doctor" or even "human" again.

Muriel Baal's ridiculous explosive death cemented her boys' lives as well, in such a way that distanced them further from each other. For one brother it was simple: Frank came to profoundly hate life. For the other it was not: Del fell into hopeless awe of it.

It is possible that Del suffered something of a religious experience as he wrestled on his brother's back. When he was at the end of the struggling chain that began with his mother, it was as if the collective panic, the outrage (or perhaps it was his mother's

soul), flowed through his family and exited through him. The
energy was of such purity and magnitude that one second after it
passed he could no longer conceive of or even recall it. But it had
worked to give him wide, sad eyes for life. He took to asking
himself and others, Why death? Why life *or* death? He began to
read books on reincarnation and astrology, and grew gentle and
needy with the opposite sex, and though this seduced some of
them at long last, seduction no longer gave him satisfaction or
pride.

If his mother's death caused Del to make public a raw heart, it
worked on Frank in more invisible ways. For him the death had
been an explosion of rage and color. His mother, bleeding so red,
lying on a scatter of white two-by-fours he'd been told to fix.
The hues of his life intensified: the pink and orange of his anger
became scarlet, and the gray wash of his guilt became indelibly
black. Outwardly he grew mute. When he did speak it was
usually to vent spite or nonsense or humor, but it was a humor
too dark to make many smile.

That fall Frank went to play semipro basketball in Turin, Italy,
and Del accepted the scholarship to Ohio State. Frank didn't
explain his choice, and Del didn't ask. Their farewell had neither
fireworks nor tears.

They were apart for four years, and they wrote very few
letters. Perhaps they didn't need to, which is the pleasant as-
sumption, or perhaps they didn't want to, which is less pleasant.
In any case, when they did write they didn't seem to relate
anything very important. One postcard Del received said only,
"Hey Beak, quit smoking the other day and my head's a jerky pile
of shit. The dagos are getting faster than ol' Frankie because all
they drink is wine. Or maybe I'm too old to run. Anyway, I hate
this fucking game." The photo on the card was of Mona Lisa, on
whose forehead Frank had scribbled a careless swastika.

A postcard Del sent Frank said, "The other day I ran into this
girl who told me I looked like Ichabod Crane. I thought it meant
she liked me, but I looked it up in the library and decided I'd been

insulted. You look like Ichabod too, and I guess you fit in with all those beaky Roman statues over there. I got lucky last weekend but she was drunk, so I didn't put a notch on my Bogart belt. In fact, I think she thought I was someone else." Del's card was of a vast yellow field of wheat backed by a royal blue afternoon sky, nothing else. He didn't draw on it because he thought it was beautiful, and he hoped the stark, pure lines and colors would help clear his brother's head in the midst of all that noise, dirt, and history. He had also purposely withheld news of how very sick their father was, not wanting to worry him.

When their father did die the explosion was surprisingly minor. If guilt had let them admit it, they would have acknowledged a strange kind of relief, one that didn't contradict their love. Frank's guilt was extreme; he'd been overseas four years and hadn't once come home.

Del graduated with a degree in Physical Education, with a specialty in Match Arbitration—that is, refereeing—and returned to Vancouver. Within several months, Frank joined him there.

They were reunited outside a coffee shop on East Hastings Street, downtown. The day was rainy and dark, but such was the twins' apprehension as they neared the rendezvous point that each raindrop, bum, and rusty car seemed somehow alert and tinged with neon. The moment was a shock for both of them. Meeting his brother's eyes, Del thought he was looking into a mirror. His stomach flipped, and his life flashed before him. He'd heard this happened to you when you die.

Frank looked down quickly too.

CHAPTER SIX

The Party

*My body, which is an omni-sided lens, cannot abide
parties. People shout and hop, they flirt like puppies,
they discuss lotteries and sports. My body-lens, being
what it is, focuses this array of fecal energy in the core
of my Self. This brings me close to death. I cannot
help it, containing multitudes.*

— Felix d'Amboise

Typically, Wally Kenny arrived early to his own surprise
party. He'd been told eight-thirty, but he showed up at six
with a pot of oyster sauce fettucini, claiming in a husky voice
that the Lions had a pre-season game tonight on TV and he damn
well couldn't bear missing this. Del was touched by the gesture.
He knew Wall hadn't watched a game in years.

Del, Mary, and Wally sat sucking up pungent gooey noodles,
watching madmen butt heads, and Del was allowed to elucidate
on what sort of job the ref was doing, which players were the
famous violators of rules, and so forth. Del was keyed up for this
new season. His first assignment wasn't until the next weekend,
when he would fly to Toronto to officiate the Argos versus
Calgary.

Though the three had a pleasant—surprisingly pleasant—dinner in Del's new den, the surprise nature of Wally's party had
been ruined. But Wally had an idea and it worked: he hid in the

den and when all the guests were assembled in the living room, out he popped, shouting "Surprise!" at them all.

The party's tone was clearly one of reunion. A mix of high-school chums, ex-Hodads like Wally who had moved from the valley to the city, sports friends, gay friends, and working friends—somehow most of them knew each other, at least casually, often carnally, and Del had never seen such a display of back slaps, hugs, coy eyes, and genuine smiles. There were no snubs or open hostility, at least not yet. But it was early, and no one was drunk. Nor had Frank arrived.

Del was pleased to see how happy Wally was, how his old pal was moved almost to shyness. Wally's early rounds of the party were quiet and sincere; he seemed less cartoony, less self-consciously a queen. Some of this likely had to do with his new friend, Melvin his name was, a huge man who hung behind him like a scowling bodyguard. Melvin, Del noted, had the body of the archetypal middle-linebacker, combining equal parts grace and threat. He looked to be the sort who didn't tolerate overt sissiness in the company he kept, so it was no wonder Wally adapted to his lover's ways.

In one of those sudden mirrors life sticks in one's face, Del saw a parallel in his own world. He'd just walked into the kitchen, happy, and there was Mary at the sink, knowing it was him, having heard his footsteps perhaps, and Del felt the instant tension in the room that smelled like electricity and tasted like pencil wood.

They were still in their cold phase. Shallow smiles and light talk pretended nothing was wrong while huge unease floated beneath them like a whale adrift under the house. This phase had lasted a week now, ever since Mary's slip of the tongue. Was it a slip of the tongue? It had to be. "Divorce" wasn't the sort of word you used once then didn't mention again—if you really meant it.

Mary hummed as she washed plates and coffee cups. Her hands quick and true, she was in her speed-hostess mode, scooping up dishes and ashtrays and washing them before their contents had cooled. Mary enjoyed this role, and the thanks she sang

Del as he passed her a glass sounded friendly enough. He bent and gave her an experimental kiss on the back of the neck. Mary's hands became briefly stuck in the suds, but that was her only reaction, a largely unreadable one. Lord, thought Del, they were in urgent need of a long talk. But wasn't that the catch-22 of marriage, that when they could talk they didn't need to, and when they needed to they couldn't? Perhaps they were in-stinctively waiting for the right time, an unforced, shared mood where they could be calm, not picky, and smile sadly together and agree that life and marriage were absurd and that the best tack a couple could take was one of kindness.

Del hoped the friendly talk happened soon, because they hadn't had sex in nine days. Nine and a half days.

Returning with another load of dishes (and requests for seven tequila shooters—things were going to be sparky before too long), Del met with the ghastliest of Saturday night kitchen apparitions. Fraser had arrived through the back door. His eyes were huge behind his glasses, his grin desperate and apologetic as he confronted Mary. In one hand he clutched a dirty blanket, in the other a can of Campbell's Turkey Vegetable soup.

"I'm *home*less, they threw me out into the *future* and it's party night in Mrs. Baal's house!" Fraser raved. Though he grinned as always, his eyes were frightened. "I'm the happy wanderer but I lost an accordion!" he shouted.

Mary took his soup and blanket, sat him down, and coaxed enough normal talk from him to conclude that he had been ejected from his group home. Something about a fight with Lulu, and broken dishes. Mary had Del phone the home, and it was confirmed that Fraser had in fact pulled a butter knife on one of the staff and had indeed been thrown out.

"The poor disturbed fellow," said the stiff voice on the phone, "is as of now a free agent. We've had it up to here. He *will* not normalize."

Fraser had been given thirty dollars and told to return in the morning for his clothes and record player. Fraser was eighteen, legally an adult; he had no family anyone knew of. He knew the bus routes, he could order a hamburger, he knew the emergency phone numbers, he knew how to ask policemen polite questions. He had a caseworker with whom he met twice a week, and now his life, it appeared, was in her hands. This meant, both Mary and Del knew, that Fraser would either be found a placement in another group home (an unlikely possibility after tonight) or be committed.

"I brought my bed to your Mr.-and-Mrs.-Baal party," Fraser said to them. He pointed nervously to his blanket. His hair stood up greasy and spiked, unintentionally punk.

"All right, Fraser. Tonight you may stay here. In the guest room. As payment you can vacuum." Mary explained this in calming tones, though she too was upset. "And tomorrow we will workshop the childish behavior that has gotten you into trouble."

Fraser hooted ridiculously and hugged them both. Mary gave Del whispered instructions to keep him there in the kitchen to settle him, and she would circulate and explain his presence to the guests. So Del and Fraser were left alone. A raunchy but nostalgic Janis Joplin tune roared in the living room, and Fraser tapped his foot to it, out of time.

Del got him a cranberry juice, which he sipped, staring down into space, that grin on his face, that private joke Fraser had no way of explaining to normal minds. Though this quirky silence lasted a good minute, Del felt comfortable being there next to him. They had always had a connection, a quiet affinity. Of this Del was proud, much in the way people whom dogs take to are proud.

Height was one bond, especially for Fraser, who often greeted Del with the shout, "Tall rules!" There seemed to be other ties, never acknowledged, but Del wondered whether in fact Fraser was aware, or even capable of, the sort of unspoken warmth he told himself they shared. They often traded a kind of sly eye contact, for instance, but maybe Fraser's eyes were simply sly all the time and had a sly pact with everything they gazed on.

Del recalled the incident of a year ago or so. Did Fraser think of it too? It had been "grocery training day" for Fraser, meaning that Fraser had to correctly select and pay for the items on the group home's shopping list. A sudden crisis in the retarded world had called Mary away, and Del found himself ripped from his den work to take Fraser to the Safeway. They had an okay time of it, Del giving advice on brands of ketchup and which cereals had so much sugar they killed lab rats. Fraser pushed the cart, said beep-beep in crowds, and gave a goggle-eyed hello of communion to every bored housewife he passed. He appeared to feel a bit sorry for them. Sometimes he shouted, "The wide world of shopping!" Later, the "wide" became "wild." As the hour progressed Fraser grew tired of making race-car noises and turned into a comparison shopper extraordinaire, surprising Del with a knowledge of kilos to pounds ratio and the like.

Though Fraser was a delight, Del's mood was bad. He resented being taken for granted, ordered from his den by a stern wife. True, Del would do anything for Mary, was often aggressively generous in fact, but it was her blunt manner that sometimes nudged him over the edge of feeling generous to feeling put upon.

Nearing the group home in the car, Del absentmindedly cut a car off at an intersection. Four young ruffians in their battered Camaro honked long and loud, and, pulling up beside him, they cursed and gestured and sneered. Del surprised himself by giving them the finger. He'd never done that before in his life. The magic finger sent the hoodlums into a hormonal rage. Hanging out of their windows and screaming, they suggested Del pull over to have it out right now.

Del made a calm right turn onto the group home's street, checked in his mirror to make sure they hadn't been followed, then parked.

"That sure was an excited car," Fraser said as they unloaded the bags.

"That's what's called making a mountain out of a molehill," Del told him. His heart was still pounding and his skin was clammy, reminding him of those few schoolyard times when some hero challenged him with calls of "Lurch" or "Stork."

"They looked ethnic," Fraser added.

"No, Fraser, they were just angry," Del said.

Del was in the hallway going out for another load when Fraser passed him and said, "The mountain car is back."

The Camaro had circled the block to find them. Now three doors were opening and three pimply toughs oozed out while the driver revved the engine in a steady, sinister way. Del edged back inside. Feeling as in a dream, or more that he was living out some kind of bad movie script, he found himself picking two black leather gloves off the hall table and pulling them on.

"Follow me," he told Fraser, and then stepped out onto the bad-movie porch. Still carrying two bags of groceries, one of which sprouted celery leaves, Fraser followed.

"Can I help you gentlemen?" Del, who had never won a fight, who hadn't swung his ridiculous arms in anger or fear for at least fifteen years, said this in a steady velvet tone. He realized he was grinning through steely slits of eyes like Clint Eastwood, and he found too that he was pounding one gloved fist into another.

The driver had joined them, and the four took up legs-apart stances on the group home lawn. The leader, not big but tattooed and muscular, shouted, "Learn ta fuggin drive, ya bone-rack chickenshit ass-ho," and the like.

To Del's amazement, the movie script had him suddenly advancing. As he did so his velvet voice crooned, "Maybe you want to kiss my hand and make up." At the same time, interrupting him, Fraser yelled, "We welcome the excited mole car!"

The four teenagers looked confused. Del took a couple more steps, pounding his gloves in rhythm. Behind his smile, below his smacking hands, his big toe shot bolts of pain up his backbone, and his heart became a fluttering dove in his chest. Reality threatened to penetrate the movie script; panic was stiffening his limbs and unbolting his nerve. But then Del had a sudden inspiration.

"Put your groceries down now, *Fraser*," Del said loud enough for the others to hear, emphasizing the name for reasons known only to the scriptwriter. Fraser put the bags down and came to Del's side.

"Take your shirt off now, *Fraser*," Del said, continuing to pound his fists and stare down on the four hesitant faces.

Fraser, smiling sloppily and letting loose a choked guffaw, removed his shirt to reveal a long torso, as skinny as Del's but sharply defined by muscles that constant hypertension and craziness had burned of all fat. He had several sores on his stomach and a streak of purple eczema across his chest.

"Let's relax now!" Fraser shouted at Del. Del couldn't tell if Fraser knew a fight was brewing, but Fraser had of his own volition removed his glasses and tucked them like a knife into his sock. And there he stood, goofy, agitated, and myopic to the point where his world had become nothing but a vague landscape and angry ethnic blur. But most important, Fraser looked like the sort of creature who, giggling and feeling no pain himself, could kill any size of fighting man with deft thrusts of carrots and wedges of cheese into soft parts of the body.

As a last straw, the seven other group home inmates—one a girl in a parka and toque (it was August), another a boy in someone's flowing mauve robe—had gathered wide-eyed and silent on the porch.

When the car drove off Del gave them no final finger. He felt neither proud nor relieved, so disturbed was he by the brave and foolish stranger he'd momentarily become. He'd reminded himself of his brother. He'd *become* Frank. Now his panic and fluttering heart had returned, and as he removed his black gloves the brave stranger just as quickly faded into hazy unreality.

He did, though, clap Fraser on the back and suggest they have a beer.

"We showed them, didn't we?" Del announced after his first shaky sip, welcoming any camaraderie this odd man Fraser might muster.

"All independent young adults go grocery shopping," Fraser said, "then relax."

So Fraser's comprehension of friendship remained a mystery to Del, though they had managed to consume three or four friendly beers apiece that day before Mary finally got back from her crisis.

Del opened Fraser a beer now. Party noises roared in from the living room. Fraser stood clutching his blanket. If ever there was a time a soul needed a beer . . .

"So," Del said, stupidly.

Fraser took the beer, smiling as always, but his smile was polite, and his look said he knew a stupid attempt at conversation when he saw one.

"La, ti, do," Fraser said.

"I mean, so how's life?" Del tried again.

"La, ti, do. Re, mi, fa, *so* . . . la, ti, do. I have a very good sense of humor."

Del looked hard at Fraser, the surprise and suspicion in his eyes unintentional, the question, Why are you playing at being retarded? unvoiced. But Fraser's face was blankly goofy.

Mary returned and Fraser let himself be led out into the party. Del wandered out as well, resuming his duties as host. He brought a drink, emptied an ashtray, and spoke with a forlorn gay man who'd been excluded from a whispering inner sanctum. He put on a record (the best of Gene Pitney), aware that his function of controlling party decorum and pace was about to end. Soon the party would be its own headless creature: the wits would rule the couches and chairs, the lovely would seduce in shadowy corners, and the bullies would command the stereo.

Was Frank coming? Wally would be hurt if he didn't show. Frank was one of Wally's best old Hodad buddies, the two of them—wasn't this funny?—ranking one-two in the girl-chasing department.

And Del felt a slight pang himself. It had been months since Frank's last visit, since they'd last stared each other in the eye and, as always happened, acknowledged that vast nameless thing. And hopefully he'd bring Laura. He and Frank could set the girls to talking and go off by themselves and be joking and cynical about women. He was definitely in the mood for his brother's dark slant.

Del located Fraser, who stood just off from a circle of folks
who were arguing about recipes or restaurants. Del caught the
phrases "*fresh* cilantro, dammit" and "the properly deveined
prawn." Fraser had picked up somebody's drink and listened and
nodded violently while purposely rattling his ice cubes. He
seemed to have some notion of the "cocktail party." It occurred
to Del that he should take Fraser up to Pender Harbour to visit
Frank and his friend, the strange and philosophical Felix. Take
Fraser off Mary's hands. What an eccentric foursome they'd
make, what a messy volcano of styles! But maybe no one would
know what to say.

The record bullies were taking over as expected, and most
were in nostalgic moods. Stones, Kinks, Beatles, even Neil
Young. At the start of each song, barely three notes in, a head
would lift, wince, and say, "I haven't heard *this* thing in *years*."
And Del, wandering, caught pieces of conversation, all of which
began with:

"Remember the time you and Mark were so drunk that . . ."

"Remember when that old car of Del's broke down and we
were stranded with nothing but . . ."

"Wasn't it *you* who wore that devil costume that Hallowe'en
when . . ."

How Frank would hate such talk. Maybe it would be better
after all if he just showed up tomorrow for a quiet beer, maybe
catch a college game on the tube. Frank had announced to more
than one such party that they were all necrophiliacs, in love with
what was dead and gone. A couple of years back he'd almost
started a middle-aged brawl after shouting at the host and his
wife: "Nothing left to live for, you fuckin' dying losers?" Frank
could be so damned absolute at times.

Del kept a random eye on Fraser, who appeared to be mingling by design. It was odd yet predictable how people reacted to
him, how he made some nervous, how some were repelled and
backed out of his range, how others were too loud and friendly,
and how some, incredibly, talked to him in something like baby
talk. Wally Kenny looked at ease with him. His eyes shone as he
told Fraser a joke, and Fraser laughed. Fraser now held a glass

with only ice in it, and this he tinkled with undying flair. When Fraser took up position at the fireplace, Del was left shaking his head. In his own version of the raconteur, elbow propped casually on the mantel, Fraser rattled his cubes nonstop as he grinned out at all of them.

And there was Mary, dancing. Del joined a bunch of chatting women and pretended not to watch his wife while he watched her very hard. Finding himself a bit too tipsy too early, he now sipped slowly. Mary was dancing with Malcolm Smith, an old romantic partner, a handsome though now paunchy literature prof. He and Mary had sparkling eyes for each other as they shared stories over the music, their faces close. Nostalgic stories? Remember-the-time-in-the-back-seat stories? It didn't matter, Del declared in a whisper to himself. For if one could not conquer jealousy and achieve perfect trust after eight years, it spoke for a pathetic union indeed. And their union was anything but pathetic. *Look* at her: she was beautiful. Her dancer's body. Lithe as a squirrel. The creamiest skin. Whip-smart and kind. Big eyes and a smile that could fix a bad day as surely as a clean sixty-yard touchdown pass. A woman's pure power, a power beyond a man's. Del tilted his empty wine glass and slurped it back, making the noise of a kid finishing a milkshake. Some heads looked up, one of them Mary's as she walked past, her dance over. Her face—that is, her glare—was penetrating.

God, love was heaven and hell in a nutshell. He knew he was a little hopeless around her, a little timid and woebegone in the face of her moods, but that was all right. That was romance. The first time on that beach in Greece (ten years ago now?) had left him transfixed, a bug pinned, belly up and wriggling, to a square of caramel. Belly up, he couldn't eat. Pinned, he couldn't leave. And that was that.

Frank arrived at midnight, alone, drunk, and dressed in a leech costume. The woman who opened the door to what sounded like incessant forehead pounding (and that is what it was) fell back and shrieked.

The seven-foot creature loomed teetering in the door frame, its muffled voice shouting, "Hey Beak, I just rolled down your goddamned driveway!" The net fabric costume was dirty in spots and torn. Everyone was staring and laughing, if cautiously. Fraser, over in a corner, laughed with a vitality that recalled Flipper the Dolphin.

"Hug me, Del. Hug me!" Frank shouted.

"What?"

"Hug me, goddammit!"

Del embraced his brother, who used this cue to hunch slightly and squeeze out a long, high-pitched fart. Those who were close enough to hear stopped laughing, but their lull was filled by Frank himself, who roared. Good Jesus, thought Del. He hadn't heard an intentional public joke-fart since he was fifteen.

Frank did look like a leech. The fabric, gray-green, tapered to a suckerlike mouth-hole above Frank's head. The air surrounding the leech smelled strongly of fish. Frank toppled to the floor and began wriggling himself out.

"Yeah, it's great, eh?" Frank, appearing now, said to no one in particular. "It's one of these filter nets Fisheries uses to scoop up plankton. I just popped the collect-jar off the end. It's for Hallowe'en, but I figured I'd try it out. Hey *Wally*, you *ass*hole," Frank shouted, "happy birthday or what*ever*! You *poo*-pusher!"

Wally Kenny, reddening, smiled weakly for a few friends and shrugged. Frank turned back to Del.

"Yeah, Fisheries was docked right by me so I just—" Frank saw Mary. "They sailed one day and just sort of left it for me on the dock."

"As long as it doesn't have a serial number on it," said Mary. She spun on her heel and walked away.

Jesus, thought Del.

By this time the party had enough of its own vigor to survive such an entrance, and it picked up loudly where it had left off. Del led Frank to a quiet corner.

"So, Frank. How are . . . ?"

But then Del found himself caught in his brother's eyes. And he suffered again, as always, the heavy flashing-past of his life.

There was no doubt Frank suffered this too, for he jerked his head in a spasm to the side, shook it, and looked down almost angrily.

"What's that, Beak?" Frank asked, not looking directly at him.

"So how's . . . so where's this Laura?"

"Laura!" Frank hooted, his nostrils flaring. "We had a little punch-out. A minor conflict. But we're still engaged." All in all Frank looked to be in a wonderful mood. His smile was infectious; he positively beamed. Del could not help smiling such a smile himself. Something wonderful must have happened.

Mary appeared and held a beer out to his brother. What a remarkable, thought Del, gesture of peace. And now Frank was grinning so hard he trembled.

"*So*, Frank. What's going on in your life these—"

"Back in a sec, Beak."

Frank and that odd trembling grin turned and followed Mary to the kitchen, hot on her tail.

Well, wasn't this something! His brother and his wife, so actively forgiving. Lord, they might even dance a dance together. Not a bad turn of events, not at all.

Del saw his wife, one minute later, racing from the kitchen toward the bathroom. She looked about to throw up. She held her hands out in front of her as if feeling for direction. She was as white as foam on a quickly poured beer.

Frank meandered slowly out of the kitchen, popping into his mouth a series of smoked oysters off a plate. He followed Mary with his eyes, looking more thoughtful now, but still manic and atremble. He was limping slightly.

Del grabbed his brother's arm. "What in hell was *that* about?"

Frank paused and studied Del a long moment before speaking.

"Well, she asked about Laura too. I guess she couldn't handle it when I told her Laura was a stripper." Frank's eyes glittered like psychopathic jewels. "Bit of the prude, eh, your Mary?"

Del's big toe shot his brain surprising little beeps of pain.

The brothers stood face to face in a corner under a swag lamp. Del held a goblet of white wine, and Frank swigged from Mr. Morgan's bottle of Jim Beam, now nearly empty. They looked identical at first glance, but if one studied them for a minute, not quite. If eyes, for instance, were venetian blinds, Del's were fully open and Frank's were angled shut just a touch. Frank's skin looked darker, and it was, and he looked slightly shorter, though he wasn't. Again, it was perhaps the angle of his eyes. And there were other differences an observer could see, or rather sense, and though sharp to the senses these differences were too subtle for words. But the brothers looked quite handsome standing there, each as if in front of a mirror, and the effect they had on observers was to make them feel that all men should have such noses. No one bothered them as they stood talking. No one would dare interrupt their sacred union, their mysterious parley. They were no doubt sharing unthinkable intimacies in tones of incomprehensible warmth.

On the contrary: the brothers talked coolly about simple things. Del ran down a schedule of when he'd be reffing on TV, and Frank promised to watch, though both knew he wouldn't. He told Frank he'd finished his den, and then felt embarrassed that he'd made a big thing out of what Frank no doubt thought minor. Frank told Del of his charters (he had a salmon for Mary out in the car) and his punk lyrics (Frank sang one from memory, Del winced and laughed). Frank said nothing about paying back Del's loan, and his mention of the rented Buick outside stung Del. Those in debt should not drive to their benefactor's house in sleek black rented Buicks. Even when Frank said, "Yeah, got me a classy pig this time," Del stayed quiet.

Nor did Del find it possible to mention how distressed he was to see Frank like this. That is, drunk, irreverent, and, worst of all, inpenetrable. He would not look Del in the eye. He made jokes out of Del's serious questions. He was snide, he was mocking, he sneered like Elvis Presley at the party snacks, at certain songs the bullies played, at Wally's faggier friends, and at certain women he'd bedded years before.

As usual over the past years, there was little to say to each other. Del's big toe had become a steady throb of nuisance. Frank shrugged at Del, and Del shrugged back, an uneasy smile was traded, and both made their way to opposite ends of the party.

Mary jumped when Del approached from behind and softly spoke her name. She whirled around with a huge, awkward smile.

"Don't worry about Laura," Del whispered. "I'm sure she's okay. It's not like a stripper's a prostitute or anything. Necessarily."

Mary's face went all blotchy and she jiggled her knee up and down. "I'm sure she's fine," she whispered, extremely quickly. Del also detected a slight slur. It seemed the hostess was relaxing for the night. Which was good.

"Take it easy on the hootch, sweetheart, you don't look well," Del said while walking away, not seeing the massive gulp of wine his wife was now into.

Del was fairly drunk himself, and an hour later much drunker. It was one a.m. and the party was just finding its legs, having the urgent, pleasant mix of reunion, birthday, and the novelty of Fraser. Though yawning frequently now, Fraser kept his ice glass full and singing. His goodwill was catching, his jokes so weirdly bad they were great (though distressing to the pot smokers), and now he had just as many people laughing with him as laughing at him.

Frank too had picked the party up, in his way. Del was glad his brother's drunkenness seemed to be taking the subtle route tonight. He watched him move from group to group, never stopping long. He watched him grab a woman's breast, but the woman wasn't too mad, and Del recalled they'd once been lovers. Frank bullied the bullies by unceremoniously pulling their choices off in midsong, replacing them with Frank Sinatra or Benny Goodman. The bullies laughed, thinking this an inspired joke, but Del knew well his brother's odd favorites: Sinatra, big band swing, the wildest, trashiest punk, and Stravinsky.

Returning from touring a batch of guests through his den, Del
noticed his brother slumped over in a chair. The thought of
Frank passed out for the night was a sad relief. But suddenly
Frank leapt up, ran outside, and returned in seconds with his
Malcolm, the uke. Jesus, his brother had been composing a song.
And he'd been too nice for too long.

Frank ripped *Hotel California* off the stereo, warded off angry
shouts with a steady hand, and silenced them all by announcing,
"This song's for *Wally*." Tottering a bit, as though his uke made
him top-heavy, Frank plinked the instrument—which had the
silly tone of a child's toy piano—and sang. The melody was
roughly that of "On Top of Ol' Smokey."

> Wally's a doll-ee,
> He do what he please,
> Ol Wally's a doll-ee,
> He do what he please.

Most everyone, Del was relieved to see, was smiling, a little
thrilled by the song's cute raciness.

> He's clean and he's fussy,
> He dress in pastel,
> If he was a Cath'lic,
> He'd be damnèd to Hell.

Half the smiles disappeared. But many, mostly gay, smiled
wider, appreciative. They liked it. But Del, knowing, put his
face in his hands. For Frank was glaring at Wally's friend
Melvin. His voice took a Jamaican turn, and the words sounded
reggae.

> He wake in da morning,
> Shit under he nails,
> Face glazed like a doughnut,
> He fun nebber fail.

The party was now divided in equal parts laughter, gasps, loud
offense, and silent offense. Del waited.

I sing for your birfday,
May youth nebber fade,
You get no mo' birfday,
If Mel's present be AIDS.

"That's *it*, my friend!" came big Melvin's shout. He reared up, but Del was in front of him before he got near. Others were standing too. The room had gotten so loud so suddenly that Frank had to shout the rest of his song. Someone had hold of his elbow, someone else was reaching around Del to slap at his shoulder, and Frank had great difficulty playing Malcolm.

You kneel like girl dog-ee,
You A-hole a mess,
You got no mo' sphincter,
You shit in yo' dress.

In the end no blood was spilled, surprisingly few enemies were made, and it was Wally Kenny who saved the day by announcing, in a tactful blend of sternness and humor, "I mean, this man Frankie Baal has to *live* with himself. My God, pity him!" Wally then gave Frank a wet comedy smooch on the cheek, and if people didn't laugh at that point at least they settled down. (The private glance Frank received along with the kiss was anything but tactful, however, and anything but friendly.)

Hotel California was soon bleating into the room again, and people regrouped into pockets of titters and drone. But wedges had been driven into the night: some were going for their coats; some, presenting coffee, nagged their spouses to sober up quick for they'd promised to drive; some were discussing taxi fares. On the other hand, some discussed ordering pizzas, and others, perhaps sensing more elbow room, began to drink and joke and party in earnest. Del was one of these, Mary another, but their reason for drinking so heavily differed from the rest: they drank because of each other, one guilty, one yearning.

Perhaps the oddest event of the night occurred when Fraser confronted Frank. Del had watched the two of them earlier, had seen how his brother was nervous around this handicapped boy, almost timid. His eyes became respectful and suspicious as a child's in church. Fraser, who was an odd sort of church, had replaced his ice cubes with dice, and these he rattled, stared at, and yawned.

This time Fraser appeared in front of Frank with a pillowcase pulled over his head. Frank didn't know what to do; he looked this way and that for escape routes, as though he were an agoraphobe and Fraser had turned into a mob.

"Hug me, Del! Hug me!" howled Fraser from under the pillowcase. He was yelling in baby talk.

"Uh, I'm Frank. Del's brother."

"Hug me, goddamnit!"

Frank leaned over and embraced the boy cautiously, not enjoying this at all. Del, who had just smoked some marijuana, which was for him a rare event, could not get straight what happened next. Rather, *why* what happened. Or how. Clearly, Frank had squeezed hardly at all. So had Fraser planned it? Was he a magician? For during Frank's embrace, Fraser's nose began to bleed, a flooding from both nostrils, and blood bloomed like crude roses on the pillowcase. Mary didn't look at Frank as she ran in to take control of Fraser and get him to the bathroom; she was stumbling now, and her face looked so overwhelmed by confusion it had become a resigned blank.

Del, in his own wobbling haze, decided that Fraser was an accidental genius. Or a neutral conduit of cosmic symbols. And he also decided—it was the last coherent thought he managed that night—that *everybody* was weird tonight. Mary looked so upset and frightened about . . . what? She avoided his eyes; when she did acknowledge him she was pathetic, shaking, birdlike. And Frank had a strange edge of sadness; he stayed untouchable, whereas usually in the span of a night's chuckles he and Frank would speak to each other as only they knew how to speak. It had begun so well, too, he and Wall and Mare watching football. Football, at least, had rules.

CHAPTER SEVEN

Frank's Party

'Tis the era of error.
'Tis the season of no reason.
—Felix d'Amboise

Things were weird enough without this Fraser freak. And how did these suburban parties persist? These aging disco-heads, these necrophiliac shindigs. It was okay seeing old pals, and Wally still had balls, but the rest . . . . Acting in love with life. Pretending the world was clean. Pretending they weren't dying and confused.

And Del. Around Mary, Del sprouted such little-kid hopeful eyes. Frank sometimes envied his brother's innocence, but around Mary that innocence knelt down and became something pathetic. *Christ*, Frank was tired of watching his brother stare moony-eyed at the wife. Del had a depressing gift for acting the sad goof who'd never been laid and wanted it so badly he moped for it. Del's goddamn gushiness. Del's goddamn *eyes*.

Frank's toe had been a blistering bitch all night. He sat by a pack of silly-drunk trivia players, watching Del stagger as he collected ashtrays. That was one sad, drunk, tall brother. He watched Mary do a desperate dance with someone. The little mink was trying to shake herself to death, pummel her nerves into ozone, go the brain-dead route. (Frank knew this urge himself.)

He would wait and see what happened next with them. She'd taken the news like a kick in the jaw, and it looked like she wasn't

about to own up to Del tonight. And the poor mink was shit-
scared that Frank was going to own up for her, and at any
moment. But that was not his plan.

All he'd said to her in the kitchen was, "Laura dances at the
Yale Pub too." That was it. Her face lurched, her eyes tried to
roll up into her head and stay there. Frank gave her nothing else—
no guilt-out stare, no sinister Frankie-smile for which he knew
he was famous, nothing. He went for the oysters in the fridge,
and Mary took off for the can.

And that was that. Frank planned no further move. He was a
neutral agent in this, a mere leaf in the wind. She'd started this
chain of dog shit and it was her choice to clean it up or get it
thrown in her face (Frank came upon the delightful image of Del
as an outraged Rototiller with long whirlwind arms spraying
bullets of dog shit at her). He laid no blame here. No, this was
clearly a case of, as fat Felix would say, causality of the bored and
selfish.

Frank sipped someone's scotch. He wanted to bolt but didn't
know where he would go. He didn't feel drawn to Laura tonight,
he'd seen her this afternoon, gotten his ya-ya's out, and that was
that. Anyway, he couldn't show up drunk at her place in the
middle of the night. She was not pleased being de-invited to this
party, though she understood that it was a messy family business
and one that her presence might mess up yet more. So, peeved,
she naturally had to get her digs in. "I see you once a month—
maybe. I take a Saturday night off but then I can't spend it with
you. I quit the good money because you want me to, but how am I
going to get my studio going? And meanwhile I'm not supposed
to see anybody else? That's ridiculous."

"I know," Frank said.

"Well, what do you expect me to do?"

"Do what you want."

Frank knew he had to talk that way, cool and a little mean, or
she'd be gone. That was the stark truth of romance. But he felt
that way in any case—cool and a little mean—because, hell, life
was enough of a draggy maze without taking on the complica-
tions of a partner. Did he want one? Sometimes, in bouts of

loneliness, or until he got the ya-ya's out. But alone he was *simply* depressed, *simply* happy. Putting two people together was to add shit onto shit. It was not so much a case of the blind leading the blind as it was the blind briefly fucking the blind, and the rest of the time the blind fighting the blind.

As Frank pondered Mary and Del, Laura, and women, the great hook of his face appeared to be darkening and sharpening itself. He had to get out of there. Go for a drive and buy some cigarets. Tonight was a perfect night to take up smoking again.

Pockets of people shouted over the treble puke-sound of Del Shannon's "Runaway," and Frank had to penetrate one of these pockets to get to his uke. He brushed by a small man who complained that he'd had his chesterfield recovered *three times* before it fit his room's decor.

"You should try a dirt-floor tent sometime," Frank said out of the side of his face. "Might learn something."

The fellow said nothing.

"Might redecorate your head," Frank added, picking up his uke. He hated not only those with fat egos, but also those with egos so slender they let themselves fall into stereotypes. Frank shot Wally Kenny an I-told-you-so look and kept walking. Wally'd had the slyest jump shot he'd seen outside of pro ball. He could have been a star in Italy.

Looking for his brother, Frank poked his head in the den to find Fraser spread-eagled on the floor beside that ugly dog Northam, a blanket twisted around them both. Frank found Del in his bedroom, out for the night. He didn't look at his brother long, not caring to see his face like that. That is, in sleep.

The air outside smelled good and sparked away some of Frank's haze. But he still wanted cigarets. He threw Malcolm and the leech costume in beside the salmon—he'd have to dump the damned fish on someone else. Revving the engine, Frank admired the classy pig's dashboard and its muted electronic display, so different from an old wooden boat's.

The passenger door opened and Mary fell in beside him.

"God, I been sick," she said, not looking at him.

Frank stared straight ahead. He sighed loud and long and put his hands up on the wheel. Mary rocked her head slowly back and forth, like a small elephant. She fought to keep her eyes open.

"We ga' talk. Drife somewhere, 'kay?"

Frank didn't move.

"Frank, ish 'e a saint, or wha'? Frank, jus' drife, okay?"

So Frank drove, burning a little rubber on the Baal driveway. They drove for perhaps a mile in silence before Frank said, "I'm just going for some smokes." But when he looked across he saw that Mary was asleep, the crown of her skull pressed into the window as if bolted to it.

So he drove. And suddenly he wanted more than cigarets. He wanted to see downtown on a weekend night—the lights, the drunks, the hookers, the weirdos—that of which Pender Harbour deprived him. So it was a surprise to him when, after buying smokes, nearing the entrance to the freeway south, he cranked the wheel hard left, made the ramp, and stomped the Buick's heavy pedal to the floor. Suddenly he was zooming south toward Washington State under freeway lights that zipped overhead in time to his eighty-per. Frank laughed, shook his head, and reached under the seat for a fresh bottle of sake.

It attested to Del and Mary's marriage, and the image they projected as a couple, that though he was asleep and she was gone, the party continued. It attested to Del's fellowship that someone before leaving wrote with Mary's lipstick on the bathroom mirror: *Del, we'll be watching you on TV next weekend*! And it attested to Mary's generosity that the fridge was raided without guilt, and food cooked and eaten. But, drunk as people were, the dishes got washed and put away, which perhaps attested to the silent side of Mary that few dared take for granted. And, attesting to the Baal house itself, or something that the walls exuded, the odd young man Fraser slept the first safe and peaceful sleep he'd had in years, though his bedding was a den floor, a stained blanket, and a dirty dog.

Frank loved driving at night, nothing visible but his own head-
lights flooding into absolute black. It was a lonely act, but it had
the vitality of motion and the romance of fate.

He thought of nothing in particular. Not of Mary, not of Del
nor Laura, and certainly not of why he was driving, or where he
might stop. Perfectly relaxed, his mind grew wide as the night;
thoughts and images danced through his awareness like fish
through a moonbeam in a deep black lake. He thought briefly and
fondly of other night travelers: Kerouac, Céline, and Poe. He
was excited, he was in love with the sake he swilled with
romantic abandon, his spine rang with that sleek silver light that
hides in the soul of nights—that sneaky light hidden in the heart
of tar, that light stored within the darkest grapes, that light
flashing mutely inside a black raisin.

He saw the ghosts of antelope shoot out from the roadside; he
saw silhouettes of bowler hats coming at him in headlight glare;
he let a cigaret burn down into his fingers to see what pain was
like at this time of night; he made up a song about deformed
babies, which began, "Lots of little nippers, with naught but
rubb'ry flippers, no wedding rings have they"; he challenged the
border guard with a lie and a daring eye; his throat was raw from
smoking so much so soon, and he gargled a mouthful of sake then
spit it out through the open window except the window had only
looked open and everything spattered all over the place. When
he giggled insanely, the car swerving, Mary coughed and
moaned beside him and Frank remembered where he was and
what he was doing. But soon Mary was snoring again, and once
more Frank's mind went wide.

He stopped for gas just north of Seattle and used the toilet,
peeing in a trough shoulder to shoulder with a fat trucker. Frank
smelled of booze but was under perfect control, macho and tall.
Frank knew the trucker liked him because of this. Frank loved
the States. Their cigarets were harsh, their politics were loud
and blind. What wonderful naiveté: because they were the
toughest kid in class, they didn't need to get to know the other

kids. The tough kid in the other class—Russia—they hated
through rumor alone. They bumped shoulders in the hall whenever possible, but they wisely avoided each other at recess. Frank
decided there in the gas station toilet that he himself was more
American than Canadian.

When he returned from paying, Mary was sprawled in the
back seat, snoring a woman's snore. The uke was tangled in her
feet (Frank moved it) and the salmon lay alongside her leg. Her
skirt had traveled up her thigh and her panties showed white and
were edged with several blatant hairs. Her thigh looked like the
salmon's earthly cousin: muscular, smooth, thick. Frank felt a
certain swelling, sat and considered the meaning of this swelling
and its possible consequences, then kicked back his head and
laughed. Over the next few miles he found himself voicing cheap
story lines:

"He turned suddenly off onto the dirt road, parked, and
fucked his brother's wife. He fucked her hard and she wanted
it."

"Slowly his hand worked its way under her panties and into
her celestial pudding. She groaned her husband's name, then saw
it was Frankie, and she groaned *his* name louder."

"He licked his sister-in-law full on the face and then punched
her lights out. He fucked her in a ditch, and when he was done he
threw money on her tits and left her for the banditos."

"The tall, mysterious gentleman casually plucked off his leech
costume and said, 'I *am* the ambassador.' She wanted it more than
ever now, and it was more than she could bear to gaze, unfucked,
upon his stately sequoia."

Frank screeched laughter at the end of each of these and
thought up some more before he tired of them. He recognized
that his mind was sharp as a razor and at the same time sick as a
bad clam. He knew too that because of the huge quantity of
alcohol he'd consumed over the past days, the huge quantity he
consumed tonight was making him not so much drunk as crazy.
There was a technical name for the chemical condition he was in
but (as he reached for a new bottle of sake) he could not
remember it.

What a thing it would be to screw his brother's wife. He would never be excused for such a deed, not for all of eternity, not by Satan himself. His brother, the saint. Del, Mr. Goodwill, warm as bathwater, cozy as cupcakes. If there was a God, he was on Del's side, and Del would inherit the earth. Frank shook his head, partly out of love, partly out of hate—he wasn't clear on the proportions of each.

He couldn't cleanse his head of a picture of Del's face and its wide-eyed, benign concern for everything, like a Jesus freak in an airport. How many times, like tonight, had he seen his brother so woeful and yet so ready to break into that stupid joy of his! That pathetic guffawing joy that exploded on his face whenever anyone treated him *nicely*. Sometimes Frank expected this joy to take his brother crashing through the wall, to send him on a laughing freestyle swim across the lawn, trailing a yellow streak of joy-forced piss on the ground. The party would hear him out there, whooping with glad exhaustion, whooping kindly, calling to them with goofy warmth.

No one could dislike Del. And if Frank kept thinking about him, his toe stub would pop his shoe.

Connected to all of this, Frank considered now, was the fact of his kidnapping Mary and driving her to . . . where? They were now twenty miles north of the Oregon border. It was five-thirty in the morning and, yes, there was light on the eastern horizon, a purple, depressing light. Perhaps he and Mary were driving south into Oregon at five-thirty in the morning to figure something out about Del. Perhaps they would figure out whether it was in Del's best interest to be kept blind; or perhaps they would agree that it was time for Del to realize that his marriage was a great hole in the ground into which he would fall if he didn't wake up.

He would let the mink sleep some more and then he would talk with her. He was getting a little tired himself, and therefore drunk in a sloppier way. At the last stop he'd bought coffee, more smokes, and (being out of sake) a bottle of California red, and not only was his driving now swervy but he once dozed. He'd jerked awake when a bug the size of Jackie Gleason (as he described it

to himself) exploded on the windshield. A look over his shoulder
assured him she was still asleep. Her breath had the dead-tide
smell of stale wine, and the low rasp of her snore was a bit comic
for a woman so small. He cracked the window to clear the air and
possibly his head. Competing with his dozy drunkenness was
the first stabbing of hangover, like thistle behind the eyes.

He took another look at her. God, this was actually all very
funny. Everyone thought she was a saint too. Her mothering of
all those unfortunate retarded types. By night a stripper in a bar
where mechanics yelled and drooled, eyes clinging to her pussy
and nothing else. What a weird minky woman. Frank laughed
again, and it was not unsympathetic. She was as selfish as the
best.

Mary woke to a disturbing set of circumstances. It was six in the
morning in Oregon, she lay in the back seat of a rented Buick
idling on a dirt road, and her brother-in-law was rapping the
bottom of her jaw with a knuckle.

With Mary coughing and snorting in sleepy disbelief, Frank
circled them back to the freeway, headed north, and when they
passed the sign saying Welcome to Washington, Mary laid her
head on the dash and moaned, "We *were* in Oregon."

"No stores were open," Frank said. But Mary's look indicated
that she neither got the joke nor remembered how the drive
began.

"Oh, God," Mary groaned, her head back on the dash. "I
don't know anymore." She fell quiet then, and her body went
tense. She said, "Frank, what happened last night? Did we—you
and me—"

"You mean you don't remember?"

"*Frank?*"

"I have to tell you you were great. The best fucking sister-in-
law I ever screwed." Frank looked over at her and shook his
head, sneering. "No, we didn't. What do you think I am?" He
paused. "I thought of it, but I think lots of things." He paused
again. "And what do you think *you* are?"

"That's . . . sort of my problem, these days."

They stopped for coffees-to-go. Mary returned from the toilet with hair combed and face washed. This morning she looked much older than she was, and Frank saw on her face the beginnings of wrinkles that would deepen and go with her to the grave.

They resumed the drive north. Frank cleared a phlegmy throat.

"Okay. I have some questions that—"

"What time will we get back?"

"Eleven. Twelve."

"Maybe Del'll be asleep. Maybe Fraser will be too."

"Maybe. I have some questions. I don't want to torture you, but I have some questions."

When Frank asked Mary if she still loved his brother, she said "Sure." When he asked her if she'd sold her body for money, she said "No." When he asked if she was going to tell Del about her stripping, she said "I don't know." And when he asked if she planned to continue her secret little life she said, "I don't know what I'm going to do. I might do anything."

Then Mary asked Frank a question.

"Are you going to tell Del any of this?"

"No. Everything's up to you."

Mary stared out at the rushing, rather boring scenery. Then said, "Well. Okay. Can I tell you everthing, then? You know Del, you know me too, in a way. It's funny we've never talked much. Because maybe you'll understand."

Mary studied Frank in a way that showed this idea was new to her, but that it made sense. And Frank, sharing this short stare with her, knew he hadn't seen these particular eyes before. Though devoid of cheer they were not devoid of humor. They looked almost wise. He thought of smooth stones under water. There was no guilt in her eyes at all.

Frank nodded.

"Well then, here's what it's been like."

Mary talked for an hour, perhaps two. Frank listened and drove. He nodded at times, and sometimes his stare was grim. He

sipped wine, but only enough to keep his hangover from swelling and settling to the jagged state. As he listened, his toe stub
was sort of hurting, sort of not.

Mary described her life with Del. She described his heart, his
joy, his goodness. She told of her slow decline into boredom
with him, and how her discovery that she needed adventure in
her life had caused her great guilt. But she had "seen through"
her guilt. Lately she had had several affairs. Nothing lasting, but
with the oddest men. "Spicy men," she called them. She had had
a brief lesbian affair with Ruth, her dance teacher. Ruth was also
a stripper, and it was on Ruth's dare that Mary first tried the
stage. The naked stage, so to speak.

"It was *fantastic*," she declared to the window. Then, to him:
"Frank, you know me well enough to know that it's against
everything I ever believed in. Stripping! Strip *tease*. I mean,
really. Men staring at your tits. All of that disgusted me, all my
life. And it *still does*. That's the point, I think." Mary fell silent,
considering.

She took up Frank's bottle and sipped from it, twice. Then,
finding words, she grew excited and began to gesture with her
arms. "When I first did it, it was like stepping off a cliff. It was
like being in outer space. It began as a dare, a joke, and suddenly
it became a *huge* joke. An inside joke that . . . reality and I were
playing with each other." She paused again. "It's like going
insane and then being able to come back. It's like I can see
everything about myself when I'm up there. Taking my *clothes*
off. I mean, *think* about it! You're in this huge, outrageous joke.
You feel your body, naked. You feel disgust, like a voice yelling
at you, but you're in the joke, you can't stop. You just dive. It's
like . . . free-fall. Your sweat is like ice on you. You feel the men
in the room, they're just sort of *eating* you. You hear their voices,
you hear your own breathing, fast, like you're sprinting. It's
wild. You can hear your cartilage pop when you flex into each
disgusting move. God, Frank, when I finished and left the stage
that first time I was crying and laughing, all at once."

Mary's outburst had drained her, and now her eyes settled back to the dashboard of Frank's rented car. "So I don't know what to believe anymore. About goodness. Or . . . spice."

"Or Del," Frank added.

Mary nodded slowly, closing her eyes. "But I don't want to leave him. I don't want him to leave me. Because I don't feel *bad* about doing what I've been doing—the affairs, any of it. But I feel like *shit* lying like I do. I'd love him to go and find excitement too, but he won't. He doesn't want to. He's excited enough . . . at home."

Mary smiled and lightly embraced herself. "And I *don't know*. Because sometimes when I go to him it's the best spice of all. You know? His goodness."

"Sure. Why not," Frank said.

"But usually it's like living with . . . your brother."

"Right."

Mary hooted and put a hand on Frank's arm. "I mean *one's* brother."

"I knew what you meant."

Extremely tired now, Frank didn't know what to think. This mink was no simple bitch. Nor was she entirely forgivable either. But he knew too well the niggling concepts she fretted over: goodness, morality. Frank used to play with them himself. He remembered how they shrieked, then withered, in the presence of spice, easy danger, and lust for vertigo.

Frank sat and mused on all of this. In the meandering sludge of his thoughts he pictured women in general. Images of Mary, images of Laura. Laura, so casual, so natural in her immorality, and trying now to be good. Then Mary, who was basically good, exploring immorality. Laura boring, Mary daring. And it occurred to him—a kind of tired surprise—that he might have done better with someone like Mary. Better, in any case, than Del. Mary fell into that class of smart woman who had the balls to explore her passions absolutely. Like nuns. Hookers, strippers, degenerates (the smart ones) were all like nuns. Nuns, though, were onto a safe route, whether they goddamn knew it or not. No one, even in this modern godless age, ever really *sneered* at nuns. Strippers and hookers, though, these jammy gals went through each day as the targets of society's rotten tomatoes, and yet they carried on.

Pretty hard on a husband, however.

In response to Mary's long story, Frank managed to offer up only this:

"Good and bad are stupid, small little words, I agree."

He was nodding on the edge of sleep, so he stopped sipping wine, no longer knowing which way it would take him. Mary offered to drive, but he refused.

"But you're falling asleep, Frank."

"We'll make it."

"Here. This will help."

Mary reached across and laid her hand on Frank's crotch.

Frank jerked up, instantly awake. He looked at her. Mary wore an inscrutable smile, and there was humor in her eyes.

He turned his face to the road. He did not bat the hand away. And, yes, he grew quickly hard. Del had a beautiful wife. She was . . . *a mink*. And so much more beautiful now, to Frank, because she had used surprise.

His mind, his poor booze- and fatigue-ravaged mind, reeled with possibilities. He was hard, he was horny with the astonishing *dirt* of this. Del's wife. Del, whom he cared about. He didn't care about anything else but Del. This was his spicy chance to not care about *anything* anymore.

Mary caressed him, the lightest touch, a maddening feather.

And Frank felt a sudden physical gap between his ears, a shocking *pe-twang* as of a snapping ukulele wire. He recognized this to be the shock of him dooming himself. He knew that if he carried on with this act, a doom-dread metronome would *tock-tock* in his head forever, would count off the foul moments of his days until he died.

"That's the kind of excitement I mean, Frank."

Mary had taken her hand away. It had been on his lap perhaps five or six seconds. Mary was no longer smiling.

Frank sat up straight and was awake the rest of the way. His mind and his penis were outraged, each for different reasons.

Mary's hand rested chastely on her own knee, and it was as though the bitch's hand was on a Bible. The mink had given him a lesson. The bitch had tested him.

They didn't speak the rest of the way. Frank ran out of money and Mary had none, so he had to barter the salmon for gas at a station in Bellingham. The owner had a scale in the back; he weighed the fish, paid Frank the market rate, and subtracted a 20 percent profit for himself. Frank liked people like that, people who were public with their greed.

Del and Fraser were asleep when they arrived. Mary threw a blanket on the couch and rumpled it to look slept in. Frank got five Aspirins from her and drove off, somewhere.

CHAPTER EIGHT

The Decoy

*Life is made up of two things only: Purpose and
Distraction. Life's Purpose, which is to achieve
resolution of a series of tasks given us, meets head-on
with Distraction, a force that allows constant
avoidance. We may owe a million dollars, we may also
have cancer, and yet life's movie—a rush of images
that is as colorful and as inane as a Donald Duck
cartoon feature—lets us forget. Thus 99 percent of
people (or those who lack a body-lens) are distracted.*
                                        —Felix d'Amboise

Few of the 37,364 people in Toronto's SkyDome paid much
attention to the five tiny humans standing way out in center
field. And hardly any of the thousands more who watched on
TV—except for Mary Baal, who watched at home; Frank, who
watched from a Pender Harbour bar; and Wally Kenny, who
watched from a scowling Melvin's bed—paid these five much
mind.

Up close, they weren't tiny. At six five, Del was not the tallest.
And the four who huddled around him—two in blue uniforms,
two in red—wore such outrageous false shoulders that Del was
rendered painfully skinny as well.

"You call it, Blue," Del said in his most authoritarian growl.

"Head," whispered a near-feminine voice from inside a blue
helmet. Del knew Toronto's co-captain, Lazlo his name was, to

be the meanest free safety in the league, and as so often was the case, only the meanest kept their helmets on for the coin-toss. They probably liked to be thought of as machines, faceless. And it was funny how everyone said "head" now, instead of the plural. A few years ago, only blacks said "head."

Del thumbed the dollar loon high and it sparkled bronze in the autumn sun as it flipped over on itself then landed, heads.

"We kick," whispered Lazlo.

Del cleared his throat and clicked on his hip-mike for the first time this season.

"Toronto wins toss, elects to kick off. Visiting team to receive." Some half a second after having said them, his words boomed back at him. The voice satisfied him, for it sounded deep, fatherly, and unbiased, the somewhat bored voice of an overseer, not a participant. Del had practiced and honed this tone for hours. It was Del's own little tradition to leave Calgary nameless—his one concession to the home team. From now on it was blue jerseys against red jerseys, and neither the boos and cheers of fans nor the complaints and pleas of players would crowd his eyes as they penetrated the tangle of arms and legs to catch those taking liberties with the rules.

Calgary quickly worked up a 17-3 score. And though Toronto's fans were brutal to referees, today's game would be easy. For again Toronto had a weak team, its only entertaining feature a rough defense. And, sharing the coaches' belief that if any team had the bad manners to beat you it damn well had to pay the price, the fans actually rejoiced when Toronto committed late hits, unnecessary roughness, or mauling the quarterback. So for Del it became a task of trying to help Calgary escape with their victory and a minimum of cheap injuries. He got into trouble with the fans just once, when he ejected Lazlo from the game for starting a fight. They booed long and loud, and erupted again the next time he tried to use his hip-mike, but they were just having fun. They loved it that Lazlo had saved their collective face by punching someone else's. (And once more Del marveled—it was an emotion tinged with disgust at the human race—how the illusion of a "home" team so completely seduced

fans. In fact, Calgary had three Toronto-born players, and
Toronto had but two. They each had a scatter of men from all
parts of Canada, and the majority of the biggest and best were of
course from the States. Lazlo was a white cracker from Georgia.
The black rookie he'd slugged—J.P. Grimes—was a big-eyed
Florida boy. But they roared as if Lazlo were a street kid re-
cruited from an alley in Leaside and Grimes were a redneck
rancher from the foothills of Alberta.)

Within minutes of the opening whistle, Del had easily slid
into the technique he called spacious instinct. Those first couple
of years he'd had to learn how to do this, how to let his eyes relax,
his vision widen enough to include both the central action and
the periphery. He had to watch not only for the fumble but also
for that infraction downfield, that red arm reaching out and
grabbing that blue jersey. And then, faster than thought, his hand
would have the fluorescent flag out of his back pocket and
thrown. It was only after play stopped, when he'd conferred
with the other refs and then snapped his mike on to say, "Defensive intereference, number forty-five, fifteen-yard penalty, first
down repeated," that what he'd seen reached the level of rational
explanation. No, his real job was instinct. It was a job of clear
eyes and relaxed mind.

So it was important to maintain that relaxed mind even between plays, to listen neither to complaints nor to boos. To
achieve this, Del let his mind wander. Last year, his thoughts had
often turned to the book he was still planning to write. It was
going to be a great book, a book that would appeal to sports fans
and intellectuals alike. He had consulted Felix on several possible titles, the choice of which depended on how the book took
shape. One, *The Whistle in the Eye*, would suit a book that
focused on the psychology of the job, the split-second transfer of
eye-information to an act of instant judgment. If this tack got a
bit mystical, a bit poetic, it would be called *Zen and the Art of
Arbitration* (and Del had located some haiku he could include, as
they seemed somehow to relate). *The Gridiron Solomon* would be
right if the book took the more traditional form of a series of
insightful anecdotes.

Today, when his mind wandered (by halftime the score was 24–6, so it wandered easily) it moved to the events of the past week. His wheezing body, for one, reminded him constantly of last weekend's party. He hadn't remembered even going to bed. He'd awoken crucially hung over, and Mary had greeted him sleepy-eyed from the couch. Leaving Fraser to make toast (the poor guy had burned a whole loaf of raisin bread), they'd retreated to the bedroom on Mary's suggestion and made wild, painful, grunting love. She'd laughed throughout, and afterwards cried. Then laughed again, shaking her head. She held him like a baby, and cooed. Del was excited by all of this, and touched, and worried by her explosive mood, her swing into craziness. She reminded him of Frank, when he was overtired, punch-drunk, and confused. And then she'd slept away the whole afternoon. When she awoke it was as if nothing had happened: she'd erased the morning's passions and was frosty to him again.

Then the week began. They didn't say much to each other about *it* (their impasse had achieved the looming stature of an "It" in Del's mind), what with Del taking part in the last preseason ref clinic and Mary busying herself with Fraser's plight. Fraser stayed with them until Tuesday, when he was taken to a halfway house in Burnaby, where his future was to be assessed. On Tuesday night Mary ventured a terse "Be patient with me, Del, it's a difficult time." On Wednesday night Del tried his own "Mare, let's just be kind." On Thursday Mary, smiling, said, "Why don't you be kind to both of us and just chop my head off?" This resurgence of humor, black or not, Del took as a huge step in the right direction.

The minute flag was up, so Del let pass two straight holding calls. The game had turned sloppy, even for this early in the season: with the score 32–12, both teams had their rookies and subs in and each play was an overeager mess. Tired veterans went through their paces, sidestepping injury, waiting for the gun.

Oh, he hated games that fell to this. The clutching, the grabbing, each play a showcase for the gray areas of the rules. It was a time when the best players were hindered by the shoddy, when the Lazlos could punch the Grimeses and get away with it.

Del knew he'd catch it from Head Official Tuck for kicking Lazlo out of the game. In his capacity as head, Tuck could not say to him plainly, "Bend the rules, boy," or, "Lazlo is Toronto's hero, you idiot. You don't kick out the hero," or, "Attendance and TV revenue keeps the league barely alive and pays your salary. Lazlo's worth five thousand fans a game and at least one corporate sponsor. You idiot." Instead he would use a bureaucrat's innuendo—that is, lie—and say, "I don't think Lazlo's expulsion was warranted, young fellow. From where I sat, it was more an elbow than a true punch. Young fellow." He would always repeat "young fellow," this expression being rich in rebuke and warning. It was nothing to Tuck to pretend he hadn't seen what everyone else in the stands saw clearly, and loved: Lazlo landing at least two savage uppercuts. He, the head official, who was supposed to be Mr. Eagle Eye himself, would call it an elbow. "From where I sat" took on a rich meaning too: there was a hierarchy in the excercising of rules.

Del hated Tuck and Tuck hated Del, who perhaps made the older man feel guilty. That's what Del liked to think. In any case, they fought constantly over rules.

"You tryin' to change the game of football, young fellow?" This would punctuate their more fierce arguments, his tone suggesting that Del had vandalized a statue of Christ with a chisel. Tuck was fiftyish but reminded Del of a pugnacious baby. Seeing his picture in a group shot at Del's once, Frank had said of him, not knowing who he was, "This guy looks like he makes his kids go *bowling* with him."

The fact was—though Mary was unaware of this—in his brief career Del had received two official letters of reprimand from Tuck, both for the crime of "frequent on-field judgments of a questionable nature." Three such letters were grounds for suspension. Del knew that Tuck would love to fire him if he could.

Del told himself he knew what he was doing. He knew he had the best eyes in the league and arguably the most exact knowledge of the rules. And Del loved these rules: not so much the individual rules, which were, after all, arbitrary and man-made, but the rules in general, and his feelings for them were much like a scientist's for chromosomes, or a duke's for his ancestral lineage.

Even children saw the need for rules. Though their spontaneous backyard games were breeding grounds for bullies and bosses, and though their rules were changed every minute on a whim and with a shout, even they saw that without structure their game would be no game at all, but chaos turning over on itself. In rules there was the chance, the slim chance, for purity.

One could see it in hockey. A local sportswriter friend of Del's had labored with his calculator and rule book and concluded that in modern pro hockey an uncalled infraction took place on the average of every twelve seconds. According to the book, a player could not impede another skater's progress unless that skater had the puck, and yet interference—with stick, hip, a grabbing hand—had become part of the game. According to the book, a player could not contact another while carrying his stick above shoulder height, and yet it was now rare to see such a clean check. And who had allowed this? Certainly it was the players who had over the years strained and pushed at these rules and bent them all out of shape, but it was the referees who had allowed the bending.

And so with football. The rules were exact, and clearly written. Holding, offside, offensive procedure—a child could understand these rules. And so why did refs allow such bending? And why did Tuck demand it? For "expediency." Del called it laziness. To allow "interpretation." Del called it error. And why, unless they were afraid of being judged by the unerring light of stark truth and purity, had the Referees' Association continually vetoed the use of instant TV replays to aid them in making a call?

Del had lobbied, he'd written letters, he'd called meetings, all under Tuck's angry eye. He'd tried two experiments—for which he'd received the two letters—in two games, both preseason contests, where he'd tried to perform flawless arbitration. His iron hand (iron whistle, iron flag) had resulted in hard-fought,

low-scoring games, where brawn and honest will won out over
trickery. And Tuck had assailed him after both games. "Young
fellow. That was boring football. There were only sixteen first
downs. You tryin' to change the game of foootball?"

I'm trying to *save* the game of football, was what Del wanted
to say.

And so came the letters, which Del took to be sanctions of the
breakdown of rules. An official stamp authorizing chaos. The
letters depressed him utterly, for he saw them to be larger than
his career, larger than football. They were harbingers of purity's
final gasp. For if you could no longer find rules in a game, where
could you find them? In 1989 Del could see the small victories of
chaos everywhere: in society, in law, in the family, and in the
way a modern woman confronted a modern man, in marriage.
Laziness, mistruths, gray areas. The rule book lay somewhere
out there in society's garage, lost between the firewood and the
Hula-Hoops.

But Tuck didn't accost him after this game, which meant Del
had again succeeded in his dangerous straddling of his own rules
and the league's. He showered slowly, and with a blast of cold
water he shocked the general Toronto malaise and mugginess
out of his system. Though he'd allowed chaos at the end, he'd
worked a good enough game, and had walked off the field and in
through the tunnel with head high and his face properly and
professionally bored. A pack of groupies—tall, short, black,
white, pretty, plain, but all with the same vacant eyes—stood like
weeds outside Toronto's dressing room. One of them gave Del a
second look. She had Mary's height and hair, and even something of her unintentional sauciness. But she was not very good
looking, despite her youth. What was going on in her mind?
Was a referee a sexual prize simply because he had been on the
field with the football players? Was he a father figure? Was it
because he'd been on TV, his voice booming throughout the
stadium? Was it a strange new kink for her drug-bored days?
Wouldn't that be something if refs became the next hot item!
Del imagined himself wading like a striped stork through
throngs of budding-breasted young things, fearing for his

clothes, his chastity. The fatherly arbitrator as sex-god. This of course would mean that not only referees but also game-show hosts, news anchormen, high-school vice-principals, and the like would now have more young gals than they knew what to do with.

As was often the case, Del's imaginings of this subject caused stirrings in his nether zone. There were six others in the shower with him, all refs, so Del crouched over a bit and spider-walked his way out. He passed a cubicle, hesitated a moment, located the barest trace of an urge, then went in.

But sitting there on the toilet he felt instantly foolish. He stared down at his penis, shrunken back now by the porcelain and metal sterility of the cubicle. He pinched a fold of skin between thumb and forefinger and wiggled it: it flipped like an absurd, goofy little thing, as dumb as rubber, as primitive a creation as a clam neck. His scurries to masturbate had become so habitual, and lately so unrewarding. And he could no longer simply blame Mary. No, he knew that, like a boy, he was using it to relieve life's pressures, as of loneliness or acne. And once again Del blushed deeply, recalling the events of Friday afternoon.

After showering and packing for this Toronto trip, he'd had a couple of hours to kill before Mary got back from work. He'd imagined a (possibly) congenial and (hopefully) romantic dinner and then she would drive him to the airport. Turning on the tiny black-and-white TV they'd let Fraser use all week, he stretched full length on the couch, his head propped on an armrest. A seniors' golf tournament was on. The screen was indeed tiny (how did myopic Fraser watch it?), so Del plucked up the TV and placed it right onto his chest. The day was hot and he wore nothing but his undershorts. The match was boring, his mind wandered; he must have been absentmindly fooling with himself there behind the TV, for suddenly he was hard. And then his shorts were down and he was masturbating. He began by watching the golfers treading calmly around the greens, but decided such a fantasy-object was just a tad too perverted. So he closed his eyes and pictured first a rainstorm catching a dozen young

Dutch girls at play and forcing them into a warm, dark barn; then his vision became one of a single Arabian breast, the wonderful curve of it. He wasn't sure what "Arabian" meant exactly, but the word played a large part, and the breast was tawny and the tiny ebony nipple tasted of tangerine.

He hadn't heard Mary come in. At the closing of the door he bucked in shock and the TV leapt an inch off his chest. What a sight he must have made! His straining face propped toward a TV golf game, behind the TV his hand madly pumping; then his struggle to get his undershorts up, his whole body going crimson, his attempt to do the impossible: that is, to pretend he hadn't been caught masturbating.

But Mary's reaction had been the biggest surprise of all. "You're so *ridiculous*!" she'd cried. She was smiling. Then laughing. Then hugging him. "You're . . . *great*," she whispered, giggling in his ear, laughing *with* him, genuinely pleased, and Del managed to squeeze his red face into a smile for her. They made love then, for the second time that week, and as on the hung over Sunday, Mary was wild, and by turns laughing and upset.

So she *liked* it that he did such things. She'd been so excited, not because she'd caught him but because he was capable of doing something "ridiculous." What an odd thing to want in a husband. He'd been spending his last ten years trying *not* to act ridiculous in front of her. So did she in fact want a clown? A gargoyle? This fight of theirs, this impasse, whatever it was, had forced on him glimpses of an unknown Mary.

Del finished dressing and gave a high-five (this gesture they'd borrowed from the players, and it too had started with the blacks) to the other fellows, some of whom he'd see at next weekend's Winnipeg game. He would have loved to join them for postgame beers (another ritual taken from the teams), but he had to catch the next flight to be on time for Mary's father's birthday party—his sixty-fifth. He enjoyed going to the Millers', perhaps because Mary got along with them so poorly. At her parents', Del became Mary's confidant, her strength, her shoulder, at the same time becoming the Millers' sole bridge to their only child.

It was funny how things repeated themselves. If life didn't follow cycles, it at least hinted at patterns. Exactly five years ago, for example, they had had a similar prolonged silent struggle. They had spoken of separating. Del could no longer recall what had started the fight, or why it had continued for as long as it did, but he did remember how Mary had been distracted from it: that Pope fiasco, that bizarre event. It had worked on Mary to make her forget the fight, or perhaps it made her see that marriage was a safe, sane haven after all. In any case, at one point she had wanted a separation, and then suddenly she did not. As now, there had been no discussion.

The Pope's visit. What conclusions could be drawn from *that* fight? Del, reclining as best he could in his second-class seat (his knees were tucked up a bit), soared a mile high over what looked like a Canadian wasteland and pictured the events of five years ago. The details were easy to recall, for as a whole they had something of the color of a Walt Disney cartoon.

Mary had just finished a night shift at the group home. She was new at the job and it drained her. And Del, having just that year been promoted from field judge to referee, had that morning returned from Ottawa, where he'd reffed his second professional game. Since both of them were so tired it probably wasn't a good idea to resume their fight—rather, their discussion about separation. Two nights before, it had seemed quite clear that Mary wanted one. Del was equally clear that he did not, and so he wanted this talk resumed.

Mary sat across the table holding up a newspaper barrier (the color comics; Mary never read the comics) like a parody of the bored, unresponsive husband. Del faced Peanuts's autumn kickoff. At the bottom of the page Charlie Brown was somersaulting onto his back again, Lucy having yanked away the football yet one more time. Lucy . . . Mary. There it was again: life supplying mirrors for any possible mood.

He would start things off lightly.

"Ahem." He tinked his egg dish with his spoon. "Ahem."

But the phone rang, and Mary hopped to answer it, slamming Charlie Brown, Lucy, Archie, Andy Capp, and the rest of them down with a significant amount of force.

"Oh, hi Mom!"

Chipper Mary. Amazing how they can turn themselves off and on. Del tried to hold down his own anger. She'd been working at her social work job two months now, and until this fight came along to yank the football away, he'd been looking forward to this free day together, picturing the two of them cruising up to Cypress Bowl, perhaps hitting a pub later that night, perhaps making leisurely love later still. He loved making love to her. After four years of marriage. And what could she possibly find wrong with that?

"Father's *what*?"

But she *would* find something wrong with it. And she'd made him angry with what she'd said two days ago. She was smiling when she said it. Perhaps it was her version of a joke. "When we got married," she said, "I was marrying a good man, and you were marrying a good fuck." Oh, that hurt. It implied that he was nothing but a shallow sex maniac. It simplified them so. It also implied that he was not a good fuck.

"Father's the decoy *what*? Mother, *get* serious."

She'd argued that they didn't communicate, that they hadn't developed as friends, and that Del didn't mind this as long as he had plenty of sex. And Del countered that they *were* great friends. They shared the smallest details of living, they accepted each other's social tics, acted as each other's smiling critic, and so on. Hadn't sex broken the barriers to all that? Opened the hidden doors? And as for the notion—was it a feminist position lately discovered by Mary, was that it?—that men and women could truly mingle without the physical mingling, Del had no idea. But who could deny that, though the borderline was a bit hazy, women lived in one country and men another?

"They're at your house now?"

Del watched his wife. Some argument with her mother, and Del noticed again the transformation she underwent when talking to her parents, her face pinching, petulant, a teenager again. Hand on hip. A near sneer. Sexy.

"That's-ridiculous-Mother-I-can't-believe-he'd-do-any-thing-so . . ."

A coltish teenette whining on the phone. The long black hair with its hint of henna, hair that almost graced the top of her ass. Delicious.

Maybe her complaint with him wasn't feminist at all, but stemmed from that insane adolescent urge to merge with a lover totally, impossibly. Maybe her heart had finally realized it had failed in this, and the urge had moved upwards to her head, found words, gone rational, gone cold. Mary, you shouldn't be thinking, you should be feeling. That's what women do so well, so why deny your gift? Maybe if you let me put my foot down a little more we'd—

"We're coming right over."

Del felt better in the car. More self-assured, in control. It might have had to do with the small space, the size of him, the size of her, the simple fact that he had the wheel. It would be a good time to continue their talk. Mary sat quietly erect, her hands folded in her lap like a child, eyes flitting at passing objects. But by the time Del had established his pose of cool driver, by the time he had confirmed his strategy and was about to speak, Mary turned to him.

"Del, drive faster, okay? You wouldn't believe what they're doing to Father."

Mary told him about her mother's call, and suddenly his marriage-plight was nudged aside by a fantastic tale. It all sounded unbelievable, and Del's questions sounded much like Mary's to her mother.

"Your father's going to be the decoy *what*?"

"The decoy Pope. They want father to be a bloody decoy Pope."

The Miller house, a modest pink bungalow, had its place along a row of other houses that differed only in color, but all falling into a careful range of pastel. Given this neighborhood, the two white limos parked nose to tail in front of the Millers' might as well have been a sign: Something Extraordinary Is Happening Here.

A dark man in a suit stood at the front door. He looked to be a kind of guard. Indeed, he said nothing as Mary and Del approached, and stepped in their path as Mary reached for the door.

"What—?" Mary stared at the man incredulously, and looked ready to lash out or cry. Del spoke up.

"We're the . . . this is Mr. Miller's daughter. I'm her husband. We came to—"

The door opened and Mary's mother leaned out and waved.

"Oh Mary, you came! Come in, come in! Hello, Del!" Mrs. Miller was hissing with glee. "They have your father in the bedroom. He'll be so glad. I'm making tea. Oh, it's all so strange." She had turned into the house and announced this to no one in particular. Mrs. Miller had a very long neck, and, while it usually reminded Del of a swan's, this afternoon it seemed to be bending in the wrong places, sideways and too quickly. Del and Mary followed her into the kitchen.

"Mother, this is too much." Mary's rage had not subsided after the door guard. Her mother poured tea.

"Oh, I know, dear, but don't be difficult. Please. I think your father's mind is made up."

"Made up? Does he even understand what's happening?"

"Oh, I think so, dear. He seems quite happy."

"Mother, that's not the same thing."

Mary ignored the proffered tea and left the kitchen. There soon followed an exchange of voices and several near-shouts. Mrs. Miller handed Del his tea, met his eyes, and slowly shook her head. The neck was graceful again. It looked as though Mrs. Miller considered this eye contact charged with a shared understanding, but Del felt only more awkward.

"She used to get so mad, that girl. Only it was never at the . . . right person."

Del nodded for her.

"I mean, if she was mad at somebody at school she'd come home and yell at her father. Or me. Then she would close up and nobody would know what to do."

Del's nod was brief and stilted this time, for he was a little shocked to hear his own dilemma with Mary so accurately summed up. But of course Mrs. Miller knew Mary too. He considered saying something to her about him and Mary. He kept quiet, though, sipped his tea and moved his eyes as if to see the voices that echoed from down the hall.

Del hadn't known Mary's father for long before the stroke. Even so, to Del's mind the stroke didn't seem to have changed him much: he'd always been shy and quiet, he'd never stood out from the furniture. Del and Mary would seat themselves to begin a Sunday visit, Del and Mr. Miller would trade last night's hockey scores and that would be that, the night's one concession to manliness. Otherwise the Miller household was a household of women: loud women's voices, a woman's obvious and well-meaning humor, decor that showed a woman's taste and touch. And low-cal, salady stuff for dinner. (Mrs. Miller had from the start reminded Del of a stern, efficient waitress who by her strength of character alone deserved to own the restaurant.) At the Millers', Del always felt a bit shy about his height and booming voice.

Then the stroke, the hospital, Mr. Miller's convalescence. There was no paralysis, no loss of speech or sight. Perhaps his words came slower now, as if carefully considered. Yet, after a year had passed, Mary and her mother talked constantly about his "lack of progress." After two years, mother and daughter conceded to each other one day in tears (as Del sat up nervously) that "his progress had stalled." Mr. Miller wouldn't get any better.

Del found the whole affair strange. Aside from the usual creepings of age, the present Mr. Miller seemed little different. He still watched a lot of TV, not really watching. He still, as before, puttered the day away in his vegetable garden, pausing long moments to lean one hand on his rake and stare off at the distant North Shore mountains. When he finally moved, the birds that had settled around his silence would whirr off to safety. Del sometimes caught Mary watching her father sadly, and he'd try to tell her that there was nothing wrong with silence, nothing wrong with inactivity. For all they knew, Mr. Miller might be a very meditative man who simply kept things to himself, and what could be wrong with that?

Del tried telling Mary all of this—that little had changed—but she would consider for only a second before saying, "You didn't know my father." True enough, Del would say. What he didn't say was that he suspected Mary of harboring false memories. Idealized versions of the tawdry. It was so typical, everyone had false memories: the carefree childhood, the Aprils that bloomed so early, the pack of perfect friends, the magical trip to Europe, the Friday nights of fifty-cent gas and cars that ran for ever and played radio music that was actually good. And Mary had this one: a father she remembered as witty, deft, and in command.

Del was no psychologist, but it was plain as day to him that Mary idealized a former father so that she could feel more guilt. For Mary blamed herself from the start and called the stroke "my own damn fault." There'd been an argument between Mary and her mother, about birth control. Mr. Miller was with them, watching TV. After years of lying to her mother, tired of her prying, Mary had blurted out that she and Del had never tried for a child, that she was on the pill, that she didn't want any damn kids, that she didn't give a shit what the Church said about anything, and that she would have an abortion if she *did* get pregnant. Like many parent–child spats, Mary found herself exaggerating in anger. The fact was that at this time she was considering a child. But in any case, one of them happened to look over then to see Mr. Miller struggling silently in his chair, eyes bugging, unable to rise.

Del had long ago decided that Mary's guilt was identical to Frank's. Their mother, the loose balcony rail. Yes, his brother's and his wife's guilt was equally unvoiced, equally unwarranted, equally self-destructive. He had told Mary this, and though she said nothing she seemed to take it to her depths, considering.

He could hear her voice, loud again, down the hall. It was time to see to her. He excused himself from the kitchen, tiptoed down the hallway, and listened at a door. He heard nothing now, pushed his way in, and stopped, startled. Sitting meekly on his bed, and shirtless, Mr. Miller was staring into the darkness of a closet. A man who could have been the door guard's twin was measuring his shoulders and arms with tailor's tape and whispering numbers in Italian to another at his side, who scratched them down on a pad. A seamstress was already at work on a large white robe she had spread on her lap. Mary sat staring death at a man who held the room's central chair. She didn't break her stare as she spoke to Del from the side of her mouth.

"Come in, Del. Meet Mr. Rigletti."

The man smiled and appeared about to speak when Mary cut him off.

"Mr. Rigletti is in the Pope's security and he wants to—"

"*Liaison* for *foreign* security, madam," Mr. Rigletti broke in. He had a smooth voice and a smile so disarming Del couldn't decide if it could be trusted.

"—he wants to use Father as a target for crazies who think they're shooting the real Pope." Mary looked straight at Del now, and as she spoke her chin quivered and tears came. She pointed to her father. "And they've shaved his head like some . . . death row . . . electric chair . . . *victim*." She began to sob. Mr. Miller made to look at her, but turned quickly back when he felt the Italian's tape measure touch his neck.

Mr. Rigletti rose and said, "Perhaps the three of us should go to another room and talk."

They settled in the living room. Mrs. Miller delivered tea, moving and disappearing quickly like an efficient waitress serving a business lunch.

For some time no one spoke. Rigletti sat with a professional blend of gravity and grace, and, watching, Del realized suddenly that he was a dead ringer for Ricardo Montalban. It was Mary who broke the silence.

"May I ask you a question, Mr. Rigletti?"

"Of course." He said this as though the word "child" were tacked on at the end, priestlike.

"Are you a Christian, Mr. Rigletti?"

"Catholic. Of course." His voice had the texture of plums rolling slowly in syrup. Strangely enough, Del decided that this was the voice of a man who could be trusted more than not.

"So please tell me then," Mary continued, "if, according to your belief, it would be of less . . . importance . . . if my father were killed instead of the Pope?"

"Yes," Mr. Rigletti said without hesitation. "It would be of less importance. That is my opinion. It is theologically an interesting point. Practically speaking, however, it is common sense. Though no one speaks of these things, it is a fact that even here in your quiet country there are men trained and willing to throw their bodies in front of your prime minister in case of—"

"Mr. Rigletti, is my father in danger? Has there been a threat on the Pope's life?" Mary maintained a businesslike manner, but her reddening neck and rigid posture revealed to Del a precarious poise.

"Unfortunately, madam"—Mr. Rigletti tried a sympathetic smile—"in my position I am not at liberty to say."

"*Mr. Rigletti. He is my father. Is he in danger?*"

The Italian shrugged.

"All right, Mr. Rigletti. I'm no Catholic. My father is miles more important to me than your damn Pope." Mary spoke more slowly, staring the Italian in the eye. "The Pope can go to hell." He didn't flinch. "And maybe your mouth is closed, but mine isn't. Unless you tell me what I want to know, in ten minutes I'll call the papers, and tomorrow every crazy in Vancouver will know exactly which Pope to shoot at."

Mr. Rigletti sat quietly. He appeared to be weighing her threat, perhaps weighing a lot of things. He sighed and reached into his jacket for a cigaret, which he lit slowly, and blew the match out with his first long exhalation of breath. Surprisingly, Mr. Rigletti smiled.

"Very well. For his Vancouver visit, there have so far been twelve threats on His Holiness's life. Eight phone calls, four letters. In Ottawa there were over twenty. In Montreal, nine. In Latin America," he looked up, shook his head, and smiled again, "we stop answering the phone."

Mary looked over at Del for some kind of help, but now it was Del's turn to shrug. The Italian continued.

"So it is very hard for me to answer your question. I am sure both of you can understand that, if it is your intention to kill a person of importance, the last thing you will do is call that person and inform them of your intention. So. It is impossible to tell. The incident in Rome? We—at least my office—had no fore-warning. We were very lucky. His Holiness is a strong man. And now His Holiness must drive around in that queer car that shields him from the world he so much loves." Rigletti paused to nudge the ash from his cigaret. On the end table he noticed a wedding picture: Del and Mary. After considering it for a moment he looked up at Mary, then at Del.

"But let me tell you what is important here. As I have told Mary, our usual surrogate, himself Italian, has taken sick in Montreal. He loved his work, but it looks as if he will die a natural death. So we searched the congregations of your city for the right man. Your father is the right man. It is more than a question of height, and appearance, and age. We searched for attitude. Some we questioned were proud, too proud. But your father was simply delighted. He is a Catholic. But most of all he is a good man."

"Mr. Rigletti," Mary was close to shouting again, "my father has had a stroke. He lives in a daze. We don't know where he lives or what he thinks. 'Simply delighted'? Don't you mean 'simple'? Isn't he the perfect man, the perfect dumb follower religious hotshots everywhere try to grab for their damn we-fear-God Church"—Mary's face was red, her eyes wild—"so they can all avoid reality together in one big happy damn family?"

It looked to Del that Mary had only now discovered her own helplessness. He wondered at his wife. Why couldn't she just let her anger go? Del, for his part, found Rigletti reasonable enough, and the whole affair remarkable to say the least. Amus-

ing as could be. Fortunate! A lottery ticket, a blessing. And yet
here was the daughter of a fortunate man writhing in some kind
of hell. Her arguing had taken on the nasty and insane stance of a
little girl who had a stranglehold on a doll she didn't really want,
except that another child had it.

"His intelligence is not the point," Mr. Rigletti said quietly.
"The point is this: in one gesture, taking place next Saturday,
your father can serve humanity, can serve his Pope, can serve his
God. This he knows, I am sure of it, and this makes him very
happy."

Happy? wondered Del. Yes. So it seemed. Mr. Miller had
looked content sitting there on his bed, being measured. Still, it
was hard to say when, or even if, Mr. Miller was ever happy.
Moving slowly in his garden amongst the vegetables, prodding
here and there with a gentle hoe as if to nudge along the slow
lives of beets and carrots, he wore a constant, witless smile. It
was the smile one finds in children's book illustrations—not the
smile of a king or a sun, but of a giraffe or a two-dimensional
fish. Since his stroke he'd developed crow's feet around the eyes,
yet whether this meant anything positive about his brain, Mary
had told Del one day, there was just no evidence, and such a
conclusion was naive.

Mr. Rigletti leaned forward in his victory. His tone became
yet more gracious and sympathetic.

"I can at least tell you that the danger to your father is very
small. Security will be the same for him as for His Holiness. I
admit that this is part of the deception. But there will be men
surrounding your father who will be willing to put themselves in
front of him to protect him." Mr. Rigletti paused significantly.
"Men who won't even know your father's name." He paused
again. "Christianity is the practice of sacrifice."

The Italian then did an unexpected thing. Reaching over and
taking up the wedding picture, he asked, "Have you no
children?"

"No." Del blurted this out, his voice breaking hoarsely. It was
the first thing he'd said. Mary didn't look up.

"So. Yes. When you have children, you will understand sacrifice. Your father has served you well, and now he has the good fortune to serve something larger." Mr. Rigletti smiled. Then he blinked and his brow lifted and broadened as happens when a speaker self-consciously changes the subject. "Yes. So. Do you intend to have children?"

Del's and Mary's response was identical: they turned to one another to see what the other would say.

The question sat them up straight in their chairs. But Del was surprised more now by Mary's eyes. She had been startled out of her anger and was looking at him with fresh and innocent eyes; seeing him, in truth, for the first time that day. Del felt like waving, but that was precisely the kind of joke that lately rubbed her wrong.

They stared for a moment more. Children? Their fight. Separation. Both had forgotten, and now the foul bird of this memory arose, shook off its sad ashes, and stood between them in sharp focus. Del realized then why this afternoon's pope commotion had been for him not a dilemma but a sweet diversion. He saw too the source of the anger Mary had diverted and aimed at a father, at a go-between, at a vast and innocent thing called a pope.

In her black beret, Mary herself looked like a terrorist. Her poncho hid her arms, and could also have hidden a machine pistol, or grenades. She wore too that look of black duty: not, in this case, a duty of deadly politics, but rather one of having to witness the peril and humiliation of her father.

She shivered though it wasn't that cold, stared straight ahead, and took no notice of the scattered crowd of a thousand or so, their cheerfulness, their murmurs of the Pope's arrival. Even when the helicopter—the first one, the decoy—appeared as a faint noisy dot to the east and heads turned to squint and gasp, Mary continued to stare down, her eyes fixed.

"Want to go up closer?" Del asked her. "Take everyone up near your mom and church friends?"

"Everyone" meant Mary's group home people. Officially they were on a field trip to "greet the Pope." This was Del's first meeting with them. He'd been introduced to a large girl, Lulu, a bucktoothed Shelley, an expressionless Lars, and another who smiled constantly and laughed for no reason, Fraser his name was, and he was new at the home. Del was touched by their loving dependence on his wife; for her part, Mary was stern, but, like a good mother, she touched them often. Del did not envy Mary her job. People stared so. This made him stand a little straighter himself, the defiant dad to these misfits.

The helicopter drew near. As the noise grew louder and people all around began to jerk and gesture and clap and shout, the young fellow Fraser let out an absurd "Halleyoola!" The first word he'd said all day, it was unclear whether it was meant mockingly. To Del it seemed so. But Fraser kept it up, and now Lulu shouted it, and so did Lars, though in an unfeeling mono-tone. Fraser and Lulu began to compete with their shouting, and while Fraser's rang with mischief, Lulu's soon roared with exuberance and celebration. She shouted "Halleyoola!" with such desperation that her neck puffed and showed blue veins. She would have fallen forward had Mary not caught hold of her. Mary yelled in her ear to stop, but Lulu continued to roar even as she lurched in Mary's arms. It looked to Del as though the poor girl had never been so happy in her life—her smile was huge, and painful in a way that revealed she rarely smiled.

The helicopter was right overhead, perhaps a hundred feet up, and deafening. Some in the crowd hunched involuntarily. Del saw many praying and crossing themselves. The piety on these faces was impressive, and though Del for a moment felt humbled, this gave way to smugness. He couldn't help feeling a bit embarrassed for them. This, the largest event in some of their lives; they hunched and prayed because his father-in-law hovered over them in the sky. Well, he decided, they could enjoy their version, and at the same time he could enjoy his. It was the closest he'd ever come to the privileged side of international intrigue, so why not enjoy?

He wished Mary felt the same way. She still hadn't looked up. As Del watched her he recalled something she had said at a party, years ago when they'd first met. With all in the room lightly drunk, the game in progress was to confide the worst part of your own character. Del had announced that he was a potential wimp (Del thought this a bravely unwimpish thing to admit). When her turn came to describe herself, Mary said with sly humor, "If you throw one gopher under me, I'll throw two porcupines under you." Del never asked her whether these words were hers or not. He'd found them sinister in a quirky way, and they pretty much summed up that part of Mary Del now had to admit he was afraid of.

He'd tried, but it had never helped, fighting fire with fire. This past week, for instance, Mary's mood had been hellish. She hadn't budged on her father. She wouldn't talk about their own quarrel, their pending separation. Finally, fed up, Del said to her once after breakfast, "So do we split up *before* your dad gets shot, or later?" Mary said nothing, but made a slow job of putting on her coat. Then she looked at him and said, "Love wouldn't let someone say that." There was a loneliness in her eyes. When she left, she closed the door so softly it stung Del's skin. And of course he felt rotten. Small, red-faced, a thief with immoral pinching little hands. He'd tried his gopher, and now felt distinctly porcupined.

The helicopter had scarcely settled when two bodyguards clambered down and surveyed the crowd with dark, all-business scowls. One signaled, and five more came out, followed by the decoy Pope. The crowd began to roar. It was more of a howl. Even at that distance Del could see Mr. Miller lurch back, startled. But then, remembering his coaching, the old man went into his routine of serene papal gestures. The masses fell silent as he crossed himself, then knelt and kissed the ground. Del looked around and decided Mr. Miller was doing a good job, for in many eyes there shone that light that signified faith and love and hope. Mr. Miller had hardly regained his feet when he was steered into the waiting bubble-car. And so the affair was over. People began to chatter, some to disperse. Del saw that already a second helicopter was visible, a speck in the east.

"Want to stay and see who is the better Pope?"

Mary stared after the bubble-car with its guard of limos and flashing police cars.

"I hope somebody shoots them both," she said.

There was plenty of good liquor, supplied by Mr. Rigletti, and at the party's peak some forty souls stood in rooms and hallways lifting glasses high to toast the man of the hour. The guests were church friends, relatives, neighbors, official but now jovial Italians, and anyone else who had somehow caught word of the decoy Pope. All eyes were on Mr. Miller. He still wore his Pope's robes, and sat center stage in the living room in an almost regal La-Z-Boy recliner, drinking wine from an enormous pewter goblet. On the floor beside him lay an ornamental censer, a gift from Rigletti, and though its incense had gone out, clouds of pungent smoke hung in layers. Mrs. Miller raced about opening windows to the autumn night air, explaining her reasons and apologizing to everyone.

Mr. Miller held court. He had kept up his papal pose and was giving blessings and a very sincere laying on of hands to any of the playfully sacrilegious who, smiling naughtily, came to kneel at his feet. It seemed a night of excess but also of tolerance. Del, for one, was enjoying this decoy Pope scene thoroughly until he realized—and his spine crept—that he could not tell if Mr. Miller was acting, or serious, or what.

Wearing his wide, graceful smile, Mr. Rigletti approached the decoy Pope.

"I am compelled to ask you, Mr. Miller, what possessed you today to so magnificently kiss the ground?"

"*Yes*, dear," said Mrs. Miller, now at his side as well. "That wasn't in the practice sessions at *all* as I recall."

Mr. Miller looked up at them and seemed for a moment confused.

"I . . . wanted to," he said.

And then he laughed what was for Mr. Miller a raucous laugh, and Del felt relieved. For if the old man had come out of this day with his sanity yet more in question, Mary's sour stance would have been vindicated, and she would have had cause to keep up her bad mood for years. As it was, she was still not herself.

Though there were good signs. This party, all the people, all the eager questions directed her way had brought her out a little. During the past hour Del had twice heard her laughter ring out, and this simple, familiar sound worked on him as though to brighten the room. The door to Mary was open, and now he had to slip his foot in.

Del sidled her way and arrived just as Mr. Rigletti sat beside her. Del took a seat at her other side. The Italian was shaking Mary's hand.

"Excuse my manners," he said, "but always I must ask certain questions of an intelligent atheist. An atheist who is also a good person."

Mary said nothing.

"So. Please. I would like to know your thoughts on my religion, madam. I understand it was once yours, as well. If you would be so kind." The Italian wore a tender, almost tearful look, and Del found himself hoping his wife *would* be kind.

"You've heard it all before, Mr. Rigletti," Mary said. "But it seems to me that your religion is wishful thinking. It seems to me . . ."

While Mr. Rigletti nodded and smiled politely, Mary unburdened herself. She was civil, Del was glad to see. For his wife's fall from Catholicism had been fast and bitter, and sometimes it showed. She resented the threat of Hell that had loomed over her adolescence. (Del recalled that during the crucifix scene in *The Exorcist*, Mary's laughter had been too feverish, too delighted.) Her birth control pills she kept on the kitchen sill, not so much to remind as to display, even when her mother came to visit. When she switched TV channels and happened on the glossy face of yet another evangelist her response was not the normal tired laughter or sad incredulity. No, Mary could not turn the channel without a stiffening of her shoulders and an acid comment. Del had once caught her hissing at one of them when she thought herself alone.

But Mary kept her emotions reined in as she ran down the opiate of the masses argument, whereby religion was a placebo, a sham tonic for old age, for the naive. If there was any saving to do, Mary said, one could save only oneself. "Religion," she concluded, "misses the mark."

"Misses . . . the 'mark'?"

"It's off the target."

"And this target is . . . ?"

"Well, you know. Truth, I suppose." Here Mary had to smile, having found herself in the arena of huge concepts, or banality. "Anyway, religion just gets in the way. Of truth." She smiled a little wickedly. "Like TV."

"Ah ha!" the Italian shouted. He looked over at Del to make sure he was listening. "So! This is interesting. For we both agree the target is truth. Truth with a capital T? Yes. But after this we are in opposition. For you, religion obscures truth. But for me, for a religious man, it is the things of *this life* that obscure truth." Mr. Rigletti looked tired, but bright-eyed and giddy and most pleased with their talk.

"Yes! and do you know"—the Italian began waving his arms now, and Del had to grin—"do you know we share more? It is this: we all of us think that finding this truth will make us very happy. Yes? Ha-ha! And so anything that gets in the way of this happiness makes us very angry! Ha-ha-yes! Religion makes us angry, fathers and mothers make us angry, TV makes us angry, and so do husbands and wives and children and sex!"

Mary shrugged, not caught by the Italian's enthusiasm. Del watched the two of them. Mary, frowning and certain. Mr. Rigletti, smiling and certain. In a flash of recognition, Del saw their stubbornness to be identical. It occurred to him too that there was maybe no truth at all, at least not with a capital T, and that all that mattered here was the difference between a smile and a frown.

This thought did nothing to cheer him up. It seemed too simple, too . . . wimpy. There was something about Rigletti's smile. At certain angles it reminded Del of those yellow happy-face stickers one sometimes still saw in car windshields or on the lunch boxes of fat girls, that smile sinister with happy ignorance.

Mr. Rigletti rose with a final little laugh, leaned over, and squeezed Del's knee. "I will stop attempting to convert your wife. You would be angry with me if tomorrow she became a nun." The Italian gave them both his perfect bow and then strode away, pausing now and then to make formal goodbyes.

Mary did an unexpected thing, which was to sigh, lean, and rest her head on Del's shoulder. Almost as though she had forgotten.

"Oh jeez, Del, I'm tired."

"Yeah." Too tired to fight anymore, is that what she meant?

"I've had quite a week."

"Yeah." Was she saying it had all been her fault? A bad mood? Could something like splitting up get shoved aside, just like that?

The Italians were waving, laughing, going out the door. Mrs. Miller, her neck a swan's, stood in the door frame blowing kisses at them.

"Del, I think if we approach this thing with no expectations we have a pretty good chance to—"

Someone was ringing a bell and shouting.

"His Holiness Mr. Miller is going to bless his garden! He's going down to bless his garden!"

They'd relit the censer and a neighbor stood poised with it in front of Mr. Miller's chair. Everyone went quiet.

Slowly, supporting himself on the chair arms, Mr. Miller rose.

The old man looked tired, Del thought, but so happy. Unabashedly happy and proud. As he made his slow and formal way past, following the clouds of incense, Mr. Miller had one arm up to his face and smiled as he studied the fabric that draped his wrist and that shone as only subtle elegance can. Some applauded as he passed. Wearing his silly gentle smile, Mr. Miller looked up to them for a moment but then shyly returned his grin to the fabric, in disbelief of all this good fortune. Staring thus at his arm, he followed the incense out the door.

"Watch his tomatoes grow now!" someone yelled. A few guests laughed. Some were following him out to the garden.

Mary had been watching her father, hardly breathing, a sad little smile, her eyes hinting tears. She did not look at Del as she reached across a frightening few inches of space and took his hand.

Was this it, then? wondered Del. Did the drama end with nothing but this? Here was Mary at his side again, Mary who had gone to battle and seemed to have lost, who with a sad and dull sigh had resigned herself to her father's embarrassing state, and who with the same sigh had just now resigned herself to a safe old life with Del.

He looked down at his wife. Even her blood had given up, her face was white. Del felt empty, and this emptiness bubbled to anger at seeing their fight drifting away in mere forgetfulness. The gash would turn into a drab thick scar, not healed tissue but dead tissue. Mary was smiling up at him, probably trying to communicate something. Del did not smile back. He was picturing the face she would wear later that night, when they were home and in their bed and he was penetrating her: it would be an ignorant face, a face that rode life too blindly, and the smile it would use would be her father's.

But that was five years ago. And tonight, Mr. Miller's sixty-fifth birthday party, attended by four people only, was a dull success. Mrs. Miller had herself slowed down considerably of late, and so husband and wife looked more like a couple. Mary tried hard to keep the party cheery, and Del joined her in this.

On the way home in the car, Mary said she'd enjoyed him on TV. She was friendly, but merely so. Her airport embrace had been the same, friendly. No loving, special, sexual signs. It occurred to Del that a merely friendly—cousinly—wife was worse than an angry one. At least with anger there were sparks, a hidden fire. Forlorn, he watched her drive.

She turned to him with a cousinly smile, and news.

"They're letting Fraser come stay with us for a while. For two weeks. I told them I'd wait, to check with you."

"Sure, Mare, that's fine." Del nodded to himself. "Good old Fraser."

He was glad, though, that Fraser wouldn't be there tonight. He was exhausted from the party, the flight, the game. He had also decided that tonight was the night he would get up the balls to finally have it out with her. He had reffed a good game. He was confident in his judgment. He would find out if the word "divorce" had indeed been a slip of the tongue. If not, well. He would discover if her problem lay within their marriage, or outside of it. If she had hidden problems of her own. If so, he would referee her problems for her.

The phone was ringing when they got home. They could hear it ringing in the driveway; it continued to ring until Del got to it, his toe, all of a sudden, hurting.

"In a jam, Beak," was what Del heard before he'd said hello, before the phone had even touched his ear.

"Money, Frank?" Del sighed, a conscious degree of censure in his voice. But his brother sounded sober this time. Alert, almost chipper.

"Talking *bail* money this time, Beaker."

"Jesus, Frank. What did you—"

"You won't believe it. They arrested me for getting shot."

CHAPTER NINE

Hell

The perfect Nihilist is a scrawny black worker ant who in a bad mood has strayed from his colony. The perfect Eternalist is a pretty blonde girl who, knowing she is dying of lymphatic cancer, takes a smiling bite out of a garlicky kosher dill. The perfect Empiricist, as embodied here in Your Observer, is everything else but these two.

— Felix d'Amboise

Frank had underestimated the power of symbols. The fury he had unleashed by his violation of symbolic objects was similar to that in the States, in the 1960s, when governors, cops, and agents provocateurs were tipped over the edge of rage as they watched war resisters dip the American flag to a lighter, igniting it. In Frank's case, the symbolic objects were fraternity mugs.

In late June, Mr. Morgan, his wife, and his thirty-two-year-old son journeyed north from California to their cedar-and-smoked-glass rancher in Pender Harbour, and there found a scene of wanton malice. Not much taken, but so much destroyed. Mr. Morgan turned to his son, Kirk.

"Who would do this?"

"I'll find out."

Mrs. Morgan scurried about her cozy country cabin, as she sometimes called it, shrieking and weeping.

Kirk Morgan was a policeman in San Francisco and had seen countless such zones of destruction. This one reeked of adolescent spleen. As with most vandal-robberies, it looked to be a battle of juvenile hormonal imbalance versus the innocent symbols of wealth and authority. Kirk Morgan could quote from the *Journal of the Psychology of Crime*. He had studied hard. He had just been promoted to the rank of detective.

Father and son stood before the fireplace, staring down at porcelain shards. Mr. Morgan had been Delta Upsilon, and so had Kirk, following his father in a tradition that had become much scorned by the time Kirk reached college age. Thus campus life had been difficult for him and, because of this, the glue binding Kirk Morgan's heart and pride to Delta U was stronger even than that of his father's. The two mugs had been identical, all except the gilt-incribed years: '49 said one, '75 said the other. Staring down, father and son said nothing. They clasped hands. They trembled. Both men were self-conscious; they were very much aware of their hands touching and their bodies trembling. But they knew that such a response was the response of honorable men. Men like Mr. Reagan, their long-time governor and their former president, who at such a time as this would also have trembled, chin up, in quiet bravery and resolve.

"I'll find out," said Kirk Morgan, loud enough so his mom would hear him too and be comforted.

He had lots of time. He had taken a bullet in the left tricep and had come north with his parents to finish his convalescence. (He was up to sixty push-ups a set; forty-one more to go.) The caliber of slug they'd dug from his flesh was the same as that which, years before, had almost felled their president. His father had written Washington with this news, joking respectfully about the criminal mind's inability to find bullets big enough to bring down big-hearted men.

Kirk Morgan had with him various manuals and sleuth kits. He set right to work. No fingerprints showed (Frank had worn gloves), and there were no clothing fibers to speak of. But the angle of damage caused by the fireplace poker indicated a left-handed culprit. Kirk Morgan popped the lid on his can of ShoeSeeker powder and dusted strategic areas of the floor. The imprints of large—very large—work boots emerged.

"We are looking for a tall adolescent," he announced to his mom and dad. "He may have a slight limp."

Things were going so well that Frank Baal could not help but be suspicious. And, as during other suspiciously tranquil times in his life, the Black Spot rode too close to the surface of things, so close he could almost see it.

When Frank was a boy he'd seen a cartoon in which a man owned a magic black dot. This dot he kept in a briefcase; he could enlarge it or shrink it at will and he could fold it up like fine, limp leather. The magic of the black dot was that it could become a hole: whenever the man wanted, he could toss the dot on the ground or stick it to a wall and step through. His hand would reappear to pull the dot back in there with him, and it too disappeared. Young Frank would see this and think, where was the black dot now? Both the man and the black dot were vaguely evil. Frank sensed that the black dot was always there, some-where, shining like a pool of ink under the surface of things. It could be anywhere. It was somehow everywhere.

This image had followed Frank into adulthood, and it became real the way wind is real, felt but not seen. "Seeing" the Black Spot under things was to be aware of shadows, as under build-ings or trees or saucers on a tablecloth, but the Black Spot was darker than any shadow and impossible to see. Yet each spring it was in the new leaves and in the grass, it was in the eyes of friends as well as enemies, it was in the sad lilt of birdsong, it was there in tinfoil, it was in the middle of mashed potatoes. It was even behind the sun. Seeing the Black Spot under all things was a little like the experience of seeing a child smile while knowing this child was someday going to die.

Frank could sense the Black Spot most clearly when he was hung over. The world, sharply lit and cut like an angry diamond, had an unseen but undeniable background of inky black. He'd told Del about the Black Spot once, years ago, but no one since. Del had listened closely, had asked him if he was hung over

(Frank was), and then suggested cheerfully that he join him for a jog and a sauna.

In any case, though the Black Spot was floating under things, wet and inky and far too close, this past month had been a jewel. He had seven thousand in the bank, the most he'd had since he'd lost his inheritance. He'd fenced his goods safely and well, then returned to Pender and chartered a lone white-haired man from Alabama, an eccentric and hilarious codger who fished as patiently as a Buddha and brought with him bottles of the best bourbon known to mankind. They caught nothing, imbibed like father and son, and the man paid him double. He'd been a small-town mayor, now retired. Frank decided that the Deep South might be worth a visit someday.

Then Laura came up to stay with him for three days and nights, and things got even better. Still ambivalent about her, he hadn't wanted her to come, but when she arrived she was cool and bored, and this made Frank want her more than he'd wanted anyone in years. They cruised islands, they drank and fished, they joked and nuzzled each other like squirrels. On Laura's dare, they made a bet over who could stay naked the longest. The weather was perfect, so they fished naked, cooked naked, and slept naked. In a secluded cove, as Frank hauled the anchor in hand over hand, his balls boomping his inner legs, Laura snuck up and sprayed a mouthful of sticky lemonade all over his bum. Frank had to dive in to get clean. When they needed gas, Frank stayed in the cabin the whole time, passing money out the window, taped to a stick. They anchored and fished far from other boats. Once, though, as they romped on the afterdeck, their rods unwatched and unthought of, they looked up to see a Chinese man and his family, packed into a rental skiff, trolling closer and closer to them. The man couldn't get enough of bare Laura; he steered their boat in a dwindling spiral around *Tammy*. The wife crouched mute in the bow, her face showing alarm and shame. They trolled so close that all three lines snagged on *Tammy*'s anchor rope. Thinking they had simultaneously caught three monster salmon, the family pulled and pulled with their broom-pole thick rods, bringing *Tammy*'s anchor off bottom.

Furious, Frank pounced forward, pulled in enough rope to locate their shiny, ridiculously huge lures, and then cut their lines. While the man shouted at him, Frank dug the lures out of his rope and, after standing and waggling his penis at them, plopped the expensive lures over the side.

In the end Laura won the bet when Frank had to don pants and shirt to make a trip for tequila and limes. He wanted the tequila more than she did; also, of their two bodies, Laura's certainly deserved to be barest longest. She had a young body, a marvelously minky, mellifluously meaty body. Her wise look—those eyes of a telepathic cat—made her body seem younger still.

For her prize Laura demanded he write her a serious, raging love poem. Frank rolled his eyes, but then went below. Two minutes later he handed her a napkin with this on it:

> If I had the sharpest knife
> ever seen
> that could cut you
> but not hurt you
> I would slice you open at the belly
> and eat my way to your heart

Laura was silent for a moment. Then she said, "Do you mean it?"

"No," Frank said. He smiled at her darkly. "It's bullshit. All poems are bullshit."

"But it's kind of beautiful."

"Fucking right."

"Fucking right," Laura whispered back.

They stared at each other now, wearing identical wry smiles. This was a coy game they had begun to play these days: staring, exchanging brief words, three or four possible meanings teasing back and forth from eye to eye. This game got the best of Frank an hour later when Laura, a forkful of baked beans poised at her mouth, surprised him by saying, "I love you."

"Well, I . . . love you too." Frank couldn't look at her as he mumbled this, and when he did look up he saw her ironic smile. What was she thinking? He wished he hadn't said it at all. At the same time he wished he had said it much better.

"I love to fuck *you* too," she said next, her smile and eyes giving nothing away. The game was on.

Frank hesitated, then replied, "Fuck you *too*," an acid edge to his voice, his smile and sneer at odds. He couldn't think of anything else to say. But he got her back later, blurting out "Let's get married" as she was brushing her teeth. Her arm froze, her body locked. Then Frank swatted her ass and hee-hawed with delight, and Laura tilted her head and nodded, a you-win look on her face.

So her stay was perfect. Frank even felt . . . serious. If the truth were told, for a while there Frank could visualize nothing better than the two of them paired up for good, pooling their finances and sailing off into unknown but ever-delightful waters aboard *Tammy Wouldn't Die*. They would continue to live and play as they had these past three days. They could wrest a decent living from the sea: catching fish, catching crabs, selling them to tourists and thankful widow ladies; selling stolen VHF radios, radar sets, loud-hailers, dinghies made of teak. The sea, especially where rich Yanks moored their high-tech plastic yachts, was bountiful indeed.

In fact, life was so colorful and so good that Frank began to feel dreadful. For he knew it was all bullshit. His romantic daydream, Laura's visit from the start, their relationship to begin with, his fat bankbook, his seemingly rosy life in general—it was as full of shit as a bad poem. The Black Spot was everywhere, and he wasn't about to be taken by surprise. He knew he was being set up.

The first omen was his summons to appear and pay a fine for indecent exposure, laid by the Coast Guard. The chink fisherman voyeur had ratted. Actually it could have been any number of boaters, or perhaps the Coast Guard itself who had seen them—Frank's memory was a bit blurred.

The second omen was not so much an omen as a disaster. It involved a scheme Frank had plotted for months, whereby he had convinced the local merchants' association to give him ten thousand dollars for services rendered, all in one nice, tidy, legal cheque.

The idea had come to him at the bar. Fishing had been off for years, and so had the weather. Rich tourists were booking their fishing trips farther north at Rivers Inlet and Stuart Island, and tourism was down 50 percent, and everyone who called Pender Harbour home could talk of little else. Pushing in the door to the pub toilet, Frank noticed as if for the first time the washroom art: a painting of a male sasquatch indicated the Men's entrance, and a female, complete with huge hairless breasts, indicated the Women's.

Frank's idea was absurdly silly, a slice of plot from a TV comedy, but it was simple enough to work. He approached the merchants and seduced them with a speech, the gist of which was this: "For a fee of ten thousand dollars, to be gathered amongst yourselves as you see fit," he said softly, lounging macho like an oil-fire troubleshooter from Texas, "I will raise your business volume by one third over the next six months. Anything under 33 percent and you don't pay me a penny. I trust you."

Frank was certain they would all win. He'd seen the documentaries, read the stories: eccentric pseudoscientists and monster hunters ringing the shores of Loch Ness; sasquatch hunters flocking like buzzards to each sighting or set of footprints in Washington, Oregon, or nearby in Agassiz. Frank calculated it would take two, at most three sightings to bring them en masse to Pender Harbour, the next Sasquatch Capital of the World, where they would buy groceries, film, rent cabins, hire pack horses and all-terrain vehicles. Days off they would charter boats like *Tammy*, manned by seasoned skippers like himself.

Frank needed a partner, one who would not go blabbing his secret in bars. And the only man he knew in Pender who didn't go nightly to blab in bars was Felix d'Amboise. The flabbing francophone he enticed with the promise of a new typewriter. Though Felix was confident his now thirteen-volume work would be attractive to any publisher in whatever form it was delivered, he decided it would be an act of kindness to render the thousands of pages of pencil scrawl into a more legible script.

And so it happened that on a bright Sunday morning, Felix, as instructed, rode the Greyhound from Pender Harbour to

Sechelt. The bus was filled with a good mix of witnesses: retirees, children, loggers. Felix was to spot the sasquatch after rounding the wide curve at the bottom of Drala Mountain. A week away was Felix's birthday, his fête—in town he would feed, exhaust, and defile himself, and when he returned he would learn how to type.

Frank waited in the tall grass, hidden behind a tree. He would step out when he heard the bus gear down at the corner. His costume was a minor masterpiece. He'd spent little on the badly made gorilla suit; he'd chopped the face out and rolled the shiny polyester fur in mud and cedar mulch, which added the necessary twigs, bark, and Neanderthal smudge. His face he'd just now blackened sloppily, creating the impression of scattered hair and stupidity. He pulled the platform-sole boots on, adding five inches to his stature. They were silver with rainbow heels, from the obnoxious 1970s; he'd found them in a Goodwill store, dusty and absurd.

He would keep himself fifty yards from the road. He'd give the bus a good ten-second glimpse, then move into trees to loiter, showing an arm here, a leg there, and finally run off into the underbrush.

Felix had comandeered two seats, one for each buttock, and enjoyed his drive by writing in his notepad. There were plenty of empty seats around him as well, because since his bath was a mere week away he had not sponged himself off of late, to better experience the contrast of dirty and clean. In the two miles from Pender to the rendezvous point he was able to write this:

> While in a hostile foreign clime, G.I. Gurdjieff made money by painting drab finches with bright colors and selling them as a more exotic species. He made sufficient gold to flee and sustain himself until his next adventure with questionable commerce. He went on to become a noted teacher and sage, perhaps Saint. Having not yet achieved certainty as to whether engaging in amoral tomfoolery is a necessary prerequisite to Sainthood, Your Observer has embarked on an escapade of questionable commerce which

They came to the corner. He raised his dark, goatish eyes, aimed them at the forest, caught a glimpse of Frank, pointed a loafy arm, and called: "You, driver. A yeti. I believe I've spotted a yeti."

The driver gave Felix a curious glance in his mirror, but kept driving.

"Stop! I tell you I can see a sasquatch!"

Some people looked out the window too, but more were staring at Felix, who had begun to sweat, his vision of a typewriter fading into haze.

"I'M HAVING A HEART ATTACK! STOP AT ONCE!"

The bus finally stopped, and Frank had only to run a hundred yards to get himself back in view. Felix took his hand off his heart and brushed people aside to point once more. "It's a sasquatch! It can be nothing else!"

So the people did see a sasquatch, and Felix's typewriter came back clearly into focus. Two duck hunters, whose pickup had screeched to a stop behind the bus, saw a sasquatch as well, and they too had visions of dollar signs, headlines, and a trophy to end all trophies. They got a shotgun down from the rack and pointed before Frank made it to the trees.

It was Frank himself who ruined everthing. He took only a single pellet in the ass; it went in and out and didn't hurt much at first; he could easily have run and hidden. As it was, he was lucky he wasn't shot again. For the hunters had by rote reloaded in seconds; the sasquatch was now screaming and coming *at* them; it was only when one hunter recognized the screams to be a string of swear words that he grabbed his buddy's gun barrel and pulled it down.

Frank, running at top speed with a grotesque limp, howling like a sasquatch might in fact howl, burst forth from the bushes, leapt a ditch, and charged them, clomping in his platform shoes, wobbling a bit at the ankles. The hunters had just made it into their pickup when Frank launched himself, sailed several long yards, and kicked in their windshield. He landed badly, his knee twisting under him, his head banging back, his bleeding bum screaming louder in his ears than his voice was.

Frank took the morning's events to be the second omen, as foreshadowed by the ever-looming Black Spot.

The third omen took place that afternoon. After leaving the hospital, where he had his BB hole patched, his scrapes and bruises cleaned, Frank went to the Pender police station to press charges. He was still seething, and so he didn't notice the subordinate speaking into the phone in whispers. Nor did he wonder why the cop asked him if he was left-handed, how tall he was, and what shoe size he wore. Cops, like all bureaucrats, were blind to the light of day and had to ask all sorts of inky questions. Nor did he see the man in the track suit, blond, muscular, and about Frank's age, who entered quietly and stood behind him. He didn't see the man nod to the desk officer, or the officer wink back.

Kirk Morgan had made friends with the Pender Harbour police force. In the course of investigating his parents' burglarized house he'd helped the locals bring to justice several juvenile crooks. And though it turned out that none of these kids was connected to the crime at his parents' house, he knew he was on the right track. Joining the RCMP guys in the bar after hours, drinking beer with them and watching girls, letting drop tidbits about real crime in a real American city, Kirk Morgan persuaded them to keep an eye out for a tall fellow with big feet. He told them to watch for someone with eyes that were spiteful, deranged, and "as mean as a teenager's from a broken home." The Pender fellows promised they would be on the lookout. This Morgan chap had worked felonies the likes of which they'd only seen on TV, and his words carried weight. Indeed, the staff sergeant, who'd had a few beers too many, straightened his shoulders and said, "We'll be on the lookout," and some of his younger cronies were a bit embarrassed for him. Kirk Morgan, though, felt perfect rapport with this sergeant. He nodded to him sagely and added, "Good. Keep your eyes peeled." He and his father had written to the headquarters of Delta Upsilon and new mugs were on the way, but they wouldn't be the same.

They booked Frank on the vague charge of public mischief.
This, Kirk Morgan explained to them, after they led Frank away
(screaming like a sasquatch again), would hold him long enough
to allow them time to search this wacko's boat for stolen goods,
and especially for a pair of large work boots (boots that—though
Kirk Morgan didn't know it—still lay in tall grass under Drala
Mountain, where Frank had abandoned them for the silver
ones). Morgan had no doubt that this Baal creep was his man. It
was now up to him to collect the ponderous pile of evidence
needed to bring a conviction. He'd begged the RCMP fellows to
let him into the cell with a phone book and a rubber hose, where
he could have a good go-round with the bone-rack and get all the
evidence he needed, but these northern candies had turned him
down, and turned him down quickly. They seemed to think they
were English bobbies or something.

Still, Kirk Morgan had no doubts. He'd seen the man's eyes.
Such eyes should be photographed and used for the cover of *The
Psychopathic Criminal*. He'd find the boots. He'd get him. He
knew who he was and where he lived. He could be followed. It
was only a matter of time.

Frank's fourth omen had to do with his brother Del.

Things hadn't been so bad when he was first thrown in jail: he
could scream, he could rage. He knew that he'd be out of there
soon, that the silly charge was as much a cartoon as the prank that
had initiated it. So it was almost fun to stand there in his cell,
wearing those damn silver boots, shouting cartoon bile at the
cartoon cops. When he calmed down enough to see the humor,
he got creative and sarcastic, yelling, "*Get me a preacher and then
I'll hang peaceful-like!*" and other such things.

But no one laughed or paid attention, and as he quieted more
his mood sank. God, he thought, there might be some kind of
fine. They'd taken his damn fingerprints, and his days of dealing
in hot goods might be over. And then there was Laura. Once,
early on, when he'd tried giving her an obviously purloined
stereo, they'd had a fight. Not over legality, but morality, for
when he'd accused her of being at least as much a criminal as he

was, she asked him, "Frank, can you name me one person I've hurt by what I do?" It also turned out that Laura was outraged by all drugs, scorned drunkenness, and thought both cigarets and caffeine should be illegal. *Women*, Frank thought: they were as consistent as the flight path of a bat.

He brooded over the exchange he'd had with the desk cop, when he was arrested, before he went crazy on them. At first he'd thought it was a joke, but when he saw it wasn't, he asked if there was any law against walking in the woods dressed like an animal.

"Your partner told the hunters the story. Your fraudulent enterprise."

"Those bird-heads shot *me*, goddammit, why aren't *they* in jail?"

"You caused a public conveyance to stop on a major highway. There were children on the bus. A second motor vehicle narrowly avoided collision. They shot at what looked to be a dangerous wild animal near the bus. I would have done the same myself."

The desk officer's face moved not one muscle as he stared Frank in the eye while saying this. He wore a mustache that, though it spanned his entire length of mouth, reminded Frank of Hitler's.

"They were going to press charges themselves, for your destruction of their windshield. Your partner convinced them that you'd pay them for it."

It was here that Frank began to shout.

"I don't have to tell you this, mister," the desk cop said, and an awful naugahyde cool in his voice silenced Frank, "but not only are you on the card for indecent exposure, you are also under suspicion of breaking and entering, theft, and destruction of private property. If I were you I would shut my ugly mouth and pray."

So what did they know? And how did they know it? If he'd sold goods to an undercover cop they'd have nailed him right there. Had someone seen him in action? He'd hit maybe five or six houses in the past year. Which one had he fouled up in?

Frank mulled over these thoughts and his mood dropped
lower, slowly but as absolutely as a dry leaf wafting down the
depths of a dead well. He'd been given his one phone call (God,
this cartoon was just like a bad movie) and he'd by turns been
trying both Wally Kenny and Del. Wally, though a real estate
lawyer, would at least be able to tell him what to do. And Del, it
went without saying, would not sleep until he saw his wounded
brother freed. But neither was home. Frank recalled his brother
had a game out east, meaning he'd be home later that night. And
Wally, the nelly who could have been a hero, was no doubt out
somewhere having his poo pushed.

There was nothing remotely romantic about the Pender Harbour police station, with its set of tiny cells stuck out back where
most buildings have their incinerators or garbage bins. It smelled
of new paint and government, and the colors were gray and the
drabbest possible green. If a refrigerator could think, it would
think better colors than these. Nothing was written on any wall;
the cot sheet was clean but had no smell of good laundry. When
it became afternoon, then evening, the bored cop who brought
Frank his dinner seemed almost like a friend to him, if only
because he'd broken the gray and green boredom.

Frank stared at it, the gray. It could have been white, but it was
gray, the color of the Black Spot seeping up to the surface world
at last. It tried to hide by mixing with the other colors, and in
doing so it darkened the entire world.

Just before midnight, when Frank had resigned himself to
suffering an all-night sit on a hard cot, face to face with the Black
Spot, his brother finally answered the phone. The effect Del's
voice had on him was that of being a child and having your father
wake you from a nightmare; it was the same as diving dusty and
hot into a brilliantly cold lake.

An hour earlier the bored nightshift cop had walked out of the
edge of the Black Spot to tell Frank his bail had been set at a
thousand dollars. Frank decided this wasn't bad, for what friend,
let alone your twin brother, would think twice before coughing
up a mere grand to get an innocent man out of jail?

Frank blurted out the bail and was about to launch into his sasquatch story, knowing Del would enjoy it, when his brother interrupted him. Cold and curt. As though Del too—what a heart-stopping thought—had just arisen out of the Black Spot.

"I don't want to hear about it, Frank. And hang on a second, okay? I'm going to have to talk to Mary about this. We're not getting on lately and I want to see that this doesn't start another fight."

Frank heard his brother's phone clunk down on the countertop.

His stomach fell and for seconds he couldn't breathe. Del was hesitating, he was consulting with his slut of a wife about whether or not to bail his own brother out of jail. His own goddamned *brother* in jail, his brother's life falling into the blackest hole, and he was asking *permission* of a wife who'd had her spider hand on his brother's cock only last month and had taken it away to fuck with both their heads at the same time, he was *hesitating*, he wasn't running over, worried for him, rushing over to get him out of there.

Frank couldn't stand it for more than a second, waiting for Del to consult with Mary. He hung up. He was sweating a sudden sour odor. It may have been a delayed reaction to kicking in a windshield, but his toe stub began to bleed. He hadn't even told Del what jail he was in.

Other than a good bout of extreme, slightly rough sex, or the next bottle of sake, or perhaps a sly tune plinked out on Malcolm the Uke, nothing could nudge Frank out of the Black Spot doldrums like a good argument with fat Felix d'Amboise.

The two men sat in Felix's cabin, several days after Frank's release from jail. Today's argument started when Felix began lecturing Frank on the philosophical and spiritual benefits a True Observer (Felix had that curious knack for pronouncing capitals) would gain from a period of incarceration.

"Do you know what 'pontificate' means, Felix?" Frank interrupted.

"Don't be foolish. Of course."

"Do you really?"

Felix stared at him, his eyes a rheumy emperor's, his nose up so that Frank could see into the nostrils.

"If you *knew* what 'pontificate' meant, you wouldn't continue to goddamn *do* it."

"Don't be absurd, I—"

"Let me finish." Frank stared him down. Felix's foot shifted, and his eyes lost their regal luster, if only for a second.

"My point is this. Wouldn't you say that, for example, if you knew what the word 'anger' *meant*, if you really understood anger, every angle of it, you would then be free of anger? You would never be angry again? Felix?"

"I understand your point very well, my friend, but—"

"And you agree with it?"

"To an extent, yes, but—"

"Do you? Because, if you did, then you'd have to admit you *don't* understand what 'pontificate' means, Felix—because you continue to pontificate. You pontificate endlessly."

"But of course," Felix said, shrugging and turning with a bored look to the window.

"Nor do you apparently understand, truly understand, the words 'vanity,' 'pride,' 'egomania,' 'absurdity,' 'gluttony,' or 'food.' " Frank was rising to a hugely good mood. His back went straight and his long nose flared its wings. "Look at you. You don't even know the meaning of the word 'food.' What it's for, what it does, why it's needed. You eat too many potatoes, you fat fuck."

"My friend—"

"Other words come to mind. 'Health,' 'decorum,' decency,' 'arteriosclerosis,' 'judgment.' "

"Mr. Baal."

Frank stopped at last, flushed with victory, breathing hard.

"I know these words, my friend. I know their meanings perfectly."

Frank's smile remained on his face, though the muscles that had put it there had gone tentative. It was impossible he hadn't won, and yet there was something foreboding about Felix's languid sneer. Something in his slightly shifting body reminded him of a whale lolling satisfied in its own element.

"Your little point, and your little lecture, was surprisingly bright. However, Frank, you have failed to consider the word 'choice.' You have not considered the simple act—simple, that is, for those of us awake and watching—of choosing our actions. You tried hard, my friend, but the simple fact is that—"

"I don't believe you for a second."

"—I *choose* to pontificate. I *choose*—"

"Bullshit."

"—to eat potatoes until I can eat no more. I *choose*—"

"Prove it."

"—to eschew middle-class notions of health, and dignity, and propriety. I have chosen my vanities. Proof?" Here Felix stuck his bullet head forward, narrowed his eyes and hissed in the most obnoxiously dramatic, pontificatingly Gallic way, his accent emerging as strong as a smell. "The proof it sits in front of you, my friend, in the person of Felix d'Amboise, who has chosen what he is."

Neither man said anything for some minutes, though they looked to be on the edge of an argument still, had there been anything more to argue about. In truth, Frank was feeling more gentle than usual. Felix was feeling rather meek himself. For though nothing had been said (and Felix was suspicious of Frank's kind silence) it was no secret that Felix had deserted his friend, had left rather quickly at the first sight of the police while Frank lay there in his sad costume, having been shot by those absurd *sportifs de canard*. Felix *had* gone into his *fête* can for one thousand dollars when, after midnight that same day, the officer appeared at his door bearing Frank's request for bail. He had deserted him, yet Frank was being gentle, even generous: he had paid Felix back his thousand, in cash, this very day. "For your private party this weekend, Feel. And thanks."

Felix's desertion had been duly noted, but Felix's desertion was nothing like Del's. No, when Felix's money came at last, and Frank was released into the night, the fact that it had been Felix's money and not Del's caused the bells of Frank's anger to ring yet more clearly, yet more bitterly. He wasn't mad at Felix, at least not very. He was being gentle with him because Felix was part of his plan.

The catch to living on a boat—especially a hulk of a questionable breeding like *Tammy*—is that it moves and makes noise. The constant rocking (as if one were in the belly of a huge soft-shoed beast, out strolling), the incessant creaking of sour wood on wood, the croaking of wet, near-rotted ropes gone taut, the shriek of boat hull on rubber tire dock cushions: most people not only expect these sounds but find them romantic and, after a first night, soothing. But there are those who in certain moods resent the world to begin with, and upon whose mind such quaint domestic belchings work like sandpaper, like a moron's nails on a blackboard, causing moods yet more foul to blister and rise. Frank Baal had suffered thus for a week. And he wasn't such a loner that he was content to suffer alone. His plan was to take everybody by the hand and lead them all to Hell.

Laura, Fraser, Felix, Mary, and Del.

Laura, because it was time she found out who he really was.

Fraser, because it was time he was baptized into the world of normal sinning souls.

Felix, because he lived in fiction.

Mary, because it was time she learned that there were consequences.

And Del because he was a fool. One could not hesitate to bail out a brother and then not expect the truth of things to come roaring in. It didn't *matter* that Del had later called police stations around the province to find him, had wanted to drive up immediately with the money, had begged Frank to quit being stubborn and let him pay his bail. None of that mattered. Anyone could pay bail. Only a brother could do it properly.

So Frank was going to take them all to Hell.

Of course, he knew it might prove to be no big deal. When he'd finished with them, Del and Mary might simply make up and decide to be more honest with each other. Felix, Fraser, and Laura might just have a strange, perhaps memorable night out.

But Frank liked to think he was taking them all to Hell.

It had not been hard to ascertain that Mary was continuing her lying, spicy life. A call to Laura, who checked with the booking agency, confirmed that. Mary, who now wore a cowboy hat in her act and went by the name Lil' Regina, was dancing—that is, showing her pubic hair to strangers—that Friday at the Yale Pub. Frank phoned Del next, told him he would be in town Friday and asked him to join him for a beer at the Yale. Just like old times, he added.

Del sensed he was being forgiven. "But I can't, Frank," he said on the phone. "Mary's at dance class Friday night and I'm looking after Fraser. I'm not sure if it's a good idea if Fraser—"

"*Sure* he should see what real life is like, Beak. He deserves to see a naked woman by now, poor bugger. Bring him along."

"But the *sexism.* Fraser is developing along certain lines. He's obsessive. We have to consider role models and that sort of thing."

"You're afraid of what Mary will say, eh, Beaker?"

"The hell I am."

"Also, I'm bringing Felix. The four of us can discuss you and Fraser maybe coming up for a holiday on *Tammy*, a little cruise. Wouldn't Fraser like that? And Laura will be at the Yale too. How many role models do you want?"

Frank knew the mention of Felix would sway his brother, who admired the fat man so. And it did. He and Fraser would meet them at the Yale at eight. Now Frank had only to convince the huge hermit to accompany him to the Yale as well. Which is why he sat in Felix's cabin, being more gentle than usual.

"C'mon, Feel. You'll be in town anyway."

"But for my *fête* alone. I have a strict schedule. All my minutes are planned to excite certain of my organs of sense at carefully plotted intervals. My Dionysian itinerary does not include guzzling swill with longshoremen in a room smelling of beer and excrement."

"Look, you selfish bastard, I'm doing a delicate thing with my brother tomorrow night. I am going to confront him with the hard fact that his wife is a squirtbag. For some reason he respects you greatly." Frank watched Felix inflate with a deep breath, as if he were inhaling a vast treasure of food. "Don't you think he deserves the support of friends at a time like this?"

Felix considered this, then shrugged.

"You still want the fuckin' typewriter, Felix?"

"Your often crude language demonstrates a very telling difference in the way we think. I draw as an example the word 'fucking.' You say it often, which shows adjectival laziness and is bad enough, but when you say it you drop the *g* and say 'fuckin'.' My friend, you talk like a peasant. Indigenous to the area, but no excuse. I, on the other hand, say 'fuck*ing*,' and I use the word sparingly in the cuisine of my language as I would a rare and piquant spice. But I must say—"

"You are one fat fuckin' asshole."

"—that I would enjoy a typewriter, yes."

The Yale Pub was the kind of place where no one looked twice at a table around which sat, say, a pretty woman, two hook-nosed twins, a supercilious fat man, and a young fellow with thick glasses and a bent forehead. And if other tables held people who at first glance looked normal enough, a second look at their eyes revealed minds giving birth to naive schemes, minds leaning at precipitous angles, minds dying for the second time that night. The Yale was newly renovated and the strippers had been upgraded. The management had hoped to get rid of their former circuslike clientele, but now amidst new cedar paneling and ferns and mirrors, it was clear enough the gargoyles had simply come back to lounge in splendor, as if a favor had been done them. The same old waiters, paunchy yet stiff in the same institutional shirts, banged endless wet glasses of bad draft down in the same old way. There were hardly any women in attendance. And tonight, before the stripping had even begun, the Yale lost one of its few women when she stood up and strode out in a quiet rage.

Laura had been enjoying her time with Frank and Felix. But when Del and Fraser came in and joined them, Laura sat up, confused for a moment, and then, when she understood, she stared hard at Frank. Frank, unsmiling, his eyes severe, introduced her to his brother. Laura said hello without once looking at the twin. She just stared at Frank. And then, saying nothing, she left.

Well, Frank thought, she has seen me for the first time.

"What was that about, Frank?" Del asked.

"God knows, Beak. PMS maybe. You know women. Better than I do probably."

Del nodded. "Yeah, I guess so. And by the way, Frank, not a word of this to Mary, okay?" He motioned his head toward Fraser.

"Right."

Felix, his teeth clenched and his eyes closed, squirmed in his chair. Though the inner shift of his guts was not noticably visible, throughout the barroom the menisci of several hundred beers shivered.

Del and Frank ordered a pitcher of beer. The first glass they raised in a toast to each other and then drained in one go, their adams appling madly. It was their traditional opening to a night's drinking, first observed after basketball games. Felix sipped his Perrier. Fraser, subdued and unsmiling, drank tomato juice. Del explained to the other two in a whisper that the poor fellow was being tried on a new antipsychotic drug, a combination of two different chemicals in fact, and couldn't drink. Occasionally Del would lean over to ask, "How ya doing, old buddy?" and Fraser would shrug. Over the course of the night Fraser got up to go to the bathroom a lot.

Del finally had to admit to himself that he was having a good time. He hadn't been to a strip club in years, since meeting Mary in fact, and he hadn't expected to find himself in one again. He was married; he'd absorbed enough of Mary's feminist view to understand that striptease, the very notion of it, was not only sexist but sick. And even if one didn't find it philosophically offensive, even if one found it sirring and lust-making, why would one want to subject oneself to all that stir and lust with no means to relieve oneself?

Still, his brother had a point. It could only be good, couldn't it, to take in all aspects of life, to see it from all angles, good and bad, like an artist? This was no doubt Felix's reason for being here as well. Felix d'Amboise—he didn't drink, didn't smoke, didn't (well, poor chap, this was understandable) womanize. Del decided to ask at an appropriate moment whether Felix was a feminist sympathizer as well.

Yes, his brother was an artist in his way, and he shouldn't be so quick to criticize the odd avenues Frank's life sometimes took. And, Lord, the sasquatch thing had been truly funny. Even Mary had laughed.

"Look, Frank," he'd said early on, just after Laura (who *was* a pretty one, a real mink, as Frank would say) had gone, "I'm really sorry you got pissed off on the phone. I guess I kind of thought you were pulling another sort of fast one. About getting shot and all that."

"No problem, Beaker."

"But anyway," Del asked, head down, still a little ashamed, "what was it like? In jail."

"I wrote a song," Frank said in a Texan drawl, "while doin' time." Frank thought for a minute, then sang in a mournful country drone: "I bin shot, and I bin alone. Where there ain't no song, to sing ya home."

Del saw his brother was being mock-dramatic, of course, but his eyes remained weirdly serious, almost accusing.

In fact both Frank and Felix were acting oddly. Very sober— though his brother was matching him beer for beer—for a celebratory Friday night.

The Yale's dim light got darker, and the dancing began. The night's card consisted of Tara, Bunny Blue, Lil' Regina, and René. Tara, who skipped to the stage now to the background of an old David Bowie song, looked about twenty-five and had a cute, flat, Asian face. For the last ten minutes of her half-hour set she lay entirely naked on a fluffy rug performing glue-slow bum raises and leg spreads. What looked to be a college crowd had come early for seats up against the stage. These young men hooted and elbowed each other through most of Tara's act, but when she served up her vagina to their eyes, so close and yet so far away, they sat silent and stiff.

There were half-hour intermissions between dancers. Del and Frank toasted Felix's birthday. (Fraser raised his tomato juice, but didn't appear to know what was going on.) Del gave Felix his warmest smile and sincerest eyes, and wished him many more.

"Thank you," Felix said to Del. "And aren't birthdays odd. For no one is, how should I say, *ecstatic* to be alive, and yet each year we celebrate a condition—aging, in a word—that makes us sigh more than smile."

Del nodded his head significantly. His brother, he noticed, had groaned and turned away. Well, yes, it *had* seemed a bit of a speech, perhaps prepared, but his brother was too hard on Felix at times. Frank would do well to listen to him more.

Felix was still talking. ". . . and parents of all cultures started the custom. For we can bet the parents are much happier than the fresh *bébé* on the first day of its life. It wails, it knows it is in Hell. But we see now, in life, that it is a hell with a purpose."

Frank groaned again, and Del watched him lurch up and walk to the toilet.

"On birthdays, we celebrate being human. Yes. As humans, we have the unique chance to fulfill a destiny, which for some of us is a monumental responsibility indeed."

Such an odd one, Felix d'Amboise. So ugly, and sometimes he smelled. There were people who didn't care what they looked like, and people who wanted to look like they didn't care. Which type was Felix? Certainly the former. He was a pedant, to be sure, but a pedant worth listening to. He'd intrigued Del with the first words he'd said to him, back when they first met in Pender Harbour, when Del asked him why he'd come to English Canada.

"English has conquered the world, and I have come here to conquer the English language," he'd announced. And Frank, who had just made the introductions, groaned then as well.

"And I discover it to be a ridiculous language," Felix had continued. "Take your word 'God.'" He had pronounced the word again, emphasizing the consonants. "It is a closed sound, yes? As such, it leads the mind to a closed concept. Better a more open sound. For God is open. Better the sound 'boo boo.' Better yet: 'oboy.' Or perhaps the resonant 'sassoon.' You might convince me of the existence of a sassoon, but you would never pull the wool of a *God* over the eyes of *Felix d'Amboise*."

"I'm thinking of starting that referee book soon," Del told Felix now. "I'd love to have you look at the rough draft."

"My honor," Felix answered, and raised his Perrier, which shook slightly, Del saw. The stout fellow was more nervous than Del had ever seen him, and he decided that, for all his talk, Felix likely couldn't abide birthdays.

Bunny Blue took the stage, and Fraser, Del was glad to see, was loosening up some. His usual smile would light his face on occasion, and when the dancer went into her first twirl he called out a babyish "Yippie!" Which was perhaps appropriate: in her fuzzy jumper of baby blue, complete with bouncy cottontail, her teenage face and plumpish parts, Bunny Blue's shtick relied on her dangerous young looks.

Del found himself peeing side by side with Frank, into urinals that dripped and smelled, where a man's nose was assaulted with a blast of mothball tang whenever his spray hit and melted the deodorizer. Del repeated the lame joke about how one only rented beer, and Frank grunted in agreement. Standing there, intent on their bodies' draining, so close their elbows could have bumped if they had let them, an awkwardness floated up between them as tangible as the smell. It was, Del told himself again, identical to the self-consciousness one felt looking in a mirror. He had never told his brother of this comparison he'd made; Frank would have found it corny. How Frank hated sentimentality. How Frank hated to blush. Always making a joke of things serious, as he was now: pushing himself deeper into the urinal, Frank mocked a fear of having his penis seen.

Why the extra awkwardness between them tonight? On such nights Frank could talk more intimately with a stranger than he could with his own brother. So why couldn't Del summon the courage simply to say to him, "Frank? Let's talk." He knew very well why. Because Frank would say, "About what?" and look away. And maybe he was right. What would they talk about? Did they really need to talk about anything? Maybe they were that close.

But no. That was Mary's excuse these days too. What about? she'd say, and the stabbing silence would continue.

Del got in a good joke as he and Frank, staggering just a bit now, returned to their table.

"Maybe your life needs a good referee in it, Frankie," he told him, grinning wryly, a Frankie kind of grin. Del liked that kind of joke best; it was first and foremost a joke, and it was second of all an invitation. It was also the closest he could come to an open declaration of love.

Del and Frank sat down just as Bunny Blue removed her pink satin G-string to reveal her shaved pubis. At that precise moment Fraser called out loudly into the big-eyed hush: "*Dalai Lama.*"

This twist-head his brother had brought in from the cold again was almost entertaining, in a scary sort of way. Frank wondered what sort of drug he was on, what it would do to a regular but adventurous sort like himself.

"What's that, Fraser? You talkin' religion again?" Frank said to Fraser, but the young man just stared down into his tomato juice.

Yes indeed, Frank thought to himself, this is my kind of world and my kind of bar, where a gal can hang her floppy shaved twat out, a retard can yell the name of the Tibetan god-king at the sight of it, and no one even turns a head around.

Frank, already feeling greenish and confused on beer, and grateful for it, decided to get properly drunk tonight. Lil' Regina was on next, the deed was almost done. He had come close to calling it all off there in the bathroom. Peeing beside Del had been horrible: Del's earnest humor, his silly jokes, his eagerness to touch and share. His brother was a goddamn one-man en-counter group.

It may have been the beer, but Frank had suffered a near-hallucinogenic vision there at the urinal, watching Del pee. There was nothing to it, he had simply glanced down there at his brother's stream. It had all happened in a flash, and goddamn if he hadn't almost started to cry. He wanted to grab Del and embrace him, squeeze him extremely hard. In one unforgiving second this sight had taken him back to the days of diapers and urine smell, to the days of sitting bow-legged in their playpen, batting colored balls around, their bums coated with poo; sometimes a diaper would come off and they would tool about with clumsy delighted fingers.

He had known this again there in the urinal. It had nauseated him with a flood of yearning. What a life this was, where one had to grow, and change, and, worst of all, remember.

His brother's peeing had also forced on him the memory of the day they parted, he for Italy, Del for school. They'd gone to the reservoir to swim. Late August, the water was cold, the day cloudy. But the reservoir and swim was a must; they had drunk beer and swum there so often, it was their tradition, their place. (Maybe, again, the primal, liquid nature of the place?) Both of them shared a chicken-fear of diving into cold water. They hesitated a long time before Frank announced, "I know. This'll make me go in." He stood there, winced, and began to piss in his cutoffs, the pee spreading at the crotch and yellowing his leg. Del whooped, delighted once more by his brother's outrage. He laughed and screeched and winced as well, and now both of them were peeing themselves. They pointed at each other, howling, pee splashing as they doubled up in laughter. Del's eyes were, for once, wonderfully crazy. And then the pee stopped and they looked at each other quietly, briefly, and both of them suffered—Frank realized now—a memory of diaper days. They swam then, getting clean, laughing tiredly, but neither said a word.

Frank decided once more that he was doing Del a favor, forcing his marriage to an end or a new beginning. Del was not happy in it as it was now. Maybe he would understand, and be grateful. If not, too bad. The world was a shitty place. And sometimes one had to act as the world's agent provocateur.

"I think we need another large jug, Beaker." The lights were on again, Bunny Blue was off, Lil' Regina soon up.

Women. Women were so squirrelly, and sometimes they were simply bad. And men were idiots for sticking around. Del, putting up with, going through such. So ball-less.

Frank recalled his one bout of horrific jealousy. Gina, the temperamental Italian cutie; they'd lived together for six months and one night she didn't come home. He'd searched all over Turin that night. They'd had a fight, a major dish-smashing, Latin-blooded shoot-'em-up, and Frank knew she'd been eyeing a professor of hers. Maybe they'd slept together already. He wrote to Del that night, all the while knowing he was building a wall of jokes to cover his heart: "I got cheated by Gina, Beaker. Avoid women, especially the good-looking quiet ones, at all costs. I had to beat off four times and shove a refrigerator up my ass tonight to keep from going insane." But that had been the last of his jealousy. From then on he sneered and mocked women to bed; he turned his back on their indulgent, lowing pillow-talk; he gave them whatever abuse and hard fantasy they wanted, and if that was not what they wanted, they were gone, and that was fine.

And the boredom of dead passion! No one ever believed it would come to that, though it always did. Boredom, and then the need for ever-increasing kinks. Frank had heard through a friend about a man who at last could be turned on only by minor diseases. Women with a cold or the flu, running noses, red and aching eyes, sneezes, headaches, moans. If he ever got close enough to them to ask, his final lust-trigger was them blowing their noses on him, sick women using him as a Kleenex. And he reportedly loved catching their colds or flu afterwards, which, it seemed to Frank, was the perfect fruition to what must have been perfectly silly guilt in the first place.

"C'mon, Beaker, let's drink this one down."

They raised their glasses just as the lights dimmed for Lil'
Regina and gulped their beers. Del won the contest by a nose
hair.

The spotlight came on and there was Lil' Regina with her
back to them, her cowboy hat on and her arms up in a crucifixion
pose. When the music began, "Stray Cat Strut" by the Stray
Cats, Lil' Regina bumped her hips a few times and then twirled
to face the room.

Frank didn't look at his brother but he heard him choke.

"Little surprise for you, Beaker," Frank said softly.

Mary started to dance.

Silence from Del. And then the pounding of a beer glass,
followed by the first of many loud, honking guffaws.

"You guys are *great*!" Del shouted. "That's right! July the
twenty-first! July the twenty-first! I forgot!"

Frank stared at Del, who was clapping him on the shoulder.

"You guys are great! My first game! Montreal in *Regina*, July
the twenty-first, five years ago today! God, I forgot! My first
game—you guys are great. Was this Mary's idea?" Del was
shaking his head and grinning. "God, *she is great*." He stared at
her lovingly. "And *Regina*. She was *born* in Regina."

Frank said nothing. It was not *possible* that the poor dumb
pathetic fuck thought they were playing a goddamn referee
anniversary joke on him.

"Look at that big old cowboy hat. Look at that slut makeup.
This is great. You guys are really great. How'd you swing it?
Laura?"

God, Del was now on the verge of thankful tears. This was
too goddamn much. Frank could feel Felix staring at him. Del
was still giggling like a goofy kid and clapping him on the back.

Frank drank two beers in quick succession.

Del howled and whooped through his wife's act. When she
took her halter top off, revealing her breasts, Del started in his
seat and looked for a moment confused, but then he giggled
nervously. "*I* can dig it," he said."*I* can handle it. *I'm* liberated,"
he joked. "This is great. And good for Mary. *Look* at her. She's
fantastic. Everybody in here thinks she's real."

Still Frank said nothing. He could not do it. He found himself smiling a quivering, rotten smile whenever Del pounded his arm.

"This is *quite* the prank, you guys, I mean, *shit*. And *good* for Mary. Thank God she's letting go. I mean, this is really wild. This is really funny."

Del was drunk on green beer and love and thanks and outrage. It seemed he was actually getting turned on by his wife, who at that moment popped her G-string and rolled her groin at the audience, as if she were scouring the inside of a barrel with her pubic hair.

"Dalai Lama!" Fraser shouted again, and then went silent, his head down in his tomato juice.

Suddenly Frank was standing. He could take no more of this. He looked down at Felix, and Felix looked up at him, sweating and frightened.

"*I* can handle it," Del was saying again. He appeared to have decided that, since his wife and brother and friends wanted him to be pleased by this, he would be pleased. So he was. "This is great. This is really wild. Mary." He shook his head slowly, transfixed as she grabbed a foot and pulled it over her head, her crotch showing darkly pink there in the center. Her eyes were made-up feline, and she appeared to be sneering at the college boys.

"Shame, woman! Shame, Mary!" Felix shouted now, pointing a sausage of a finger at the stage.

God, the idiot was trying to *explain* things to his brother, Frank realized. He grabbed Felix hard by the flab of his upper arm and pulled.

"Feel and I gotta go, Beak. So we'll just, ah, leave you here with, ah, ol' Regina."

"Well, okay!" Del rose now too. "Well geez, Frank, thanks. This was really too *much*," he said again, and as Frank dragged Felix out of the Yale Pub, Del continued to shout his amazement and thanks. Drunk and slurring now.

Outside it was cool and Frank took deep breaths to calm himself.

"Well, Frank, I must be off to begin my *fête*," Felix said nervously. "One would hope that—"

"Oh fuck off, you trained pig." Frank shoved Felix and stomped away with wide, wide strides.

He traversed an alley, stomped another block, and another, and then began to kick in car windows. Grabbing a parking meter in his left hand, he swung up and booted the driver's window with his right boot, the boot he had retrieved, along with the left one, from under Drala Mountain. He did not discriminate, he kicked cars as they came to him. He kicked in a Porsche, he kicked in a Mazda, then a Buick. He kicked in a Datsun because he hated the fact that he'd been aroused by Mary too, and he kicked in a Chev because his brother was in love and he himself was not. He kicked in a rusty old Volaré station-wagon because he was not in love with Laura and had been turned on tonight by Mary because she was unattainable, and above all men, and therefore the prize of all prizes. He kicked in a second Mazda because he realized he was jealous of Del's hellish love. He was about to kick in a second Datsun when he found himself flying through the air, landing hard on the cement, and then being kneed in the neck, pinned to the ground. Barely conscious, he felt himself being handcuffed.

"Citizen's arrest," said a brisk, efficient voice. "Try to get rough or get away and I'll beat the tar out of you and it'll go my way in court." The voice stopped, and its owner seemed to consider for a moment before whispering, "You big stupid darn creep."

Frank let himself be helped up. He was dizzy and hurting in many places. A rib felt broken. Such was his assailant's hold on him that he couldn't have struggled or fought back had he tried. Frank stole a dizzy look over his shoulder and saw a blond man in a tracksuit about his age, with an ignorant, honorable face. The citizen flagged down an approaching cop car and Frank was thrown inside.

CHAPTER TEN

What Happened after Cheops

*Twinship, so private an affair, is somewhat the
experience of an only child.*
        —from *Twins*, by Edythe Crane, Ph.D.

O nce, together, the brothers climbed the tallest pyramid in
the world.

Four months after Frank returned from Italy and Del graduated from Ohio State, the brothers again found themselves
playing basketball on the same team, this time in Egypt. The
wealthy family of an Egyptian exchange student who took in all
the Buckeye games and loved them arranged for an alumni team
to fly over, all expenses paid, for a series against the Egyptian
nationals. A full roster of alumni was hard to assemble on short
notice; at Del's suggestion Frank was invited. "He's every bit as
good as me," Del told them.

Del and Frank met the rest of the team at the Chicago airport.
Del knew most of them, others he recognized from their pictures in the gym hallways. Frank, scowling, unwashed, and with
a two-day growth of beard, carrying his wardrobe in a shopping
bag bound with a macramé belt, grunted howdy at the crew of
country, wind-burned basketballers and received open stares of
suspicion in return.

"Frankie likes to be different," Del whispered to some of the
guys he knew, and this placated them well enough. But when he
added, "I mean, *you* guys are different from him *too*," they

recalled not only that long ago Dellie had mentioned he was a
twin but that somewhere along the line they'd heard that twins
were either faggots or loco. Proof of this had appeared in the
form of this hippie hobo, Frank. Now they eyed Del askance as
well.

The team had the first-class compartment to themselves.

" 'We have done everything in our modest power,' " Coach
McPhee stood up and read from a telegram, " 'to make very
comfortable your long American legs.' " McPhee, a big-jawed
but small and balding man, sounded mocking as he read but
looked impressed despite himself. "It's first class for the Buckeyes all the way, boys." A deep-throated cheer filled the compartment, which was the size of a small dressing room.

And it was first class—for a night. They were booked into the
Alexandria Hilton and tried to rest as best they could for the
game scheduled that same night. Culture-shocked, jet-lagged,
and hot, a puff-eyed Ohio alumni team managed to prevail over
the inept Egyptian nationals by twenty-three points. Perhaps it
was this defeat that angered the rich father. But more likely it
was his discovery that, instead of the "All-American All-Star"
professional team he'd been promised by his son, what he'd
gotten was a so-so prairie alumni team. Ex-basketballers, as it
were. In any case they were relocated the next day at the Central
Guest House, a hostelry that, though not quite dilapidated, not
quite bug-infested, had no elevator, air-conditioning, or extra-
tall beds. They were issued meal tickets, which allowed them to
dine standing up at a greasy noodle-and-bean stall adjoining the
hotel. When word reached them that the rich Egyptian had been
unable to get his money back from the Hilton, that their former
rooms remained paid for but empty, and that their now third-
class treatment was nothing but petty vindictiveness, the team
took a vote on whether or not to go home. "We're here, might as
well see the mummies and stuff" was the argument that carried
the vote. In fact their plane reservations were nontransferable;
they were stuck there, like it or not, but no one wanted to admit
that. Both Del and Frank voted to stay. They played a game that
night and won by a mere eight points, and this in the face of

unabashedly biased refereeing. The next morning the team rode a cramped second-class train to Cairo—stared at by suspicious men in robes who ate goat milk curds off wax paper and held crates of live chickens between their legs—for a three-game stint and a week-long stay.

The brothers enjoyed Cairo. Frank told Del it reminded him of Rome, the Rome of two thousand years ago. The donkeys in the streets, the occasional camel, the open stalls burdened with peaches and gourds and mangoes and watermelons, some of which had burst open in the heat. Beggars waved arms like languid tropical weeds. The streets were a mix of stone, papyrus, and neon. The swarms of people—the tall, pale Copts, who claimed in their ancestry the great pharaohs of the past; the darker Arabs; the poor blacks from Ethiopia and the Sudan— were childlike, friendly, and, as Frank put it, "as silly as Italians." In searing heat the brothers wandered the bazaars. They drank endless bottles of juice and water but hadn't urinated in three days. ("It's the heat," Coach McPhee told them. "I saw a doctor. We're all pissing through our pores.")

Frank, deeply tanned from Italy and a summer on Wreck Beach, looked like a hook-nosed Semite. He bought himself a ridiculous billowing kaftan, lime green, which had printed on it, over and over, "The Wonders of Egypt." He took to wearing nothing else, and each time he wafted into the dressing room the team's reaction was split into those who thought he had a wacky sense of humor and those so disgusted by this Canadian freak in a green dress they refused to think about him at all. Coach McPhee approached him one night, regarded the kaftan, then took his eyes off it fast.

"I think it's best you didn't wear that." McPhee was used to looking up to tall people and had developed a tilt of head and confidence of eye to carry it off. But now, sweating and eyes bugged, he looked lost—in swarms of beggars, in strange food, in heat, in an Egypt of no rules, in a clutch of athletes graduated beyond his range of intimidation—and Frank saw before him a man searching for something, anything, on which to impose control.

"It's not good for the team. And it's an insult to our hosts."

"I'm wearing it," Frank told him. The stare he burned at the little coach would have been enough. "And our hosts are insulting *us*, who are you tryin' to kid." Frank was going to add, "And we're not a team to begin with," but he didn't see any point in frazzling the poor bugger's life completely all in one go. He was barely hanging on. He had sweat dripping off his little nose.

This interchange marked the beginning of the end of Frank's career with the Buckeye alumni. But he was right in his assessment of who was insulting whom. They'd once again been lodged in a dive. Their days were filled with tours that forced them to walk unnecessary miles in the heat. Their meals— indigestible noodles and beans and greasy sauce—were scheduled a half hour before game time. They supplemented this diet with fruit from the street stalls, fruit watered from the Nile, and so they spent lots of time moaning and shuffling to the toilet. The Egyptian refs carried on their blatant ways, and Ohio's best players found themselves fouling out early, their only infraction being that they scored too many points.

The worst insult took place during the second Cairo game, when the Egypt side added to their team two beefy goons whose role it was to beat up on Del, Frank, and a smaller guard named Howie Green. It was Frank who figured it out. Howie Green was a Jew.

"They're going at Howie there," he said to Del on the bench, pointing to the slender man taking yet another elbow in the neck, "and us. These assholes think we're Jews too. It's our names."

"And our noses," Del said, eyes widening.

They talked to Howie Green at the half. Howie had known it from the start but had said nothing. Frank, though, went public.

"Look," he announced to the team, "these guys are going after Howie and me and my brother because they think we're Jewish. Del and me are bigger than them, no problem, but Howie isn't. Right?"

"Are you guys Jewish too?" asked Coach McPhee, his eyes a foggy swirl.

"That's not the point, man," said Frank.

"That's not the point, *Coach*," said Coach McPhee.

"We're Swedish," Del added.

Frank and the coach glared at each other.

"Or Danish, I think," Del reconsidered.

Howie Green's teammates were seeing him with new eyes. Until now, he'd just been a regular, though quiet kind of guy.

"So what are we going to do about it?" Frank demanded.

"Nothing!" said Coach McPhee. He glanced warily at Howie Green, who had his head down. "These fellas just lost a war to the Jewish. The Seven Years War—"

"Six Day War," mumbled Howie, his head still down. Again eyes were upon him.

"Yes and, well, it's . . . a delicate situation." Coach McPhee seemed satisfied with this phrase. "It's only bee-ball, guys, remember that. And Mr. Green's man enough to look after himself. Right, Mr. Green?"

"Right, Coach," Howie said quietly, staring at the floor.

In the second half, when Frank Baal went after the goons with slashing elbows and discreet fists, sneering calmly all the while, he not only got thrown out of the game but also off the team.

"Take a shower, Mr. Baal. You can sit in the stands from now on," said McPhee. "That is not Buckeye bee-ball."

They had the next day and night off, and Frank announced to Del his plan of climbing Cheops to watch the sun set and the full moon rise. Having visited the great pyramid the day before, having stood in awe of it, Del first hesitated but then agreed with Frank's prediction that it would be wild and dangerous and spiritual. The climb would be illegal but, according to a German they'd met, the guards would merely arrest them at the bottom and take a few bucks as bribe and that would be that.

After dinner Frank and Del took a taxi to Gaza. They waited for a break in the guards' loose patrol, did the first one hundred feet of ascent at a run, found a hidden nook, and caught their breath. Frank had on his green kaftan and sandals and had just that day added a crimson fez. Del didn't look at him much.

"Present for ya, Beaker." Frank was bouncing something the size of a big toe in his hand. "Bit of sheesh."

Frank unwrapped it and hashish it was, a huge resinous wad of it. "Cost me two bucks, can you believe it?" He broke off a quarter of it, popped it in his mouth, made a lemon-face as he chewed, then washed it down with a gulp of sugarcane juice from his wine sack.

Del hesitated.

"Well, maybe things're exciting enough already," Del said. "It's a great day. We're climbing Cheops." He didn't look at his brother. "I mean, maybe that's enough."

"Yeah, Beaker, a natural high, you're right. Can't beat it." Frank used a sarcastic nasal voice, new since Italy. It made Del nervous. "As for me, I've played my last *bee*-ball game and I want to celebrate. But you're in training. A couple more crucial games against a very skillful squad of dedicated Arabs." Frank looked at Del. His tone lost some of its sarcasm. "It's just my opinion, but this stuff *is* a natural. It *lives* here. It goes with the heat. I can hear the rich ol' mummy buried under us applauding me."

Del held out his hand. He'd eaten the stuff once before and found it more profound and long-lasting than when smoked. What Frank had eaten would keep him high for two or three days. Del took half the amount and resigned himself to a fuzzy *bee*-ball game tomorrow night.

They continued their climb. The sun was falling into the desert hills. Exertion and heat brought the drug on quickly. Halfway up, Del's head felt like a watermelon whose rind had melted away, exposing spongy pink pulp and black seeds. The pulp buzzed; the seeds were sharp thoughts. No, habits. He followed his brother up, watching his groping hands and tall strides, watching the bony knees thrusting sharp green triangles in the front of his dress. That ridiculous green bag. The red fez. Del wore sneakers, shorts, and a polo shirt with a puma over the heart. How different they had become. This thought was sudden cause for panic, so Del refused to pursue that. His hands were by now covered with limestone. Ancient, ancient, these stones. What men had quarried them, dragged them here, and placed them? What were their thoughts? He'd read that you couldn't slide a razor blade between the joins, so precise was the knowledge that guided these stones' fitting. Yet scholars didn't know if it had been a labor of love or of slavery.

He stopped to breathe. He turned out to gaze. There was Cairo in the distance, under its modest Third World dome of smog. There the Nile, a flat, twisting silver snake. He looked down. Only halfway up and already the guards and lingering tourists were specks. He heard the faint bawl of a camel.

Frank, fifty feet higher, shouted down. "It'll be better at the top!" Del could hear his brother's gasping.

The apex was rounded and large enough for several people to sit back-to-back. One could sit or lie on flat shelves ten feet below. All around were candle stubs melted and stuck to stone, and initials carved in or painted. Dates: 1975, 1940, 1911. Del could not yet look out. When he did force his head up to take in the whole of what he expected would be there, his breath was sucked from him by a vista so enormous it contained—as expected—both Heaven and Hell.

Sitting back-to-back on the precious top slab, wheezing for breath, the brothers said nothing. Del calculated, by imagining his own sensations doubled, how very stoned his brother must be. Because Del felt himself to be very small. What he saw that made him so small was the entire span of human history—billions of births and deaths, scatterings of villages, towns, and cities spread over deserts, fields, mountains, continents. He had visions of immense barges drifting down the Nile, ferrying stone fresh-cut in blocks the size of railcars. He saw a billion people living, dying, taking countless billions of unanswered questions with them to the grave. He heard birth cries and death rattles echoing from prehistory's gloom, and they were identical to those cries shocking the corridors of hospitals today. He had thoughts too big to be his own. These grand understandings—made possible and precise by the hashish, but discounted for the same reason, because two minutes from now he would not remember them—had the exotic tenacity of the Sphinx and the vibrancy of the waves of heat rising from the desert floor.

"They call this the assassin's drug, Beaker," Frank said suddenly. Back-to-back, Del could feel his brother's words resonate physically in his own body. And he realized that, for the last five minutes or so, Frank had been singing "Ahab the Arab." Which he continued.

"A-hab. The A-rab. Sheik of the burnin' sands . . ."

His brother's irreverence. It was impeccable, in its way. Frank was so relaxed and slap-happy all the time. No, slap-angry. Could someone be relaxed and irreverent and angry all at the same time?

". . . wanted to ride. So he hopped on his camel name' Clyde."

The assassin's drug. Del felt nervous. This hashish was far stronger than anything he'd ever had. Could it make him do insane things? Could it make him kill somebody? Jump off this peak? He considered this. No. He felt courageous, in a way, an absolute way, but also very wise. He decided that if one murdered while on this drug, one would have to believe in what one was doing.

Del was shoved forward as Frank jumped up. He turned to watch his brother knock the fez off with a slap, then pull the kaftan up over his head and off. He stood naked, balling the kaftan up in his hands. He looked around, far off into the desert, a little nervously it seemed, as if seeing it for the first time. As if he were regarding cod liver oil, or a friend he didn't want to see. He was still singing, in a whisper. His eyes looked completely crazy.

"With rings on 'er fingers and bells on 'er toes and a bone in 'er nose, ho ho . . ."

Frank laughed, then suddenly cranked up a leg and farted. To Del, with no apology in his voice at all, he said, "Things are silly no matter where you go, eh Beaker?"

Frank laid himself down on his back, using the balled kaftan for a pillow, and closed his eyes. He appeared to go to sleep. But every few minutes he would mumble slurred lyrics to an insane song, twitch his shoulder in rhythm, and snap his fingers soundlessly. Movements like a dog dreaming. Passed out, yet antic. Del grew a little worried.

He stared at Frank's body. Naked, exposed at the top of the world, at the top of the monument that marked civilization's start. Del studied his brother's penis. It lay flaccid and white, having swelled a bit in its freedom under the sun. He had never so much as glanced at it before and now, studying, he saw it was identical to his own, even more so than their faces.

The following night Del played a fuzzy game while a foggy Frank sat in the stands, still mouthing words. They'd been forced to spend all night on Cheops. Losing all common sense in the midst of dreamy understandings that counted yet didn't count, they saw that the moon had gone down and that they had no flashlight. On their way down at sunrise they passed a French couple (over Del's protests, Frank was still naked) who climbed with excited glee until the bored looks on the twins' faces told them their adventurist *truc* was passé.

The Egyptians had not yet won a game, and with the help of the referees, timers, and goons they did everything to beat the Buckeyes in this last-chance game. Howie Green was being badly mauled. To make matters worse, the team had been hit with dissension earlier in the day. A tour had taken them to the Cairo Museum, where, to enter, one had to tread on a huge Israeli flag nailed across the foyer floor. Howie, of course, refused to cross, and a few others joined him in a protest coffee across the street. Others said they "wanted to see the mummies, big deal," and "what the hey, Howie, you're not them anyway, you're an American." Del waited with Howie, but Frank, slapping Howie on the shoulder and saying "I'll check it out for ya," pinched his kaftan up like a woman, tiptoed across the flag, and disappeared. He still hadn't slept, had been chewing little hashish pellets all day, and Del decided he was no longer responsible for his actions. Del explained this to Howie Green.

So on the court the Buckeyes were a testy squad, divided by vague loyalties, tired and dysenteric, elbowed by Arabian thugs, cheated by referees. They bickered on the bench, they botched easy passes and yelled at each other. They wanted to go home.

By halftime four starters had fouled out. Coach McPhee was by now screaming indiscriminately—at the players, the refs, the crowd, Egypt. A last ludicrous development saw them short by two players with ten minutes left to play, and not only did Coach McPhee have to pull on a jersey and enter the fray, he also had to signal up to Frank Baal in the stands. Del turned and looked at his brother, saw him smile wickedly back and pop the remaining hashish in his mouth. In a minute Frank arrived from the dressing room. He'd cut off the top of his fez, pounded its edges flat, and pinned it to his hair: a crimson yarmulke. His eyes bulged and looked in independent directions. They seemed to be two people shouting two different things.

The team huddled up.

"Let's just protect our lead," Coach McPhee was gasping. "Please."

"I'm getting those two Farouks," Frank whispered.

"Frank," said Del, "what good will that—"

"You're a chickenshit."

"Frank," Del said in his ear, "those guys, just like everyone on earth, are just trying to avoid their own pain." He was still suffering bouts of grand understanding.

"Chickenshit."

Clearly, Frank was not to be reasoned with. He was frazzled, he was in a realm of mindless reactions, titters, beeps.

He hit the first goon so hard with an elbow that snot flew from the Arab's nose. Up and down the court, holding his yarmulke down with one hand, he scored three baskets on the strength of craziness alone. Once he could have scored but, when the thug raised his arms to block the shot, Frank drilled the ball into his face. Up and down the court, a lurching dervish, limping madly, all elbows, nose, fists. He screamed during Egyptian foul shots, as players will in grade school. He fired a bullet pass to Del and yelled "CHICKENSHIT!"

Frank received four fouls within two minutes. On his fifth and final foul, one of the few he hadn't deserved, Frank refused to leave the game. He stared at the ref, smiled, and said simply, "No." He turned to take his place at the foul shot, the ref tugged his jersey from behind and shouted, but Frank swatted the hand away, turned to the ref, and roared, "NO!" The crowd went silent, but began to hoot and whistle when, incredibly, the referee let the game continue.

No more fouls were called on Frank. No more fouls were called on anyone. With seconds left and the team hanging back protecting their basket, waiting for the buzzer, an exhausted Coach McPhee patted Frank's bum and sighed a happy sigh. "You're a Buckeye, m'boy."

Not looking at him, Frank said, "Fuck off." He spun away and frisbeed his crimson yarmulke at the Egyptian team bench.

On a Saturday night six months later they were sitting crossleg-ged on the living-room floor of a rented house on Deep Cove Road playing board hockey by candlelight. Del had grown his hair now, and the candlelight had been his idea. He had left the team in Athens to tour Greece alone, and now his bearing was worldly and his skin bronze, while Frank had settled back to West Coast pale, and idleness.

They talked little this night. Their arms thrust over the board, hands grabbing and twisting the metal levers that made the men spin to clatter the wooden puck wildly back and forth. Above the board all was still, poignant.

The mood had to do with several things, all of them sad. It was Saturday night, but being new to Vancouver they had few friends and nothing to do. So, board hockey. And it was poignant because in Greece Del had met a girl named Mary, who was coming in a week to move in someplace with Del. The brothers would not live together again. Sadder yet, they had only an hour ago seen two kittens die. Randy, a pregnant cat they'd taken in, had given birth a week before. She rejected both kittens several days later. Armed with eyedroppers, force-feeding them at in-tervals, Frank and Del had kept vigil for four days, but the kittens went limp in their gentle hands only minutes apart. Together, kneeling, they'd watched the kittens die. Cooing low to them, nudging the glass teats to their clamped fuzzy mouths, they'd

seen the wonderful—in the literal sense—instant of death. So also
in the air was the ghost of their father and the question, could he
have saved the kittens? And now, though no one said a word,
over the board and clattering puck swirled nightmares and mus-
ings: their parents, their mother, the broken railing, instants of
death, their past together, their future apart.

Perhaps prodded by the proximity of death, Del decided to
tell Frank what happened to him in Greece. They took a beer
break.

"I kissed a dead man in Rethimnon," Del began, instantly
ashamed of the dramatic opening.

He told the story slowly, describing Rethimnon, his nights
there playing backgammon outside tavernas, drinking retsina,
lying on the beach by day. The hostels and the easy one-nighters
with American girls made willing by the anonymity of tran-
sience. His pace of telling was that of one recalling events,
hearing the words inwardly for the first time.

"I didn't pay much attention," he said, taking a pull on his
beer, "but there were these stories about a witch in town. She
had a corny name like Zena or Lola. They said she could read the
future, cast spells, all that stuff, and people gave her money. But
she was crazy, they said. They said if I saw a woman dressed all in
gold chains, that would be her."

One day, Del told Frank, he was lying on the beach as usual.
One of the guys he was with looked up and pointed to a commotion down the beach. A crowd had gathered about a hundred
yards away. Sounds of shouting. Just as Del noticed this he also
noticed a person standing right next to him.

"There she was, Frank. The witch." Del looked at his brother
and shrugged. "She had this canary yellow dress on that dragged
in the sand and this chain mail thing over it. Gold. She was
pointing at me, her finger right in my face. 'Boy in water,' she
was yelling. And, 'You can help.' Over and over. 'Boy in water,
you can help.'"

Del told Frank he realized immediately what was wrong.
While at Ohio he'd taken lifesaving as part of his referee creden-
tials; somehow the woman knew this. He sprinted the length of

the beach and plunged into the knot of Greeks to discover, lying at their feet, an unconscious teenage boy. An old Greek had been pumping the boy's knees into his abdomen. The sand around the boy's head was covered with the contents of his stomach: feta cheese, spinach, digested ooze. Sea water from the lungs. There was a strong smell. His eyes were open.

Del knocked the man away, knelt down, and began mouth-to-mouth. The Greeks edged back to make room for the tall American expert. Del felt his lips go snug and wet on the boy's; he forced air in, lifted his head, watched the chest fall. Again. He groped for a wrist. No pulse. The boy was cold. His eyes were open, staring into Del's but communicating nothing more than a child's glass marble. Del could taste feta cheese.

Now the witch arrived. She pushed the crowd back more, clearing a circle for herself and Del and the boy. With rattle and fistful of feathers, a parody of a Hollywood Blackfoot, she began a slow dance, moaning.

"I don't know, Frank." Del thought a moment. "I've never felt anything like it before. I've never felt so *good*. I don't know how to say it. Here was this dead guy, all this stinky cheese, his eyes staring at me, goddamned blue eyes, I was kissing his goddamn mouth, this crazy woman chanting around us. . . . I don't know. Maybe I was in shock or something. But it was like I could see . . . everything. Like having huge eyes. It felt so *cool*. *Cold*. I could see myself. Not like those out-of-body things. But sort of. I knew exactly what I was doing. I was doing mouth-to-mouth, and with *this* hand I was pounding on his heart, I could see the witch, I could feel a sand bug on my leg, here." Del tapped the back of his calf. "I could see all the people standing around watching. I could've held a goddamned conversation with them all, each one at the same time." He paused and looked up at his brother again. "Frank, I've never felt so *great*. It doesn't make sense. Here was this poor *dead* guy."

"Maybe," Frank said, "it was because he was dead. It was already over. There was nothing to worry about."

"Well, no, it was more. I felt . . . vast." Del considered. "Well yeah, maybe that's just shock."

Del saw that his brother's face was dark and pinched. Frank looked at the floor. Maybe he'd been expecting a miracle-recovery story but had gotten instead a story about Del, yet another inarticulate mystical straining at something. Or maybe . . .

"Yeah," Frank added quietly, "maybe it was just shock."

Del finished the story by telling how a doctor had arrived, how he'd helped with equipment and whatnot, but the boy had been declared dead. An autopsy revealed he had died of a heart attack. The story was front-page news, about a valiant American lifeguard who'd tried to save one of Rethimnon's sons. The next day at the hostel Del was approached by a shy, dark-haired woman. Very pretty. Mary her name was.

"Was that you on the beach yesterday?" she asked. "I heard all about it."

"Yeah."

"Want to talk about it?"

Del hadn't told Frank much about Mary because Frank hadn't asked. Nor did he now, and the brothers kept to their beer and board hockey. On the far wall the candlelight shot flickering magnified images of hook-nosed heads bent over a child's game. The rattle of the puck, a groan over a missed goal, the occasional burp. But Del thought of Mary constantly, and he thought of her now. He thought of her with his head, with his heart, and with his loins, and these three parts of him hummed their respective versions of her like a tautly tuned engine of yearning.

In Rethimnon she'd listened to his rescue story. She'd understood his excitement, his awe, his odd happiness. That night they'd slept together, but at her request they didn't make love. In a quiet way she'd mothered him, though nothing he knew of was wrong. Del found himself a little afraid of her.

He knew he sounded exotic when he gave her the encapsulated story of himself: he was a twin, sort of a Siamese twin at that; he was wandering after playing basketball in Egypt; he lived off inheritance money; it seemed a witch had picked him out of a crowd of foreigners as someone able to perform a remarkable feat.

She was small, dark, and more cute than beautiful. She didn't often smile, but when she did she meant it and it was always a surprise, transforming not only her but, somehow, the room, Del's mood, life. She was from the prairies and now lived in Vancouver. She had studied biology, then social work. She wrote painful chick poetry, she said, and then came the smile, ironic and therefore poetic. She too was wandering alone. Del decided this made them kindred souls: both of them were hand-some and friendly, neither possessed any pinched social flaws that kept others away, and yet they had chosen to venture alone.

The next day they hitched to Agia Galini, on Crete's southern shore. They set up an open-air camp on the deserted beach near the village, where, on a whim, Del bought a white lambswool rug. He tossed it out with his long arms and it unfurled lux-uriously, wafting to the sand like a veil of fleece. "I een fact bought thees to deeflower you upon," said Del, a comic French rake. It became his way with her: always shy of her, even after years had passed, he mocked his eagerness with a gentle joke, giving them both a safety valve.

Mary was lying on the fleece, her arms up to him and her smile coy, going with the joke, finding safety in obliqueness too. And they joined under the perfect sun, the purple sea at their feet lapping the sand like playful love itself. Their coyness fell away to honest fever. Del was driven mad by the sight of her sparse black pubic hair against the pure white of the wool. The faint smell of her sex tugged him right out of himself, he was com-pleted by her, it was destiny that he and she do this every day, lick and prod and love each other, on this beach.

They roamed islands, Simi and Serifos, Kos and Ios, eating kebabs and melon and egg-lemon soup, plucking pomegranates and figs from trees, sloshing retsina by night, singing songs with old men who plinked bouzoukis. They made love like hungry kids and bought each other love trinkets and toed hearts and initials in the sand. They had a sex-fantasy day and succumbed to each other's demands. Mary buried Del's body in the sand so that only his head showed. Squatting over him, her wish to be licked by a disembodied, hook-nosed head was granted. She seemed disappointed that Del only wanted her to lie there unmoving, so to copulate on her silently, intensely, at whatever speed he wanted.

But it was perfect, the union, the traveling.

"We could do this forever," Mary said once, and Del agreed, from his heart.

"But it's kind of easy like this," Del added. "When there's an end to it. You know? It's safe." Del was going back in two weeks.

Several days later Del asked her to live with him back in Vancouver.

"We can even get married or something. If you feel like it. Someday." Del said this shyly, a little afraid of her.

"You're too fucking *tall*," Mary said, then saw Del's sad, shocked face, saw that there were going to be times he could only be sincere, so she shouted quickly, "Yes! Yes!" and they were ecstatic for days on end, feeding each other sweet cakes and whispers, laughing and kissing and not caring that public romance was corny. And Del often sighed long sighs and shook his head, as though a grueling part of life had come to an end, as though some momentous deed had been done.

Del was right, it had been safer before, when their union had a time limit. It had been more possible to play. As the two weeks dwindled he grew more serious. When they walked, and though there was no reason for it, his eyes grew watchful and his body stooped to protect her.

Now Del had returned to Vancouver. It was 1975, Del had spent the last four years in the midwest, jock purgatory, and Frank had been in Italy, and they were both trying to catch up with the urban revolution. They had missed the first surge. By now the most dangerous drugs, the most naive spiritual hoaxes, and the flimsiest political whinings had died their welcome deaths, and, able to escape these embarrassing traps, they chose from what was left. But Del's choices rankled with Frank and vice versa.

In a nutshell: Del had grown long hair and Frank had cut his off.

Del read books and attended lectures on astrology, Zen, Findhorn, yoga. Politics he sampled and abandoned, deciding that the New Left was yet another complex master, and that unless all people changed first from within, any change from without was just another cage. Through these inner ways Del was treated to delightful flashes of insight. How was it that yoga, a relaxing of body, and Zen, which had no rules except sitting up straight, could seed identical gleamings? Marvelous. He suspected that if he worked hard, if he overcame frustration and Eastern paradox, within years his being could shine like a diamond, his eyes could see the hidden plan of this gaudy, confusing world. In any case, he'd be smarter. Four years of phys ed courses in Ohio didn't make one very smart. He still loved sport though, and refereeing would allow the application of certain principles he would learn.

Del didn't just want his brother's approval; it would do Frank good to be in on this. He tried grabbing Frank's attention with the most colorful stuff, which nonetheless always found Frank at his most snide.

"At this place Findhorn, in Scotland, way up north," Del would say, "where nothing but scrub used to grow, they grow these huge tomatoes, flowers, the biggest vegetables in the world."

"I hate tomatoes."

"But how do they do it? It's some kind of power spot, they say. It's like, if the planet was a lightbulb painted black and you scratched paint away at certain spots, that's where the light would shine out. There's one in Mexico, one in South America, one where ancient Babylon was, and this one in Scotland. Indians take drugs at these—"

"So *what?*" Frank's exasperated face. "And if it's so great there, if you believe that shit, why don't you just *go?*"

Well, true enough. And though Del knew that such things were perhaps a little too flashy to be important, why couldn't his

brother just relax into the speculation, the fun of it? Del's similar
outbursts on astrology always drew the same response.

"Look at us," Frank would sigh. "We probably have the same
planets and all that crap—am I right? And we're as different as a
fish and a spider."

We aren't, Del wanted to say. We are identically yearning,
we are identically scared. We have just taken up different teats.
The question was, what can we do to make things good before
we die? But he couldn't say this.

Frank, on the other hand, was not searching at all. He knew he
was in the right place at the right time. In this day and age no one
knew anything anymore, and so he could do what he wanted.
There were a thousand styles, a thousand ideas, and none of
them was true.

Italy had been a biding of time, a sneering at North America
from a distance. He'd had one salable skill—basketball—and in
one go he'd been able to sell himself, see the world, and get out of
the goddamned Fraser Valley, away from its ghosts.

The hippies in Italy weren't followers, they were spunky.
There were as many movements as there were people. Assholes
and momma's boys to a man, but individuals. Look what an old
fart like Fellini could get away with. Frank had taken to playing
the ukulele on Turin street corners, his smile changing to a blank
depending on who looked at him which way. He played basketball for money, he played the uke for the girls, he wrote poetry
for himself, he grew long hair for the hell of it, he tried heroin
for its famous sinister sleep. He was a man of colors. Different
girls, attracted to one color, were repelled by the others and so
stayed, trying to dig deeper. Frank laughed at them, and relaxed.

Here in Canada he had sold lyrics to a rock group. He had
heard his song on a college FM station and had taped it for Del,
who giggled and jumped like a boy. The song was inane, a
Zappaish ditty that went, in part:

> You buy leaves in their store,
> You dream of pumpkins in your dress,
> You want antennas for the aliens—

You're a loser, lady, confess.

You wanna baby, but no big belly,
You wear makeup behind your eyes.
So what you want? You don't know.
Your hesitation is a lie.

The chorus droned over and over, mantralike: "Better buy a weed-eater, do it with a weed-eater, better buy a weed-eater, do it with . . ." Popular music had taken one of two cheap routes: the psychedelic philosophizing had become silly love songs again, and the rhythmic trend had fallen to disco. But remaining underground, a third stream of druggy paradox had mutated anew to belches of irreverence and decadence and insult. Failed hippies loved being insulted and reminded of futility. Roxy Music was doing it in Britain. Captain Beefheart was doing it in the States. Frank Baal was doing it in Canada, if anyone wanted to listen. He was considering getting an agent.

On returning from goofy Egypt, Frank's notion was to buy a house with Del, the one man he could stand, the one man who could stand him. He envisioned a house that hosted parties, parties open to all, parties of such wit and challenge they would weed out the boring. Frank would wear a fake tiara, he would stick pins in his cheeks and draw blood, he would nudge the spines of the timid. He saw the house furnitureless save for the bedrooms, plantless save for the trees outside, where one could frolic and climb and vomit and take deep breaths before re-entry. Inside, the walls would be for painting graffiti and faces; outside, under the eaves, would be a brace of ten-foot-long papier-mâché circus cannons painted in clownish polka dots, which in the Vancouver rain would first droop like dinks, then collapse, then melt like candles down the Baal brothers' outside walls.

Stuff like that.

But Del was going off with Mary. The two would always be together. Frank would have to be polite. She wouldn't like him. The happy couple, the boring couple. The death of the Baal brothers, just when Frank was ready to give it a mature try. But this was the way of the stupid world, was it not? And if anything it would light a strong match under his gassy poetry.

So this Saturday night was for the brothers a night of small deaths—the kittens, packed still and cold in a milk carton in the garbage can; Del's recollection of cheesy death; the brothers' swansong as housemates. And when the cars crashed outside, it became a night of coincidence.

They played board hockey still. It was midnight, their eyelids drooped, their arms were automatic, and they hadn't spoken in an hour. A booming shock of impact shook the house, scraped their bums across the floor. Their hearts raced, their hair stood up.

"*What exploded?*" Del shouted.

"It's a car." Frank was already at the window, knowing.

Through the window, all was dark and still. Then they saw the black car in their front ditch, steam hissing from its radiator. Twenty yards away another car straddled the road, its side crushed in. The brothers ran outside, across the lawn, leapt the ditch in unison. A boy with blood-streaming face, broken nose, staggered from the black car. He held his head, wobbled, moaned, "My car. Oh man, my car." He smelled of beer. He ran his hand over the crumpled front, then fainted. Frank went to him. Del approached the other car, looked inside, and found it empty.

"Through the windshield," a voice at his side suggested, a neighbor he'd not met. "Or maybe it was just parked."

"No. Someone was inside." Del did not know how he knew this, but he did. Once more, he knew everything.

In the ditch water Del spotted the crown of a head. He and the neighbor, with Frank joining them too, each found a grip and pulled. As the man emerged—forties, fattish, dead—Del could feel the mashed bones and organs of the torso fall to a pile around the waist, like pulling up a sack of mud and gravel, nothing intact. The man's empty pant leg shouted of half a leg missing, gone at the knee. Strangely, there was no blood. The bleeding youth staggered up to kneel at the man's side and crooned, "Hey, man, you okay? Hey, sorry about your car, man."

Del, on this night of coincidence, was excited again. A man was dead, he had dragged him from the ditch, he now cupped the thoughtless head in his hands. He could hear the crickets begin to chirp again, could hear the very first one as distinct from the others, and now a frog as well. Neighbors' doors opening, and whispered questions around them. He felt Frank's shoulder against his, so he turned to him. Frank's face was drained of blood and sharp, as though carved in wood by a primitive exaggerator. It was Del's face too.

Del locked his eyes onto his brother's. He tilted his head and pierced his brother with his eyes, shouting silently: *Frank, do you feel it, so clear and cold, do you feel this, so vast?* Del knew from Frank's look that he was there too, Frank knew where Del was, exactly. They held the stare, their union perfect in shock and vastness, and while Frank's eyes remained steady, Del's grew insistent, pleading. Just as the clamor of new neighbors rose behind them, Frank's shoulders lifted tantalizingly slow in the charged air, a shrug. His lips traced the bleakest of smiles.

"So *what?*"

CHAPTER ELEVEN

Freedom

*Apparently there is but one rule, which is that there
are no rules. Such paradox makes this Observer want
to cease writing, and die. I begin to see paradox in the
questionable existence of potatoes. I predict that the
death of Observation will be tainted by pathos and
slapstick: Fate will pass sour wind, and Your Observer
will be gone.*

—Felix d'Amboise

Felix d'Amboise well knew that while exploring the phe-
nomenon of synchronicity, Carl Jung came to understand
that most events of coincidence are on a small scale, and meaningless in and of themselves. Jung would be thinking of buying
his wife a scarab beetle brooch, and suddenly there on the sill a
scarab beetle would land. On the surface, at least, the closest
such events came to "meaning" was a kind of minor comedy.
Jung also discovered that twins are magnets for more than their
share of coincidence.

But Felix was not aware of the coincidence that occurred late
on the night of Mary Baal's disrobing at the Yale Pub. Again, it
was a coincidence more comedic than meaningful. Perhaps even
its comedy was questionable, but not its oddity: never before had
five people vomited at exactly the same moment, each person
vomiting for a different reason, yet each person's nausea having
its roots in the same set of circumstances.

Frank, bruised, exhausted, and profoundly hating life, sat on a lower bunk in a downtown Vancouver jail. The evening had been a nightmare. Poor stupid Del. His slutty, squirrely wife. Enough was enough. He would stay out of his brother's life now.

He was alone in his cell, a large one with five other bunks. It lacked a toilet; instead its cement floor sloped to a hole in the center. He was in the drunk tank. It smelled of urine and morons and rage.

Keys clanked, the door swung open, and a young bum was shoved in. His blond hair was mussed and he staggered, but otherwise he looked healthy and well built. Dressed in a tracksuit.

"Got shigaret?"

Frank stood to get at the crumpled pack in his pants pocket. He'd give him five, shut him up for an hour.

Before Frank could flinch, the drunk cocked a leg and kneed him mightily in the groin. As Frank was falling, before the worst pain hit, before the shock traveled up to his brain and back again to his groin, he recognized the man who had arrested him.

"Like that, creep?" came the whispered voice, bubbled through a smile, no trace now of a slur. The cell door opened again, sounds of laughter, a slap on the back. Frank lay bug-eyed on the concrete, vomiting beside the hole in the floor.

Felix, alone in his posh room, felt weak and forlorn. His first night of *fête* had been disrupted. Tomorrow he would have his women, the next night his drugs, but the anticipation of these events did nothing to enliven him. No, instead of his grand repast he had been served up a feast of human mediocrity and confusion. Del had been shamed, his wife had debased herself, Frank had been mean. The specter of their ignorance had drained him so. Sitting in that insidious tavern, watching them, Felix had felt confused and timid, and merely fat. He had been helpless himself and, because of that, tainted. Outside the bar, Frank had shoved him.

Returning to his rooms, Felix ordered two family barrels of Kentucky Fried Chicken. These vessels of fowl and grease arrived—and frightened him—complete with family portions of white rolls, mahogany gravy, limp fries, pale slaw. An hour later, barely able to see over his stomach, Felix sat in his special leather chair facing the TV. Rock videos blared, and he could not hear his own moans. Empty buckets, cartons, plastic forks, and gravied napkins lay scattered, as if thrown in great haste, on the luxurious mauve carpet. The spectacle triggering his frantic waddle to the bathroom, where he commenced his painful, thunderous heaving, was that of a forty-year-old blue-and-yellow haired rock star in studded arm bands and tights, screeching with perfect insincerity to thousands of screaming girls that they would be saved by his love.

Downstairs at Mary and Del's, Fraser arose wincing from his bed. Mr. Baal—Del—had tucked him in and turned on a night-light for him, but he could hardly see. He bashed his knee on the way to the laundry room.

He loved his new bedroom, the first he'd had to himself in his life. Yet tonight he didn't feel alone. The room was crowded with whispers and crying and voices giving commands that he was too tired to obey. He knew it was these new pills. A yellow one and a black one, at breakfast, lunch, and dinner. Mrs. Baal—Mary—said it might take time to get used to them. He hoped she was right, or he would have to hide them in his mouth and spit them out later like he had the pills before, the purple ones. But he would get used to them because Mrs. Baal—Mary—loved him. She'd given him her mother's homemade quilt, there were roses on it, and Mr. Baal's—Del's—dog loved him too and slept right there where he could pet her, even though she smelled like his socks before washing day.

Fraser didn't have his glasses on and he almost walked into the wall beside the laundry-room door. He made out Northam at his feet. She lay sprawled on her back, her hind legs wide apart. "Dalai Lama," Fraser whispered, and then went into the laundry room, bent over the washtub, and threw up bile and chemistry and jagged voices for the tenth time that day.

Mary, stepping quietly through the kitchen door, had had quite a night. She had fulfilled her contract, performed her last show. The decision to quit had come a week ago, partly as a result of her talk with Frank. Explaining things had somehow exorcised them, and felt like a punctuation mark. She realized that stripping no longer thrilled with its perverse contrariness but had grown merely perverse. She would have been disgusted with herself had she not learned something large. Also, tonight she had brushed off Art, her on-off lover of the last few months. She had never really loved him, but Art had been wealthy, charming, discreet. He'd tried to get her a part—what a cliché, but he seemed sincere and able—in a local dance musical. He had cocaine and a good sense of humor. But he was empty of soul. Or something. Mary had only to compare Art to Del and the big part of her heart, the one to be trusted, moved Del's way without fail. Her doubts were still huge, but she had chosen him for now. And the herpes Art had given her seemed to have cleared up, so maybe she wouldn't have to lie to Del so much now and bar him from her bed. In fact, as she thought all of this through there in the kitchen, the idea of moving the double bed back to their bedroom comforted her. Scared her too, but the warmth of the notion—Del's good old big body, his soft breathing through that long length of lung—won out. Yes, she had quit Art just in time.

Mary saw the note taped to the fridge. She stepped up and read it. One arm was still in her coat.

"Mare—you were great. You tart! Thanks, sweetheart, for remembering. You and Frankie should put your heads together more often. It was weird, you up there in front of everybody, it kind of turned me on. Hope you're still wearing that trashy makeup. Couldn't wait for you—Fraser's still shitty and had to get him home. Come to bed, you cupcake."

Mary flattened her cheek against the cold enamel. She began to sweat. Her eyes bugged out, she shut them, they bugged out again. She lurched to the hall bathroom, fell in front of the toilet bowl. Drenched in icy sweat, her body whiplashed in a quick convulsion, images of the Yale Pub and a distant Greek beach warring in her head.

Del heard his wife come in the kitchen door. He'd been dozing, still quite drunk, the room twisting and spinning. He no longer wanted to make love, was maybe unable in fact, but tonight was funny and special and Mary had set such a stage she would expect romance. It might help if he could get rid of his stomach full of beer. Reeling carefully to the ensuite bathroom, Del turned the taps on full and knelt at the basin. He rammed three fingers down his throat, twiddled with his glottis, found the nausea point, and brought forth a gush of beer and potato chips. He was as quiet as possible and stifled the heaving reflex. It felt wonderful and sobering.

In time Mary did come to bed, but she sat on the foot of it with her clothes on and told Del everything.

Two days later, Sunday, Frank languished in a new jail cell, awaiting trial for breaking and entering, destruction of property, theft over two hundred dollars, and dealing in stolen goods. They had matched his boots with the imprint taken at the Morgan house; they had recovered a shotgun and the Craftsman drill and socket set he'd fenced. He was also charged with public mischief, interfering with public transport (the sasquatch event), seven counts of destruction of property (the Porsche, the Mazda, etc.), and resisting arrest. Frank consulted Wally Kenny, who in turn contacted friends in criminal law, and Frank got word that the proof was ironclad, that "somebody big" was behind the prosecution, that requests for plea bargaining had been laughed at, and that the big somebody had initiated so many delay tactics that Frank faced being shunted around the court system for years. A guilty verdict and a prison term were certain.

Frank felt calm, almost content. He had brought them all to Hell, and here it was. He studied the cell walls. A cushy pastel blankness, not unlike a nursery. Here, in the nursery, in jail-school, he would learn.

He had a headache, and his bruised ribs made it hard to breathe. His balls were still swollen and all his movements were slow, hunched, protective. This felt good, like justice. All was as it should be. That morning he had phoned Del and instead got Mary on the phone. She didn't know where Del was. At first her voice was as crisp as the time she took her hand off his crotch, but soon it became soft and tremulous. Del had run from the house in the middle of the night after she confessed, she told Frank. She didn't know where he was. Most likely in Winnipeg, because he had a game there today.

Then for a long minute neither Frank nor Mary said a word.

"I'm sorry we all saw you naked," Frank said then from his nursery. Mary hung up quietly, and Frank tried to imagine the expression on her face, but couldn't.

They'd taken away his belt and shoelaces, as in the movies. When he'd asked politely for writing materials, the pencil they brought was a miracle of penal engineering: a flabby pencil with rubber wood and gooey lead, so he couldn't stab his eyes out in despair. He would spend his hours and days writing long letters to Del, describing life from the inside, explaining life from the very middle of the Black Spot, how it wasn't really so bad, but warning him to keep on his toes. He would write epistles to Laura, woo her with his pain and precision. She would no longer want him, but he'd win her over with his new . . . goodness? What a riot! She would visit and they would smooch tenderly through visiting-room glass. They would be married by the prison chaplain, they would be allowed to consummate the marriage in one of those special trailers, and Laura would wait for him and have his baby and build her career in choreography. Frank decided to mail her a cheque for five thousand dollars this very day so she could get started.

He would write poetry and song lyrics. He would begin now. The Snuff had just recorded an album, using some of Frank's songs. This nudge of success had blasted the group's egos and split them up. The bass player had already formed his own group, Lunker Smallmouth, and in a letter told Frank he wanted to "go the intellectual route." He paid Frank in advance for lyrics.

In his cell, quite calm, Frank began to write a song about forcing a child's wooden alphabet blocks down the throat of a puppy.

> The A goes down the pup,
> little ache, a little ache,
> The B goes down the pup,
> little bleed, little bleed,
> The C goes down the pup,
> little cry, a little cry

He stopped writing, read the thing over, shook his head, and balled it up. Tossing it to a corner, he whispered, "*Good*bye." On a fresh sheet he stabbed with his gooey pencil and wrote this:

Kryptonite

Fall down to the music
and shake in every cell.
Lie down and face the music,
rest in heaven, twist in hell.
Your baby's lips are squeezy and full,
yet she will die, they'll dry and drop off her skull.
Lie down and taste the panic,
it's a riot, but what's going on?

The music of the spheres
they say is harmony, and gleaming.
So I wonder why supermen lie,
and disintegrate, and die,
and choose the path of dreaming?

Frank read the words over. God, he hadn't written such a mellow thing in his life. And so much explaining. It was teenage. And yet he didn't ball it up. He smiled. He was a teenage girl.

Soon he'd be writing goddamn love poetry. Or lyrics for supermarkets.

Then he laughed, realizing Del would probably like this song. Maybe he'd write songs for Del now.

"God. There he is. In Winnipeg."

It was not hard to pick out Del's loping gait from the tangle of uniformed and stripe-shirted bodies. Wally Kenny slid in closer to Mary on the couch, and once again took her hand.

"Yeah. There's your man."

On the floor at her feet the wads of Kleenex had dried. Through her crying bouts Wally had smoothed her hair and cushioned her convulsing body with his. Now she sat slumped and staring. The TV appeared to anchor her.

"He looks okay, Wally. He's running fast."

For the third time, Mary had spilled the beans about her secret life. This time, at Wally's urging, she'd let herself examine the details, exploring the anatomy of illicit sex and stealth.

"Your tongue gets addicted to spices, I agree," was one of Wally Kenny's culinary observations. "You want it spicier and spicier, and finally you can't taste the good old pasta anymore."

"So I should go on the brown rice diet again?"

"Should? Don't know. I'm not one to judge. I went for spice myself. Girls were okay. But then it got so normal. Or something. The first guy I fiddled with I felt so unbelievably naughty and horny. I've never been so shocked and twangy in my life." Wally sighed. "And now a guy feels . . . normal."

"So?"

"Well, yeah, a girl might feel twangy again now." He gave Mary a comic leer, put on a lolling-tongue idiot's face, and passed a paw across her breast. He laughed and shook his head at his joke, and Mary smiled a tired smile for the first time in two days.

"But it would be more funny than twangy," Wally concluded.

They talked about Mary's childhood, her relationship to her mother, their clinging love and screaming matches. They talked about Del. They talked about familiarity's breeding of contempt: the snores, the habits, the irksome tics of face and humor. They agreed that of course there was nothing wrong with non-monogamy save that, sadly, it hurt people. Wally cooed warmly throughout, complementing her moanings with tales of his own affairs and hurts.

"Honey. You want to hear about guilt?" he would say, waxing Jewish and matronly, holding up an arm from which dangled an exaggerated hand. It was plain that his reservoir of experience—betrayals and pleadings, tales of sadistic minds and slavish hearts—was broad compared to hers. For delicacy's sake he barely skimmed the surface of the sordid, his intent being to elevate Mary's spirit, not outdo her. Instead of analyzing her statements he merely agreed with them. His eyes were bright and alert, his arms rich with gestures.

"Honey, I know. I *know*. It's all so crazy," Wally would say.

"Wally, my life is falling fucking *apart*," Mary would say.

Wally held her. And they watched Del on TV, running, blowing his whistle. Mary studied his movements with the sad, fixed face of one staring at a portrait of a dead relative.

"And the adoption's off for sure now, Wally."

"The hearing's in a week?"

Mary nodded, her face in her hands.

"He knew nothing about it at all?"

"Only you and Fraser know. God, I shouldn't have told the poor little guy. But I knew he'd love it so much. He's been so lousy lately."

"And you can't change his drugs?"

"Unless we adopt, no. I don't even have a say in changing his goddamn psychiatrist. That's why I want to adopt. God, they're experimenting on him and they see him for twenty minutes every two weeks. Del and I talked about it a year ago. I know he'd love it."

"You going to tell him?"

"But what if he came back just because of *that*?"

"Maybe he could just come for the hearing. Pretend to be the happy couple for a day and go from there."

"He'd stay anyway. To be a father. You know Del."

Wally turned again to the tiny tall man on the TV. He seemed to be running nonstop. The crowd was booing him once more. Mary huddled her knees against her body and closed her eyes. Wally watched her eyeballs rolling under the lids, wondering what she was seeing.

"And you know what, Wally?" Mary grabbed his shoulder, grim with another idea. "Del's freaked out now, he's jealous. Someone else touching me. It's all jealousy. But *I've* been jealous from day one. It's hard to admit this, but it's Frank. I can hardly *look* at Frank. You know, for years I've had the feeling that Del sits around all day worrying, thinking, *yearning* about Frank? They hardly even *talk* to each other. But there's this big *thing*." Mary sat up straight. "This big-deal *understanding*. At least Del thinks there is. It's like I'm competing against something I can't even see."

"Like the sky. The tides. The pull of gravity." Wally mimicked a profound Charlton Heston.

Mary's eyes appeared to be pleading with the TV.

"Want to hear a good one?" Wally's voice fell to a conspiratorial hush. "I remember Del and his first girlfriend. This was in high school. He never slept with her, he was too shy to try. And then at a party along came old Frankie. Everyone was really drunk, it was a basketball something or other, and Del passed out. Along comes Frankie and he takes Tracey—that was her name, she was girly and cute—and screws her in the back yard. We could hear them. It was pretty funny, but sort of sickening. Nobody got mad at him or anything because it was their business. Del and Frank. That's how it always was. *Their* business. We stayed out of it. It was like they were one person or something."

"So what did Del do?" Mary whispered.

"He *thanked* him," Wally hissed. "For showing him what she was. Something like that."

"God."

"I don't quite know. It was *their* business. No one saw anything like an argument. But Del dropped little Tracey like a
stinky potato."

"God."

"I picked her up. Nobody knew it, but she was my last time
with a breeder. My next girlfriend was a hockey player. Name of
Bob."

"The funniest thing, but I guess it's typical," Mary said, "is
that now that Del's gone—and God, he's so mad I know he's not
coming back—I want him more than ever. Now *he's* spice.
Goddamnit."

"Well there you go. Maybe you guys needed this. You see
what he's worth to you now. And now he won't take you for
granted. As they say."

"I don't think he ever did."

"But now he never will."

Mary watched the figures on the screen scurry in their manic
patterns.

"Maybe he won't come back at all."

Wally watched the screen, considering.

"Yeah, maybe he's kicked you out of the game."

"I've violated the rules."

"He's blown the whistle on you."

"Personal foul."

Mary and Wally often watched Del on TV, and jokes like
these were too tired to raise smiles.

Referees are not noticed unless they draw attention to themselves by calling a bad game or hamming it up. One of Del's little
reminders to himself was "Be accurate, and be invisible." An
irate player will blast an obtrusive ref with "They be paying tah
see me not *you*, muth-fuckah," and the player is correct in saying
so. But this Sunday in Winnipeg any shrewd observer of referees could see that the tall one out there in center field, the head
ref, was calling a game like no ref had ever done. His speed was a
sprinter's, his style choppy and severe for a man so big. His
whistles were bell-clear and driven by a full lung. Not even the

hypercruel defensive backs emitted such nervous energy. It seemed his flag was out of his back pocket and thrown before the foul had been committed, as if this ref knew in advance. The flag was being thrown a lot.

It hadn't exactly come as a decision, but Del knew before the contest started that he was going to call a perfect game. On the field now, his mind was open wide, his eyes missed nothing. He ran fiercely yet hardly breathed. Explosive thoughts and images shoved his soul this way and that but could not nudge the diamond focus of his vision. Whistling down a play, picking up the ball, and stepping off penalty yardage, his mind would go blank and an image of Mary popping her G-string and lifting her leg would stiffen his spine and shoot juice to his feet again. He would break into a run for no apparent cause. Sometimes the image would be this: a shadowy man on top of her, his back concave with orgasm, his head arching up, jaw dropped, gasping, resembling an evil, animated fox.

No ref had ever called a perfect game before, and by halftime Del was being loudly booed. It was not because the fans felt their team hard done by. Del knew he had called roughly the same number of infractions on Ottawa as on Winnipeg. And Winnipeg led by ten points. No, they booed because of the number of penalties: Del was calling one, sometimes two per play. They were blaming him, not the players, for these penalties, for this turtle-paced game. As if it was *his* fault these players had learned to commit holding infractions as a matter of course. They booed because they had never seen football like this, football controlled perfectly by the rules. Each time Del stepped out front, clicked on his hip-mike to say "Ottawa, number sixty-eight, offensive holding, fifteen yards, second down repeated," he intoned both a lecture and a sigh, to let everyone know he was only doing his job, and doing it with perfect and unyielding authority. He was letting everyone know he planned to continue as unbiased and absolute as an electric eye. The players could trespass over the line or not.

Del knew he was setting a courageous example. To all referees, all the players, all the sportsmen of the world. But he didn't dwell on this. Nor did he care about losing his job, or that he'd caught sight of Head Official Tuck sitting in the stands. If called on later to explain his actions of this day (and he would be), he would use the name of Mahatma Gandhi, another in the line of men who had stepped selflessly into fiery action, sacrificing themselves in their role as truth's agent.

"Ottawa, number fifty-four, offensive interference. Winnipeg, number sixteen, defensive interference. Penalties cancel each other, no loss of down."

Del's plan was to change the face of the modern game, to restore its original purity. But he didn't let grandiose thoughts interfere with his precision, knowing that today's game was but a necessary first drop in the bucket of fair play.

"Ottawa, number sixty, offside. Winnipeg, number forty-two, offside. Ottawa, number eighteen, unnecessary roughness. Winnipeg, number eleven, personal foul. Penalties cancel, down over."

The players had quit complaining after the first quarter and now only shook their heads, their eyes glowering from inside their big shiny helmets. The other officials had changed tactics too, questioning him now in polite tones and jokes, but these subordinates Del overruled in a monotone, as though quoting scripture. He *was* quoting scripture. His one explanation to them was, "Now they know what to expect. Let's all tell the truth."

The fans had expected a Sunday of fun, and had so far had a great time booing. They grinned as their own and thousands of other boo-tones mixed frequencies and resonated in their chests. But soon they tired, and their boos became cranky. Before each play, whistle in mouth, Del relaxed each muscle in his face and bent down, hands on knees.

In the corridor at halftime Head Official Tuck approached Del from behind and put a gentle hand on his shoulder. He was smiling.

"This is real cute. You're gone, Baal," he said.

"It has to be voted on." Del looked down at his cleats. "I'm writing a letter and sending it out. To every ref and to the players' union."

"Oh, everybody knows what you're up to, mister. And nobody's having a very good time."

Del looked up. Something sharp and surprising sliced into his vision of Tuck.

"Fuck their good time. And fuck you, dink."

Del was not very good at being Frank. But, walking away from Tuck, he suspected he had just tasted his brother's brand of joy.

All day long the toe had been aching with the intensity of the crowd's booing; now, insulting Tuck, Del felt a wheedling of pleasure there, not unlike a feather tickling your armpit.

In the Officials' Room no one spoke. Del was liked, but considered a bit of an egghead in this redneck realm. Del knew this. He also knew his colleagues could smell a vacancy for head referee. He gladly would have explained himself to them, but what was the use? In any case, he was unable to speak. Sitting at his stall, head in hands, he suffered in the halftime hiatus an attack of images: breasts (Mary's), buttocks ("his"), jokes at his expense, Lil' Regina giving her pink nether mouth to the faces of sailors, boys ... football players. Even more acute was his suffering when the images took a turn for the better: Mary on a fleece rug in Greece; Mary mothering the chimps, their love of her; Mary regarding him over a wine glass, her eyes knowing him to the hilt; Mary curling her chipmunk body into his as they watched a Marx Brothers movie, both of them not laughing for the same reasons. Thoughts, pleas, would interrupt this flood of images.

"*Mary* ..."

"I thought she was in *dance class* ..."

"All this time Frank *knew* and he let me ..."

"Have I *left* Mary ... ?"

"Anniversary! I'm an asshole, *Frank* left me looking like an *ass*hole ..."

The buzzer ended the break, and as the men in striped shirts filed by none of them noticed Del's pinched, bloodless lips, or the tear hanging off his chin, caught on a whisker.

The second half carried on like the first. Del had to change whistles, his first was filled with spit. The fans booed less, resigned to the crawling spectacle of perfect arbitration. By the fourth quarter the coaches of both teams had filed formal protests. With five minutes left, Ottawa and Winnipeg were tied with twenty points apiece.

Del already knew his effort had been in vain. His perfect game would change nothing. Gandhi was dead, in India people still starved, millions died with dreams unfulfilled, and marriages still broke apart to the pain-packed melody of sobs and gnashed teeth. So what if perfect football was played while, in hotels, wives gave their pink fruit to strangers? What use were good intentions when wives smiled from dank hotel beds, street neon flashing off the saliva on their teeth? When poor souls like Fraser had pennies thrown their way while cruise missile scientists shuffled millions? When a twin brother led a shitty, careless life and didn't care enough to help you lead a good one? For all he knew, Frank had slept with her too. Why not? It would be funny. If they hadn't already, he would write them both a letter, suggesting it. They should, they were both made of the same hairy stuff.

His wife gone, and now probably his job. All he had left was his perfect game, which he would call for its own sake and nothing else. Rules, like vows, were meaningless unless obeyed.

One minute left to play. Del's eyes remained perfectly clear. He watched a Winnipeg halfback plunge over the goal line with the ball. He heard the fans go wild with victory. But he had seen how the other Winnipeg back had nudged his shoulder into the ball carrier's backside, a helping shove, just the slightest illegality. So he'd seen no touchdown. No ref would make that call, not on a home team's winning touchdown; Del himself wouldn't have in the past, but he had seen it perfectly, and now with face slack he waved a horizontal "No" to the touchdown and already the cheers were lurching back on themselves, not so

much boos as hoarse screams of disbelief. Del stepped into a
clear patch of field and snapped on his hip-mike.

"Wow. He called it no touchdown," Wally said, his boredom
lifting slightly.

"Yeah." Mary's eyes focused on the game again.

Exhausting each other with talk, they'd watched the game
without really watching. Something about it was odd, but they
weren't sure what. Del's voice had come on an awful lot. In their
noncommittal Canadian way, the TV commentators hinted at
controversial officiating.

"Wonder what the call is," Wally mused aloud. "Maybe
offside."

"No, wasn't offside," said Mary.

They listened as Del's voice boomed louder than ever as he
fought to be heard over the jeering roar.

*"Winnipeg, number twenty-two, blocking from the rear, touch-
down disallowed, third down."*

Del snapped his hip-mike off. Mary and Wally watched him
hesitate, then click it on again. He looked up in the general
direction of the TV cameras.

*"Mary, get out of my house and don't come back. Frank, you're a
fucking asshole."*

The tall referee clicked the mike off again, spun around, and
started walking. Then he stopped, spun to face the camera banks
again, and once more clicked on the mike.

"EVERYONE'S alone now, fucking IDIOTS."

The referee walked calmly off the playing field, the air around
him silent for a few seconds as the ghost of his last words
reverberated back and forth in this bowl of thousands. He
removed his hat—he was the only official with a white one—and
frisbeed it at the Winnipeg players' bench.

Frank strode the trail to Felix's place, feeling lightweight and
light-hearted, wearing nothing but shorts and jail shoes (they'd

kept his boots as evidence). This first day of freedom, the
Wednesday after his weekend arrest, was sunlit and breezy, and
he not only felt light-hearted but also childlike and curious. He
was a pawn of fate, not really free. He had no more choices. He
wondered what his new life would be like.

The escape had been easy. So easy he felt more like a stroller
than an escaper.

He hadn't planned it. Nor had he really wanted to be out of
jail, if the truth were known. He'd merely wanted to talk to Del.
No longer allowed to use the phone, Frank had sent messages to
Del, and to Mary and to Wally and to Felix, asking where Del
was. No one had replied. Frank didn't blame them.

When the duty officer led him out to the back hall for exercise
and then disappeared (Frank, after all, had been a timid, model
prisoner for days), Frank simply wandered as far as he could to
the back of the building, found a door that opened, and walked
through. He actually passed a couple of chatting guards. Perhaps
because he didn't really intend to escape, he didn't look like an
escaper. He didn't break into a run, he didn't skulk behind
garbage bins waiting for his chance—he merely looked around
him, said "Ah!" when he saw what he wanted, and jogged across
the street to the pay phone.

He had no change. He could have phoned Del collect, but
didn't think it would be a good idea. Standing out on the street in
full view of any passing police, his only sense of urgency was that
they might catch him before he talked to Del. A woman approached, pushing her baby and groceries. Frank had always
been a good panhandler, able to frighten citizens into acts of
kindness, and he won a quarter from her.

He dialed, and as the phone began to ring a police cruiser
turned slowly onto the back lot. Frank made no attempt to hide.
Someone picked the phone up at the other end. He knew right
away it wasn't Del.

"Hello!" answered an odd, twisted voice. It sounded like it
was being channeled through a synthesizer.

"Is this, ah, Fraser?"

"Is this Fraser? who doesn't talk to strangers?"

Frank pondered. He put himself in Del's place and tried to talk as his brother would.

"Fraser, it's Del's brother, Frank. I'm no stranger." He paused. "And anyway, I think it's okay to talk to strangers over the phone."

"You are no stranger to jail."

Frank sensed the synthesized voice was shaped through a smile.

"Is Del there?"

"In jail?"

This was going nowhere. Fraser was unable to hang onto the smallest thread of logic. And it sounded like he was doing something with his tongue, sponging it around in his mouth so that each word had a different pitch. Frank didn't want to picture this.

"Fraser. Ask Del to come to the phone."

Frank heard the vacuum noise of Fraser's head pulling away. He noticed another cruiser gliding into the lot, and someone coming out to greet it, talking quickly. He heard Fraser calling.

"Mr. Baal—Del—come to the phone!"

More silence, nearly a minute of it.

"*Fraser!*" Frank yelled. The vacuum sound filled with Fraser's head. "Is Del even there, Fraser?"

"No."

And so on. In a similar way Frank discovered Mary was away as well, staying at her parents'.

"You're there all alone?"

"No grease fires, don't play with matches, and *don't go near electric outlets!*" Fraser's imitation of Mary was eerie, as it too was synthesized and tongue-rolled. Fraser laughed heartily, then stopped, serious. "Can I change channels?"

"I think so, yes. But—"

"Cause I got no money for Bibles anyway."

"What?"

"For God. Mr. Ainsley—God—says I'm a good Christian and that I have enough money for Bibles for all my relatives for the perfect loving gift but I don't think I do. Wait, I'll check."

Sounds of Fraser going through his pockets. "No. Mr. Baal—Del's brother—you didn't *steal it, did you?*" Outrageous synthesized laughter.

"Have you *seen* Mary, Fraser?"

"She's living with her parents again and it's like a bad dream. You can't go back, you know. And I can't live there too because Mr. Mary's father is stroked again. *Maybe.*" Fraser paused. "We're *not sure.*" Again Mary's voice. "*Let's not be jumping to conclusions here Mother he might only be tired but Fraser you can't come because he needs to rest.*"

"So you're alone, eh, champ?" Frank felt stupid.

"She comes and cooks my sit-down dinner and laundry and reading drills and gets out of there *fast* because . . . *my husband is mad as toast and might get back from the Winnipeg game.*" This time a Mary-like tremor in the voice.

"Fraser?"

"Yes?"

"If Del comes, tell him to phone me at Bob's Resort, okay?"

"Bob . . ."

"Resort."

"They're going to adopt me. You are maybe my uncle Frankie." Fraser's voice had gone babyish.

"What?"

"But adoption board needs *two* good parents but Mrs. Baal—Mary—says she might only be *one* parent now so I might have to be on the yellow pills again. Mr. Wally—Kenny—says he'll be my mother too but Mrs. Baal's dress doesn't fit him."

"Fraser . . ."

"It's a joke. My sense of humor is always *acting up.* But I'm off the yellows and I'm normal again. I'm not supposed to tell anybody this. *No* one. But you're in jail anyway. And . . . *Bob's your uncle!*" Fraser screeched with laughter at his joke. "So don't you think it's back to normal? I'm really smart."

"Fraser, tell Mary—"

"Ninety-nine times ninety-nine is nine thousand, eight hundred and one, Uncle Frankie—Frank."

Frank called Mary collect at her parents'. She sounded humble, polite. She still didn't know where Del was. He hadn't returned from Winnipeg. Frank told her he was sorry her father was sick. Mary told him about Del's performance on TV and Frank said "*Jesus*." His heart went warm and then it went cold. How far would his brother's rage take him? Mary asked how much Frank's bail was, and Frank told her ten thousand dollars this time. Incredibly, she proposed to pay it. With Del's inheritance money. It's what Del would want, she said, though maybe not now, mad as he was. She too sounded childlike and awestruck, shy in the face of this new and surprising world.

It was time to go. That is, decide. Back to jail, or out there, somewhere.

"Well thanks, Mary. For the bail." Frank spoke softly. Another cruiser had pulled in, lights flashing. Three cops in a huddle at the steps. "But I don't need it. I'm already out. Sort of. Till Friday, I mean. The hearing's Friday." Frank said this mostly to himself, remembering.

"Me too," Mary said. "I was—we were—supposed to be in court on Friday too." A sad, ironic laugh. "For Fraser."

"Yeah. I heard. Too bad, I guess."

"I guess."

They hung up. Frank stepped out of the phone booth, still not knowing where Del was. Which was why he had tripped quickly behind the booth and into an alley. He walked a bit, hitched a bit, snuck aboard the ferry, and before three hours had passed he was in Pender Harbour and on his way to Felix's. He had a feeling he just might find his brother there too, hiding out. In troubled times Del would conceivably seek out Felix's brand of philosophy; bind his head up in a web of words and so allow his head to stick up calmly above all clouds. Frank suspected that at the ultimate end of all Felix-rationalizations there lay a sort of blank state.

What a perfect mess he'd made. Well, perhaps he'd only hurried things along a bit, but now all was certainly messy in the Baal sphere. His two phone calls gave indications of labyrinthine shambles. The plights of Del, Mary, Fraser—even Mr. Miller's stroke—fit easily into the pattern of his guilt.

On this sunny day of questionable freedom Frank picked his way through ferns on his way to Felix's. The ferns tickled his ankle skin, as white and unused to exposure as an old woman's breast. Still out of sight of the cabin he shouted his usual "*I wanna beer, Felix*" to let the fat man know all was well for the time being and that he had nothing to fear from his best friend Frank.

Emerging from a stand of cedar, Frank saw that Felix's weather-beaten shack had been reduced to a smoldering pile of ashes.

"Jesus. Felix."

He ran to the middle of the ash and began clawing through it. Searching, he realized, for bones. His gropings grew methodical as he crunched over to where the bed should have been. He began to claw there. The grotesque thought struck him that Felix's bones, should he find them, would look like normal bones. That is, not grossly fat. Frank picked up his head and took a great breath. He surveyed the site and saw that the fire had not been fought but had burned itself out, spreading ten feet into the grass at one end and into some drift logs on the beach, some of which still smoked. They would not be philosopher's bones, they would not be French Canadian bones. If anything, they would be squeezed bones, bones forced to perform like weight-bearing steel.

His mood lightened as he found no evidence of so much as a tooth. Then Frank saw the gasoline can. He recognized it. Red paint, rust in certain spots. It was his. That is, *Tammy*'s.

On his bad toe three blisters grew, swelled, and burst during his run to Bob's Lowtide Resort. At the head of the driveway his eyes zeroed to the dock, and he stopped running. He'd expected *Tammy* to be burned too, or sunk, or trashed, but there she was, lolling in the drink like an old-fashioned gal in a modesty-panel swimsuit. But on approaching her, Frank noticed she rode bow-heavy, as if she'd taken on water in the forward bilge. He leapt aboard, opened the cabin door, and heard a snore, then a croak, from within. The cabin smelled like ammonia and Chinese pork.

"Frank?"

Felix's question sounded more like "fronk."

The pungent francophone was wedged into *Tammy*'s forward bunk compartment like a lardy seal stuffed into a drawer. The door panel was ajar, and Frank could make out gray feet, barrel legs, and the full yellow moon of stomach.

"Okay, Feel. Come tell me all about it. I'll cook some coffee."

"No coffee." Felix spoke very softly. "Thank you. And I prefer to lie here. I am very tired."

Frank leaned his head into the cubbyhole, then withdrew. It smelled horrible. In the sulfurous light he'd glimpsed wedged against Felix's body a scatter of potatoes, cooked and now starting to mash apart, a box of Frank's crackers and a loaf of his bread, and a dutch oven full of water.

"How long you been in there?"

"Ever since . . . my lodgings . . . were consumed by flames. Two days, I suppose."

"Jesus. What happened? How did it burn? I mean, I saw a gas can— I saw *my* gas can there."

"I'm too ill to speak, my friend."

"What about your papers—your encyclopedia?" Felix got upset when it was called anything else.

"Leave me in peace. I'm ill. Close my door."

Felix's voice was so frighteningly sapped of life that Frank let him alone. Before closing the door, he noticed a tangy shit smell and saw a dribble of it on the inside rim of the porthole. He quickly closed the door. God, Felix had not moved in two days, not even to relieve himself.

Frank paced the cabin. His mind, squeezed hard from several angles, managed in seconds to sort through a complex grid of plans, possibilities, wishes, fears. The one conclusion reached, shouting at him as though flashing on a computer screen, was that above all he must not get caught. He didn't know yet what he wanted to do, but he knew he could do nothing if he was caught.

Frank cranked *Tammy*'s engine and checked the fuel tanks. Water was at two thirds, cupboards full of food, minus the starch Felix had hoarded. As the engine warmed, he found paint and brushes.

A police cruiser pulled into the resort parking lot just as *Tammy* cleared the dock. Depending on the degree of cooperation between the police and the Coast Guard—he knew it wasn't much, and it wasn't as if he had robbed banks or smuggled heroin—he knew he had from one to three hours' safe travel. The region's lone Coast Guard cutter was an old tub, her top speed perhaps a knot better than *Tammy*'s. Frank had all six illegal government VHF channels, and if spotted from the air he could monitor any radio calls to the cutter, and so even if the Coast Guard made him a priority he could zig when the cutter expected him to zag. He'd have to be alert and sleep little, but he knew he could stay clear. Four hours north were a maze of islands and inlets, with deep water anchorages choked at the tide line with overhanging cedar.

Out on the sound Frank throttled back to three-quarter speed and tied the wheel with a rope to keep *Tammy*'s course straight. Watching for planes, he brushed the entire upper deck, bridge, and cabin with sky blue paint. He chain-smoked; he hummed favorite old songs. Eyes, ears, and hands worked nonstop. He no longer knew why he was escaping. He only knew he must.

Four hours later he nudged *Tammy* up against a rock face in a small cove. Almost a lake, its entrance was blind and could only be navigated at high tide. He had spent a solitary weekend here last summer, at the height of the season, and had seen no other boats. He threw the anchor off the bow, winched it tight, and tied the stern line to a tree root. He'd heard a single message on channel 37, Coast Guard central reporting the jailbreak, Frank's name, *Tammy*'s size and color. No direction, however. And Pender's response was noncommittal: "Roger," the youngish voice said. "We'll see what we can see."

Frank flopped on his bunk for a half hour, the whole time wondering where in hell Del might be. He roused himself to cook some food. As the baked bean aroma filled the cabin, muffled sounds of unease issued from up forward. Frank couldn't tell if Felix was snoring or moaning. But he heard a loud grunt, *Tammy* shuddered along her length, and there followed sound of urine tinkling out the porthole. Then a bulbous toe pushed the door ajar.

"*I burned it myself*," Felix hissed.

"What?"

"*I.*"

"What about your encyclopedia?"

"*That is what I ignited.*"

Del wished he'd chosen a seedy motel instead of the Saskatoon Holiday Inn. He had too many choices here. The day was hot but the air-conditioner was noisy, so he had to choose either a roaring cool or a muggy quiet. The TV had cable access to one hundred and twelve channels—again, the hell of choice. He settled on "The Muppet Show" for the third afternoon in a row.

When Sunday's Winnipeg-to-Vancouver flight had stopped in Saskatoon, Del found himself following the Saskatoon passengers off. He felt vaguely criminal pretending to be one of them. But the thought of landing in Vancouver was unbearable. What if she was waiting at Arrivals, as usual? What if she wasn't? What if she was home? What if she *wasn't*? He pondered these words—what if she was there, what if she wasn't—and like so much of his life these past days, weeks, months, they read like a bad movie script. Del imagined he was Sam Spade talking to himself during the melodramatic woe-is-me part of the movie. Sam Spade, no longer acting.

He walked the miles from the airport into town, exhausted and flop-footed. The attacks of Mary's face, her thighs, her castrating intrigues were no longer able to burn his being this day. He passed motels, considering then rejecting. Should he in his movie script (he could at least be snide, otherwise it was all despair) pamper himself with room service and linen trimmings, or should he be the eager loser, chain-smoking roll-your-owns, waking up on the unshaven Kerouac floor with phlegm on his

pants, surrounded by empty bottles? In the end he decided on
two things: one, he didn't want thin walls and the sounds of
lovers delighting, and two, he wanted a phone in his room. He
decided this with his hand already on the Holiday Inn door. He
could walk no farther.

Now, three days later, the Muppets yabbered and screeched
again in their purple skin and fiery hair. Harry Belafonte was
today's guest star, and he was having a hard time pretending he
talked to sensate creatures, not these gaudy bags of lint. Del ran
his palm up his whiskers, dragging his chin skin almost to his
cheek. He snapped the top off another bottle of sake. It was fun
being Frank. He'd always hated the stuff, never understanding
his brother's fondness for it, especially this lazy room-tem-
perature way, when it tasted like Varsol. But now he understood. He'd learned these past days that when dosed down in
quantity sake gave both a calculating high and a devilish morning
after. The hangovers were not so much headaches as they were
urgent chemical panic, which is precisely what Del sought.
Apparently his movie script was casting him in a twofold mode,
that of pampered derelict, a grizzled Sam Spade on the one hand
and an indulgent Jack Lemmon on the other.

Amazing how populated an empty Holiday Inn room could
get. The dessertish color scheme, the sterile fabrics, the forget-
table paintings. Each noon fresh glasses appeared, upside down
and wrapped in wax paper. No one disturbed the quiet save the
TV and the roaring fan. The TV shot out a surprising number of
ghosts for Del to rage and giggle at. Women named Mary. Rock
songs she'd hummed to herself this past year. Music videos
bawdy and teasing with dancers who moved like Lil' Regina. Old
movies they'd viewed together, laughing in perfect harmony at
the bad dramatics.

When he turned off the TV, the room population would
grow with voices so numerous they could have crowded out a
prairie wheat field. They seemed to issue from the fan. Voices of
dead parents, young Frank, early Mary, voices unconnected to
Del's life now. There were voices from this present script, and
they were needling and bossy and whispered and conniving.

There were bleats of naive hope and gasps of unforgiving treachery, and they must have come loudly out of Del's own mouth because there were poundings on the wall, and paintings rattled. And there were new voices today. He'd sensed them before but hadn't known their source. He'd sensed them all his life—they'd been there during the diaper days. Now, after all these years, snapping on the TV again and lying back with pants down to carry out his snide plan of masturbating drunk to the Muppets, he caught a glimpse through the side of his eye who it was talking: they were tall and gray and lived in a black world that was always there, hidden behind the normal one. Their mouths were ovals that never smiled, though they were telling jokes. Jokes and nothing else. Long jokes with no punch line, they just went on and on. And as Del's back touched the mattress it arched up in fright, for he understood suddenly that these jokes being told were about nothing else but his own and his loved ones' lives.

CHAPTER TWELVE

As You Like It

*You know, fellas, Baal is oldest, most noble name in
Scandinavia. We're prehistory, if you want to know
the truth. I researched this myself. First we were war
god. Tha's right! Then we were god of fishes, and
finally we were god of only certain kind of fish. That's
the way happens. So Baals are fallen gods. Tha's us.
Or you could look at another way. Maybe you're
rising human! Tha's other side. I guess. But maybe
not. Who knows! What do you think? Ha-ha!*
—Dr. A.A. Baal, after scotch,
to ten-year-old Frank and Del

Frank knew they wouldn't get him at night, and when he
finally resigned his body to his bunk he fell into the pure
stubborn sleep of a baby who'd been kept up too late at a barking
adults' party. Such had been his past days. But no man-made
sounds reached this secret cove some hundred and fifty miles
north of Vancouver, and the fresh breeze and the kissing sounds
of wavelets on *Tammy*'s hull forced him deeper into his bed.
Only Felix's occasional wheeze from the forward cabin would
sometimes cause Frank's eyelids to twitch with worry.

In the morning, Frank made pancakes with blueberry jam for
breakfast, and then jigged a cod off the bottom, cleaned it, and
marinated it in soya sauce for his lunch. He touched up *Tammy*'s
hasty paint job, scrubbing away as best he could yesterday's

careless blotches of sky blue. He stood long minutes eyeing *Tammy*'s homely wooden lines. He loved this old boat, built the year his father was born. This blue paint was tacky at best, but it would have to do for now. He decided: when they finally caught him (for he had no delusions they wouldn't) and he was forced to sell *Tammy*, he would make the buyer promise in writing to strip off this goddamn blue and . . . but no. No need. For Del would get the boat. Who else but Del? If he wanted it.

In a spurt of thoughtless resolve Frank grabbed some paint, jumped to the swim grid, and blanked out the lettering on the transom. Allowing himself no time for nostalgia, he buried *Tammy Wouldn't Die* under several slashing strokes. He stood up, stared at the newly white transom, and considered. Then he stabbed a small brush into a can of black enamel and with steady hands (Frank hadn't had a drink in days) bestowed on the vessel a new name: *Mary Del*. The perfect innocent family-boat name. As he regarded the lettering, Frank's sneer rose naturally. This name was the perfect sour joke, its timing ironic and sinister. Yet even as he laughed he sensed in his gut that he'd chosen the name out of a kind of warmth and corniness, new to him. Frank shook his head and and tossed the painting stuff overboard.

Felix didn't speak until almost noon. Frank sat in the cabin plinking his uke. He knew Felix was awake and listening. Suddenly Frank interrupted a song and said:

"Okay. So why'd you burn the book, Felix?"

"As you can perceive, it was not an impulsive act," Felix said immediately, in a voice that was rancid, but most of all weak. It made Frank think of a cartoon mouse, and it frightened him. "I walked two miles, the second under the burden of your petrol can."

"Yeah, but *why*?"

"It took but a single match. Volume One, which contained both my definition of terms and the kernel of my intent, I doused with petrol and ignited. The ensuing volume followed its lead. And just as they were written, the order of my ideas, so they were expunged. The house followed. I didn't care about that. The world has been my house, and if the world had burned as well it would have been more than fine." Felix wheezed from the effort of his rasping speech.

"Jesus. Felix. Why?"

Felix paused, and for the only time in Frank's memory, the pause was not for effect. In the fat man's silence, Frank could almost see the flames himself. Then again the frightening voice:

"I am naught but a grain of sand."

"No, *why?*"

"I'll use your terms, then." Felix eased the door panel open with his toe, strained his scowling head up, and looked Frank full in the face. He looked demented, and less than alive. "It has been brought to my attention that . . . I am nothing but a useless piece of shit."

"C'mon, Feel. No you're not."

"More reasons, then? All right." Felix wrenched his head up still farther, and blue veins worked their way through profound layers of fat to rise bulging at the neck. "My body-lens has imploded inward. *I have seen myself.* My ideas have been deemed vacant because they are frozen in the face of the real world. My generator has discovered that it does not in fact exist. It has shut itself off. I have *seen* myself. As a result, I am a dying man."

"Jesus, Felix, you're not. I mean . . ." What *did* he mean? What was safe to say here? "It sounds like maybe you learned something. That can only be good, right? You can start a new book—encyclopedia."

"Liar. Fuck yourself."

"What?"

"I won't bear your condescension." Felix flopped his head back.

The cabin went dreadfully still. Frank studied what he could of Felix's skin, and it looked long dead, as though not blood but a sluggish gray-green water had coursed it for years. Blanket folds had left dents in his legs that hadn't sprung back.

"You knew all along," Felix continued, his voice resounding in his tiny cubicle, as though he lay inside a megaphone. "You saw me as a man helpless in the real world. Pathetic. Without courage. Laughable. A know-all, a proud man who could not hammer in a nail. A *real nail*? And you were right. I cannot."

"Well. Shit. Felix, I don't have a clue what to say."

"Say nothing. Nothing is required of you. Leave me in peace. Let me die. I have chosen to die. For the good of mankind. It is my last chance at courage."

Frank sensed he should keep the fat man talking. It seemed he gained color in the legs, at least a little, especially when he rose to melodrama and pomposity, like the Felix of old.

"So when did you discover all this?"

"Your quaint soirée at the striptease establishment. A nest of confusion, a bog of stalled souls, and I could do nothing. I, who have aspired to change . . . many things in the world, could not influence a single misguided fool. And I saw . . . that I *fit in there perfectly*." Felix broke into an evil but feeble laugh, which changed to desperate coughing. Then he caught his breath. "Do you know, Frank, the last time I attempted to operate a car I ruined it? This was in Quebec. I borrowed a relative's vehicle, declared to myself that it needed oil—such is the extent of my arrogance and stupidity, for I have no knowledge of either why or when a motor needs oil—and proceeded to introduce a quart of oil into the radiator. Not long after this mistake I fled Quebec like a coward."

"Felix, come on. A nail? A car? Big fucking deal. These are just little—"

"They are symptoms of the larger cancer. Where is your subtlety, monsieur?"

Crazy as this new Felix was, it was clear he couldn't be babied. Frank would have to tell the truth.

"Well look. *Nobody* can do what you wanted to do. I mean, change the world? *That* was your mistake." Frank forced anger. "You wanna be Hitler, maybe? So what did he manage? A few deaths. You wanna be Jesus? What did he do? Well, you got your crusaders hacking heads off Arabs, you got your Baptists burning books, you got your evangelists making coin off old biddies, you got—"

"Frank."

"What?"

"The point is, I have reached *no* one. A teacher must touch people. I have touched only myself. You have witnessed a man masturbating in a squalid closet. I am obese with selfishness. I have not done a single good deed. Any cub scout *naif* with chocolate on his face has done more for the world than the man Felix d'Amboise. Whom have I helped? No one. If I had done but *one good thing*."

Frank thought fast.

"My brother is one, Felix. Del loves what you tell him."

"With all respect, Frank, your brother would listen to any-one. He is hardly a conquest."

"You . . ." Out of habit, Frank was about to say "you fat fuck," but restrained himself. "You sometimes teach *me*, Felix."

"Oh? Tell me more, Mr. Baal."

Frank could think of nothing. Now he was caught, and he sensed Felix knew it. To lie, or tell the truth.

"Well it's true I argue with everything you say. But perhaps I'm only stubborn. Perhaps—"

"Liar."

"Okay. You've taught me by example, Felix."

"Oh? Indeed. *Incroyable*, monsieur. You are telling me you emulate my way of life?"

"No, not exactly." Frank was sweating and could not look at Felix's face. "By *example* I mean . . . well, I learn from certain things you do that . . . well, certain mistakes that . . ."

"Shut up. I know what you are saying. You learn from my mistakes. I am a reverse example. A grand mistake." Felix caught the door edge with his toe and pulled it closed. Then a final hiss, muffled. "You quicken my death. For this I thank you, my friend."

Frank sagged in his chair. He sat quietly for a while. He knew there was no reason on earth he should feel guilty for Felix's state. But he let himself feel guilty anyway. It was the easiest thing to do, for now. He wondered where his brother was. He could feel him clearly, too clearly. The sensation his toe was sending to his stomach was the kind of weak panic a thin bridge might feel if forced to stretch across a chasm that was slowly growing wider.

If you can measure love by the hate it's capable of creating, it was hard to say whom Del loved more. And though love was now hate, there was the same urge to communicate it. Not even national TV had been enough. For the tenth time that afternoon, Del cradled the receiver before he finished dialing. The first few times he'd banged it down, groaning, unable to decide what to tell her, what to shout, how to blame. Now he was putting it down ticklishly, and he giggled each time as he thought of better and better opening lines: "Mary, the sound you are about to hear is wrist blood flowing onto the mouthpiece." He would trickle a glass of water over it. "I am in Saskatchewan. I will be dead in twelve to twenty minutes. Find me." Then he'd hang up. Or: "Hi, sweetheart. Boy, did I ever just have a weird dream. You turned into some kind of slutty monster and I stayed drunk for days. Boy . . . Anyway, I'll see you in an hour or so, sweetness. Bye." He'd hang up. Or he would phone her and commence shrieking, crying, then belly laughing.

He knew this last one was quite possible. And he kept chickening out for that reason. He knew he couldn't carry out a plan. He had no idea what might blurt from his mouth when he heard her voice, whether sudden stabbings of rage would have him screaming, or whether sadness and exhaustion would have him sobbing pathetically. Worst of all, he might fall to stammering politely, afraid of her still. This possibility he could not bear.

He giggled again, blanking out this last version by conjuring another enigmatic death threat. "The next time you wear anything green, I'll be there and I'll do it. The next time you wear anything *green*, Mary."

Del's hand rubbed hard on his short beard, up and down, a new habit. The whiskers were growing out at various lengths, like a scatter of anarchic dogs let loose in an unfamiliar park, fast dogs, small dogs, dogs curling around on themselves, dogs in snarling packs, dogs alone and gray. When he'd seen these first white hairs on his cheeks he'd thought: whatever happens, I'll die anyway.

He decided again not to drink this morning, having discovered that life was more punishing—that is, clearer—when the mind was sober. How quickly the booze/sleep cycle became routine, its shift from euphoria to depression as predictable as a TV schedule: soaps, sit-coms, documentaries on the Third World. How quickly too he'd discovered the hidden corners of his brother's solitude. Frank's slant on things. His brother was right: living alone, you saw more clearly. Living was complicated enough. Living with somebody was complexity squared, mud on the lenses, a big smudge. Frank had often said as much. And Del had always responded with some liberal arts banality about learning from one's partner, you ought to try it.

Oh, he had learned from his partner. His hand on the receiver again, Del, his lenses so recently unsmudged, took clear stock of his life. He sat naked, his clothes soaking in their own filth in the bathtub. He'd been sick on himself, at least once. Blankets, chow mein cartons, bottles, and newspapers on the floor. A sports blurb, ripped out and stuck to the wall with sweet and sour sauce, told of a controversial tie game in which a certain referee left the game with seconds to play after making delirious announcements over the loudspeaker. In front of him the TV, roaring unchecked as it had for days and nights, singing cheerfully an old Beatles' melody, and on the screen handsome men and women danced and laughed with the same brand of beer, hoisting it so the label showed, laughing, such friends, living forever in a time when the Beatles were innocent geniuses, and you can have fun too if you buy this beer and make it your own. Del's own beer commercial had paid him five hundred bucks to arbitrate a shouted argument between two famous footballers (who made thousands for the ad—refs were *never* valued, not in ads, not in sport, not in life) over why lite was best—tastes great or fewer calories. How many of these handsome chugging Beatles dancers smilers laughers had cocaine habits, cheating mates, AIDS bugs blooming in the blood, kind but now feeble moms ignored in reeking old-age homes? Del's new world was indeed a clear world. His wallet lay spread-thighed on the floor, empty of cash—right, *that* was why he had stopped drinking; beside it a plane ticket ripped halfway through, an act aborted in mid-rip by the thought of too long a life in a Saskatchewan hotel room with soaps, Muppets, and a paper belt wound crisp around his toilet seat every morning. He had to act.

He dialed again, and this time let it ring. Before fear had time to swell, Mary's hello made the world clear as clear could get.

"Hello?" she said again.

"Hi, Mary." His voice sounded bored to him.

"Oh God, where are you?" Mary caught herself, took a deep breath. "So. What are you going to do?"

"I don't know."

"Are you going to . . . are you staying somewhere in town? Do you want me to come there?"

Del didn't answer.

"Do you feel like talking about this . . . what's happened . . . at all?"

"Sure. Why not."

"Face to face? Will you come here?"

Del didn't answer.

"Del, I really think that, no matter how mad you are, you are right to feel that way. But I think you should hear what I have to say. Lots of couples survive problems like this, if they're honest. I want to be completely honest with you."

Her voice and words had the controlling membrane of a carefully rehearsed speech.

"That sounded like a carefully rehearsed speech."

"Del, we *both* turned away from our marriage. . . ."

"So, you're not even going to apologize."

"I just turned further than you for a while."

"Maybe I've gone further than that. Now."

"Well . . . okay, but . . ." Mary's soft sobs bubbled through. "But we still should talk, okay? Can you come home? Can we meet in a restaurant?"

"How about the Yale?"

"Del, don't. Can you come home?"

Del didn't answer. Neither spoke for a full minute, and Del let his wife sob. He refused to consider what the sound did to him, the sobs so open, her mouth pressing wet on the receiver, crying *to* him, not away, honest for once.

"Anyway, Del. Del?"

"Yeah."

"Are you with Frank? The police have—"

"Yeah, *Frankie*! He's right here. We're holding hands. We're at the Yale."

Mary's tone grew colder. A familiar fear gripped Del's gut, but he laughed it away with a Frankish snort.

"I just wanted to tell you, if you didn't know, your brother escaped from jail."

Del started laughing. Quietly at first, but it grew throughout Mary's story.

"He was thrown in jail for lots of things he did, pretty serious, I think, from how he sounded. Anyway, the police have been here looking for him, they said he *escaped* and . . . I guess he's in trouble. So he shouldn't come here, if you see him." Mary was crying again. "God, his hearing was supposed to be tomorrow, like ours. . . ." Her crying choked off her words. "Everything's so . . ."

Del's whole body shook. He threw down the receiver and laughed into a pillow.

"Del?"

Del finally stopped laughing. He wiped his eyes and picked up the receiver with a casual grace. "Okay, Mary, I'll tell him. See you soon, *sweetheart*." He hung up.

He ran to the bathroom and began wringing out his clothes, so tightly that he grimaced and his arms shook. Tomorrow was Friday. He ran to the phone and talked to the airlines. His patience had paid off. He knew exactly what he was going to do. It was perfect, wonderful. What a joke, what a crime, what a life. Now he was the scriptwriter.

He pulled on his clothes and sudsy sneakers (he'd been sick on his shoes as well), slammed the door on his room and roaring week-gone-by, and squished down the hall. Nearing the front desk, he reached for his wallet, out of habit, but then decided he would skip out on them without paying. He winked at the desk clerk, who smiled cautiously at Del's sopping state, then double-palmed his way out the door. The script had begun well.

The bow-heavy *Mary Del* approached the old wharf at sunset, slowly, with running lights off. From where he stood on the bridge with binoculars, Frank could see no official boats, no police cars up by the store. The adjoining fish-packing plant looked deserted. Frank had landed here with Del several years ago. The place was called Bella Combe, an Indian reserve with general store and deepwater dockage. It had lived off the fishing trade for decades until that had recently died.

Frank climbed down and tied to the dock. He ducked inside to shut her down but then decided to let her idle.

"Will you bring me some water, Frank?"

Frank considered. "No, Felix. I think it's time you got up. You get your own water."

"Fine. I shall dehydrate. It is fitting that I *shrivel*."

Not only could the fat man pronounce capitals, he was the only one Frank knew who could say words like "shrivel" with perfect onomatopoeia.

"Felix. There's a store here. I'm going in to use the phone. Why don't you come up? We can buy some food. Anything you want. A walk would do you—"

"If I *chose* to rise, I would rise. If I *chose* to, I would don ballet slippers, I would pirouette along the quay, I would dance into the grocer's, I would entertain you at the *téléphone*. However, and I repeat—"

"Felix."

"—that I *choose* to lie here and die. Water or no water."

Frank reached his hand in for the empty dutch oven, half filled it, and holding his breath, placed it back on Felix's bunk.

The store was occupied by a lone man, a native who looked about Frank's age, sitting bent double on a chair behind the cash counter.

"You got a phone I can use?"

The Indian didn't respond. His eyes shifted from side to side and his face was puckered, in pain. He was clutching a wrinkled paper bag tightly against his stomach. Frank could hear the deep-throated murmurs of a family through a door at the back, and a TV announcing the CBC evening news. Then channels changed, and canned laughter from an American sit-com took over.

"Any chance I could use a phone? Calling collect."

"Maybe you buy some things first," the man grunted, not looking up.

Frank walked the three small aisles and after a minute deposited shaving cream, two cans of beans, bacon, and grape juice on the counter. The Indian brought a phone up from the floor and handed it over, still not looking, still clutching the bag to his stomach.

Frank turned his back on the man and dialed Mary. It was busy. His toe stub flared for an instant, a long-distance sort of prodding. He waited, then dialed again.

"Hello?"

"Hi, Mary, have you—"

"Del?"

"No, it's—"

"Frank—God, you sounded just like Del. He just phoned me, Frank, he just hung up. Where are you?"

Frank didn't speak. Not because he didn't want to say where he was, but rather because of his surprise at being mistaken for his brother. Nothing like that had happened for so long. Since high school. Friends saying "Hi . . ." and then peering at the face to check it closely before venturing a name. But it had been years and years. Frank felt warm, yet disturbed.

"No, right. Don't tell me where you are. They were here. Looking. Who knows about this phone?"

"That's okay, Mary. I don't care. I'm in San Francisco. So where's Del? How is he?"

"Frank, I don't know, he didn't say. It sounded far away."

Mary's voice, trembling on the verge of a sob, was nonetheless controlled. Frank could hear in it the soul of one now used to her pain. He heard in it too the true bond to his brother. He realized he'd never in all these years acknowledged this bond before, that it could be real. He realized as well that there was a good chance that much of what he'd thought about his sister-in-law up to this point was wrong.

"He sounded really out of it, Frank."

"God."

"I told him about your . . . situation, Frank."

"Yeah?"

"He laughed. He laughed for a long time, and he sounded *crazy*."

"God."

"He said he was coming home soon, but I don't think he is. I didn't believe him. I'm scared, Frank. He sounded crazy."

Frank's own fear, a fear he knew was identical to hers, forced him into silence. He felt a little jealous of her, something else he'd never acknowledged before. And, as is often the case when people share fear, the unspeakable questions hovering overhead forced them to talk of smaller things, as soldiers in their thundering trench will muse on baseball scores from home. Frank asked after Mary's father, who he learned was "stable." He asked about Fraser. He too was "the same." She had taken matters into her own hands and had thrown away his "poison," but now, on no medication at all, Fraser was getting unreachable.

"He goes on and on and doesn't touch ground," Mary said. "He's so happy about getting adopted. I haven't told him it's off. I can't. But all yesterday everything he saw was a 'present.' When he'd go to the fridge he'd say, 'Time to unwrap my gift,' and then he'd open it and scream, 'Cheese!' A glass is gift wrap and the water in it is the present. All TV programs are presents and the TV is the gift box and the cord is the ribbon. He started talking about his heart yesterday and he had this look in his eyes. I mean, I thought he might cut himself open. It would be great if he was trying to be funny, but he's not. He needs *some* kind of drug. I don't know what. But not the ones he was on. That was worse."

"Did you tell Del?"

"I almost did. A whole bunch of stuff gushed out. I don't think he caught the Fraser part."

Again they fell silent. But Frank could feel their thoughts traveling over the wire like chatter.

"Well, I'll call again. Sometime. If he comes, tell him that I want to, *have* to talk to him. Meet him somewhere. I don't know how."

"Okay." Mary sounded as helpless as Frank.

"Take care, okay, Mary?"

"Sure. You too."

Frank almost hung up, but brought the phone back to his mouth. "And . . . *sorry* about everything, Mary. Really."

"Sure." Like a trace of melody in a dirge, a note of wise mirth nudged her voice. "Me too."

Again they resisted hanging up.

"You know," Mary said, "I always wanted to say this. I should have said it to him, but I'll say it to you."

"Uh-huh?"

"I've always been jealous of you. The two of you."

"Uh-huh." Frank didn't know what to say, so he repeated himself. "Uh-huh."

"What you have."

The immensity of her statement forced silence on them again. Frank had a sudden, clear vision of himself: the phone hard on his ear, the Indian's empty store, the wide night outside. Felix crammed, sick, into his boat. Del, out there somewhere beyond, not himself, wild.

"Del loves you too, Mary. He loves both of us. A lot." Saying this, Frank saw he was trying to make Mary feel better. But he also saw that it was true. "And, well, you know," he continued, awkward with honesty, "I think I've sort of been jealous of you too. Come to think of it. I mean, to be perfectly honest. If you know what I mean." Frank was sweating as he babbled. Grinning too, a little. Very much, he suspected, like his brother did at such times.

They finally said goodbye in the middle of another awkward silence and Frank handed the phone back to the Indian. He slapped his pockets for his wallet and realized that it was back on board. He hesitated, then smiled at the man, who looked at him now. He shrugged and turned red. It was clear the Indian had read his face.

"Jeez. My wallet. It's—can I just go down and—"

"Yeah, okay." The Indian looked down, not believing him for a moment. But it was no big deal. Like a massive scar, his entire face showed he had been betrayed by the white race one more time. "Go down to your boat."

"No, look, *really*." Frank thrust his face forward. His panic felt new and absurd. Why should he care? "I *want* to buy these things. I *want* to pay."

"Sure. Go to the boat."

"No. *Here*. It's worth a hundred bucks at least." Frank stripped off his watch. He grabbed the Indian's hand, a pudgy and weak hand, womanish. He folded the man's fingers around it.

"There," Frank said breathlessly. "Actually it's probably *two* hundred." The watch was old, stolen years ago, but it was a Rolex.

The Indian said nothing. He looked down at the watch and studied it, then bent the band. His eyes lit up and he began to twist the band into its celebrated contortions, its perfect physics of sprung snake ribs. He looked up at Frank, almost smiling.

"Yeah," he said. They looked at each other, and then the Indian's face jumped, struck by a thought. "Here." He opened his paper bag and lifted a jar out gingerly, two fingers carefully pincering the lid. A gray blob, oysterlike, hung suspended in fluid.

"Appendick," the Indian whispered. Then he pointed to his stomach, a little left of center.

Frank just said, "Wow, painful, eh?" as he gathered his things in his arms. He lurched out of the store, down the ramp, and tore loose *Mary Del*'s lines. He jumped to the bridge and roared the boat away and out into the twilight. He cruised north for five minutes, too fast, he knew, in an inlet that was being logged, as revealed by the tide line of deadheads he'd had to dodge on his way in. He throttled back, paused a long minute, then shut the boat down altogether. He stood up and stretched.

Then sighing from his depths, he flung his head back and breathed, his mouth open to the budding stars. Planting his feet, he tried to think. Below, Felix coughed weakly. Frank tried harder to think but nothing solid came, nothing that gathered and held long enough to become words. Instead, he suffered a swirling of gut and nerves and blood, a seeding of thoughts as yet unborn. He recognized—a recognition so obvious and simple, and yet so new—this swirl to be goodness, the muscle of thought's young body, the force behind the bones.

He looked up again. The stars, so clear. They seemed washed clean of irony. For the first time they looked kind.

One good thing. Could it all boil down to something as corny as that? It was gushy, embarrassing. It was the logic of Saturday morning toddlers' cartoons, the Care Bears' dim pink whimperings from the deepest blind pit of the nuclear age. Neither the writers nor the kids believed it, at least not for long. *One good thing.* He thought of Del, full of good things. He pictured Del braking his old car in traffic and letting a whole string of surprised but ungrateful cars swing in front of him from a stalled lane. Del would wave to their rearview mirrors, and a few would wave back, giving Del his joy, while cars behind him honked in crescendo. Del, so full of good things they almost canceled each other out. They seemed merely bland as they rose out of a background of goodness in the first place. One *expects* the free turkey from the Salvation Army man at Christmas.

For goodness could be, should be, like magic, shouldn't it? Magic: the arrival, sudden, of the unexpected. Thunder, lightning, a blare of glory horns. But it could be quieter: a break in the clouds, the forgotten marvel of blue. That was it. And it could be noble: the strongest army suddenly putting down its weapons of its own free will. That was the stuff of it. The bully who had you on the ground but suddenly stopped punching, despite himself.

That was it. To truly do good, to reach the magic of it, you had to surprise even yourself.

Frank stood there on the dark bridge under the stars for an hour, perhaps two, unable to shove aside waves of corniness, waves of simple good wishes.

When at last he stepped calmly down into the cabin it was to find his jacket, for it was chilly out and it would be a long sail. He checked the *Mary Del*'s fuel and water. One good thing. He had decided. If he could make it to Bob's Resort by daybreak, and to the Sechelt bus station by seven, he could avoid most police.

"Come on, Felix. Get ready for a long drive. Wanna come up and help me look out for logs, old man?"

Felix wheezed and moaned, then relapsed into silence.

Back up on the bridge, under full-blown stars, Frank's blood manufactured the bones of a final, simple thought: good acts might seem to fail on the surface of things. But that's just the surface of things. Frank saw now that goodness scared the hell out of the Black Spot, and maybe even shrank some of it away.

Del took the courthouse steps two at a time, his limbs pumping madly, his tall body teetering off center, his face that of a pale, grinning Arab. Not a grin, actually, but a toothy slash that stretched ear to ear. Rasps of breath sizzled through the saliva between his teeth. His clothes had dried crisp with the creases he had wrung into them.

At the bank of glass doors he stopped short, seeing himself. He was surprised by what he saw. It struck him then that this space-age glass courthouse, a kind of Cheops of mirrors, represented perfect justice. Not the fake justice inside, not the shuffling of forms, the judges with calculators punching in six robberies times two years equals twelve years in jail; three rapes times five years equals fifteen years minus seven for earning a degree in remedial reading. No, the justice of a mirror.

Del sneered at himself in the door. He lowered his eyelids a cynical tad and they fell comfortably. How comfy this new face felt. Elvis. Today true justice—justice of the heart, years of

violations of bonds of the heart—would be served. Del pulled
open the door and strode in, slap-angry, his feet stamping loudly
on marble.

"I'm Frank Baal. B-A-A-L," he said to a uniformed old
woman at Check-Ins and Information.

"Mm-hmmm?" She turned her dumb face up to him.

"I had a . . . *trial* . . . I think. *Today*, but . . ."

She was already scanning a schedule. Her fingers found a
name.

"Here we are. Baal, F. Let's see. It's been crossed out. Did no
one contact you? Do you know of any reason why it—"

"I escaped. I busted out of jail."

"Oh. I see." The woman's hand was on the phone. She was
Katherine Hepburn now, head shaking, mouth aquiver. Absurdly, her free hand fixed her hair. Del realized: I've made her
month. Frank does that for people. This old bag's heart was
going again. Del cocked his head back and closed his eyes, James
Dean for her now.

"Better get someone . . . quick," he whispered.

In seconds an old policeman came humping across the foyer,
heels clicking, arms working, face red. He did have his palm on
his holster, but this was not quite as Del had envisioned: the
squatting ring of grim cops, guns drawn and pointing the tiny,
deadly black o's.

"Afternoon, sir," the old cop said as he guided Del's arm back
around and snapped on cuffs.

This was okay, Del thought, this was good. He was instantly
sweating and angry under the bondage. Safe now in these hand-
cuffs, he began to hint at struggling, felt the wonderful press of
the cop's hand hard on his elbow, a warning shove, a bit of
hatred. As he struggled he laughed, a manic treble note, new to
him.

"Settle down, boy," the old cop said, in control, his month
made too.

"Fuck yourself," Del laughed, safe.

Bureaucracy being what it is, Frank's escape had been noted in
the provincial court registry only that morning, the hearing

canceled but an hour ago. The event was easily reslotted. And now a second phone call to each of the principals roused them and gathered them into position: a judge; a prosecutor; the crown's chief witness, Kirk Morgan, SFPD; a reluctant Wally Kenny, who had earlier in the week agreed to represent his boyhood pal only after explaining to him that he would be useless, that the law of houses and deeds had nothing to do with the laws of larceny and vandalism.

Meanwhile, Del languished in a barred room. He *tried* to languish, for that was the right word. He spent only an hour there, but suffered. He wanted to suffer. The greater the suffering, the greater his revenge. As he stared at the deadly blank walls and then tried a practice grip on the bars, bars that bit down to the floor and boxed time so absolutely, he knew his future pain was the fire over which Mary's and Frank's guilt would rise and cook and char. This was perfect. He laughed again, savoring the treble shriek.

After his hour of black joy, Del was led through corridors to a stately oak-paneled room. Seated at stations appropriate to their roles were a judge, a court typist, and various well-dressed men, one of whom was Wally Kenny. Del's heart bubbled a brief instant at seeing his friend, but as he was led to the seat next to Wally he fell easily back to who he'd become, his eyes lidded, jaw severe, face Frankish.

"Hey there Wall, ol' doll," was what he'd heard Frank say once, and so he said it now.

"Hi, Frank. Man, you look . . ." Wally was peering at him closely. He stared and his lips parted. He seemed on the verge of a question when the judge banged his gavel, and then he hissed in Del's ear, "Frank, any hope we had of getting you off is screwed now. You should have stayed gone."

"Just keep me off the electric chair, pal." Del spoke to Wally through the side of his mouth. "Flirt with the judge, maybe. Love the pink tie."

"Right."

The hearing began with a reading of the charges, followed by statements of counsel. The prosecutor, a middle-aged, bookish type with TV good looks, painted Frank Baal as a "rural ter-rorist," a sociopath whose only passions were destruction and profit. Del James Deaned him throughout, but never once caught his eye. Then Wally, calm and earnest, politely scoffed at these assertions and suggested that the absence of a prior record and insufficient evidence were cause for a light or suspended sentence. The judge asked Del how he chose to plead.

"Guilty," Del said. As an afterthought, he decided he might as well begin now. "As guilty as *you* are."

"I beg your pardon?"

"Guilty as you are. I can see you dreaming of girlettes and playing with yourself under your robes at home and I bet—"

The judge gaveled like Thor.

"—you wake up and cringe and sweat in the middle of the night."

Del sat down but held the judge in his sneer. It was a brilliant sneer, a sneer of judgment, and Frank could have done no better. Wally slid his face out from behind his hands and looked at him. "Fine," he said.

The judge banged a final time and cited Del for contempt of court.

"You got *that* right," Del shouted.

Wally went to confer with the judge. He returned and ex-plained to Del that the hearing would proceed with or without him.

"There's already an extra fine. Maybe extra time. It's your life. You like jail?" Wally stared Del in the eye. As he stared he paused and his head tilted for a second, puppylike, but he said, "So shut up, Frank."

Kirk Morgan was called as the first witness. The prosecutor produced Frank's boots, their prints, photos of a vandalized house and smashed-in cars, fenced goods, affidavits, forms, statements, reports, and more. Kirk Morgan's suit was new, his hair short, his manner crisp as an avenging angel with his foot on the neck of the damned. The judge asked if he could identify the man he had apprehended in the act of kicking in the cars.

"Certainly, Your Honor. We've met several times." He turned Del's way, and the look he gave was not unlike the acknowledgment of a respectful rival. Del wondered who this young quarterback could be. Morgan raised an arm slowly and, like in the movies, pointed a finger. "That's him."

"And your professional opinion of him, Sergeant Morgan?" asked the judge.

"The man is, as the prosecutor said, a sociopath. I would like to add that he is unbalanced, unremorseful, un-American—"

The judge raised his eyebrows and the prosecutor coughed, to no avail.

"—a menace and exceedingly dangerous. He should be caged with his kind. With all respect, Your Honor."

"Thank you, Sergeant. Next the bench will call—"

"Your Honor, if I may?"

"Sergeant?"

"I would like to read something I found on the suspect's boat. His hideout, if I may. He thinks himself a poet." He picked up a sheet of crumpled paper. "I submit this poem as a character witness. It's called 'I Would Kill You for a Song.' "

"*You can't!*" Del was on his feet. "*That's about my brother!*"

Del was restrained. He sat grimly, head down, not wanting to listen.

"All the worse, I'd say, Mr. Baal. Your own brother?" Morgan said.

Last year Del had visited Frank in Pender and found him in a trough of depression. "Ever want to do yourself in, Dellie?" Frank had said. "I was really bummed last night, boy. Feel okay now, though. Here." He slid him the poem. He'd written it about himself.

Morgan read:

> Everyone sees your ways, your brains,
> but I know
> you're a real dink.
>
> You depress yourself then aggrandize yourself
> each time you
> dare to think

Each time you think, you think you're right,
but you've never not been wrong.
Dirt ass, fist face, lonely 'cause you like it:
I'd kill you for a song.

"I see," said the judge, cutting Morgan off.

"And there is much more. Worse," said Morgan. "The man's deranged. I will supply only titles. You can imagine, or hopefully you cannot imagine, the filth that follows." He picked up a list. " 'Pots of Piss.' 'Porno Sesame.' 'The Sharpest Knife Ever Seen.' 'Mulroney Toothpicks the Poor from his Reeboks.' "

"*Thank you*, Sergeant," said the judge, but Morgan's neck was puffed out and his face red. His voice shook as he read faster and, it seemed, from memory.

" 'Nigel's Samurai *Nose*.' 'The Taste of *Dali's Mustache*.' 'I Fucked Your *Mother*, You're my *Son*.' 'Nigel's Samurai *Cock*.' 'Sex in the Sky, *Needle in the Eye*.' " Morgan, hyperventilating, slapped the paper down and glared at Del.

But Del wasn't looking up. A wrench had been thrown into the fragile scaffold of his black ecstasy. His Frankish spark had been snuffed by Frank's own words and Frank's own depression. Well, there *would* be times of sadness. His brother's life was like that, and now so would his be. But he wasn't going to turn back. No matter how much he forgave Frank—he was forgiving him now—he would carry on. He could not go back, it was impossible. A virgin falls, abandoned; a soldier is shot, and heals painfully. Neither will see the same pastel world as before, but the world as it is really: a bag of broken glass and spiders, too bright inside, being shaken by the dumb child-god.

The rest of the hearing shuffled by, nudging dully at Del's senses. He vaguely witnessed more bile poured his brother's way, *his* way. He noticed Wally doing his best, a calm listing of legalese calling for clemency—the man had done his homework. Thanks, Wall, but I'll just spit on any pretty picture you paint for them, for that's my plan, and my nature now.

Could he be blamed for mixing up Frank's and Mary's faces in his rage? And his forgiving of his brother made the plan that much better. In one act—he saw this, and smiled, and lifted his head—he would be damning his wife but freeing his brother. The Sword of Manjusri, the blade that cuts both ways at once.

"Very well. The trial is set for a month from this date," the judge was saying to him. "Bail, given your recent foolish holiday, Mr. Baal, will be set at a purposely prohibitive—"

"Ah, *fuck* it." Del was on his feet. "I'm *guilty*. I confess *everything*. I'll take you to where *bodies are*." Wally grabbed his arm. "Send me away. I'll kill you I'll kill your children I'll kill myself you're an *asshole* judge you're an *asshole* Tuck you're an *asshole* Mary . . ."

They led Del away. Wally called instructions after him, but Del was laughing too hard to hear.

Down the corridor he laughed, shrieking a treble higher than ever.

In the cell he sang songs, Frank's.

He found a sudden memory of his silly father and homey mother, but the faces were dim now, imprecise. He laughed at this horror.

He saw Fraser and mimicked the boy's gibberish out loud. He saw his den, his dog, his life, he sneered a suburb-burning sneer. He cocked a leg and farted at the bars, for they were so much like the stripes worn by refs. He mocked Pender mountains, he snickered basketball, he groaned old beer-drinking friends, and he snorted the Fraser Valley. He conjured Mary abed with his favorite generic other, getting himself to cry. He whimpered to the so-human smell of her hair as she, with head pressed sideways, sought solace on his chest. He roared then like a courthouse lion, for other men had smelled it too. Into one palm he punched the beginnings of a bruise that would grow and grow. He sang songs in gasps of rhythm, an evil jazz, and found opening to him a hidden shadowy valley where darted—some flying at him in rage—the quick black birds of his brother's genius.

Frank leaned against the rail outside the courthouse doors, delirious with lack of sleep, feeling still the dip and rise of last night's rocky journey. He spoke with Mary. They had sent Fraser off to one side.

"Okay, Frank," she said. "Thanks for this." She kept a careful distance, but her eyes were warm.

"Piece of cake." Frank watched the cars slash by in the light rain. Mary had dressed him up in a pair of Del's bathtub-colored pants. He just wanted to get the deed done, and then sleep.

Behind them a door rammed open and a young blond man, red in the face, flew by them, brushing aside a lawyer type and an old lady as he did so. The sight of the man's face cracked Frank awake. He froze. Who . . . ? Why did he want to hide from this man? Why did he know him? Now the blond was leaping a chain fence and sprinting out of sight.

"That man's going to give somebody a *really* big gift!" Fraser shouted to them.

"We'll be with you in a second, Fraser," said Mary, turning again to Frank. "All I can say is, if this works out, he's going to be very happy."

"That's nice. It really is." Let's do it, Frank was thinking.

"He sort of knows you're not Del, but he isn't sure. You're doing a great job."

"Again. *Morceau de gâteau.*"

"And in the court. Could you be . . . ?"

"The loving hubby. The eager dad."

"Well, yes."

"I'll be good. I'll be honest, good, responsible. Sincere, self-less." He found her eye. "I'll be more like Del than Del."

They gathered up Fraser. Mary brushed back his hair for him. Determined, joining hands, they strode toward the door. Suddenly Frank stopped, stopping the others. For a second, in the door, he'd seen Del coming at him. Fraser dragging on his hand, Frank stood there a moment more, taking advantage of the mirror to once more practice being his brother. He made himself smile whole-heartedly. There, easy. Remarkable, the change. He even felt different. It occurred to him then that maybe kindness was a trick you could do with the face, and the heart was fooled into following.

In the corridor Frank didn't notice an old cop scratch his head at the sight of him, nor a receptionist gasp as he passed.

They were seated in a small oak-paneled room. A court typist smiled at them and turned back to his soundless typing of forms. Fraser sat in his dark blazer and tie, more stiffly than he'd been told. And, as he'd been told, said nothing. His eyes huge and unblinking behind his glasses, he looked like the sleepless book-worm, nervous before an exam. His hands clutched and released, clutched and released, the fabric on his knees. At one point, not smiling, he leaned across and whispered.

"What did the polite judge say to the bank robber?"

"Fraser, remember—" Mary began.

"What did he say?" asked Frank.

"Do I ever have a present for *you*!" Fraser's eyes were cross-ing and he still didn't smile. "I have more jokes if you want," he added, almost sadly.

The magistrate entered and the proceedings began.

It was easy to be Del. Say little. When you did talk, make the voice flip with glee like a boy bragging about his report card to his parents. Smile continuously.

"And how much do you make yearly, Mr. Baal?"

Mary had briefed him. He outlined Del's inheritance, the interest from it, the football salary. They decided to say nothing about the letter that had arrived from a Mr. Tuck.

"And your wife makes . . . ?"

Frank felt Mary's anger at not being asked herself. Himself, he liked this old-fashioned law business. He took her arm and caressed her inner elbow with his thumb. Easy to do this.

"My lovely wife adds twenty-two thousand to the coffers. We are comfortable, Your Honor."

The magistrate asked them their philosophy of raising child-ren. He asked if Mary could continue to work and still look after the boy. He asked why they had no children of their own. We can't, Mary said without hesitating. Smart of her, for Frank didn't know this. Was it true? Del would have told him. The more private the matter, the more public his brother went with it. He remembered Del telling a hitchhiker that he'd been impotent the night before. Eyes pleasant, he asked the hiker if he'd ever experienced anything like—

"Mr. Baal. Why do you want to adopt this young man?"

Frank sat up straight. His smile quivered. He looked at Mary and then at Fraser.

"Please be candid, sir."

"Because . . . no one else can love the lad like he needs to be loved. Because . . . he deserves something good. Because . . . it's a good thing to do."

"Well. Fine."

"Because his world is a pile of sh—"

Mary grabbed his elbow. And she too caressed. Was this a joke? No, it felt like a warning, it reminded him. And yet it was soothing. Oh, he was tired. Del had felt this touch. Where was Del, how was Del, where was that brother of his? Mary was giving the magistrate man her two bits. Frank caught the phrase "and the family-oriented as opposed to the client-oriented environment will be of benefit to his particular condition."

Now the magistrate looked at Fraser and smiled. From the judge's look, Fraser could have been a three-year-old.

"And you, young man? Fraser, what do you think of all this?"

Fraser jumped to his feet as if asked a question in school. "I think of all this." His voice sounded babyish. He stopped and looked at Mary, who smiled lovingly and nodded. He looked at Frank, who said, "Go ahead, fella."

"Okay, Uncle Dad." He looked at the judge and took a breath. "It's a *present from heaven*! You're *God*!"

The magistrate chuckled benevolently, shaking his head. He shrugged at Frank and Mary and mouthed the words, "I was warned."

"Well, Fraser. It sounds like you are a religious young man, is that so?"

"Yes," he said, too loud. He looked up and pointed at the ceiling. "I'm *exquisite*."

"Fine, young man. Now I'd just like to say—"

"It's *delicious*."

Mary stepped over and put an arm around Fraser.

"Yes. I'd just like to add that all seems in order. I've met with both his caseworkers and his psychiatrist. You are two fine people, most worthy of this challenge. For it is a challenge, as you know." He gave them a significant stare. "In some sense this was a formality. In any case, I am reassured. And so, as I sign my name to this document"—he picked up a pen and signed—"this young man Fraser becomes yours by law."

Fraser whooped and jumped and punched his fist into the air.

The magistrate rose and strode past them through the central door, erect and businesslike but grinning despite himself.

Frank thought: this life ain't so bad sometimes.

Mary whirled to face him and as she did so, Frank stepped into her careful distance and embraced her. "My darling, he's ours at last," he groaned, and kissed her hard on the mouth. The typist smiled at them. Mary was rigid, but Frank, exhausted laughter convulsing his stomach, pushed his tongue past her lips and ran it threateningly over her teeth. Pay the gal back.

First he would get back to his boat, kick Felix out, and sleep. Then he would find Del. The world could catch him when it wanted to.

It is sad to say that, throughout the twin farces enacted in the city's court of law, miles away on a boat, Felix d'Amboise lay quietly dying. Of this fact the immense man was unaware, though he had indeed wished it so. Perhaps he had been dying for years. But he was unaware of virtually everything this day. For his system was calmly closing down on itself: veins pinched thin under listless flesh and nerve endings sputtered out like a charring forest of candle wicks. As the oxygen supply to his brain choked off, a fuzzy, painless strangulation, one by one the bright glass bricks of Felix's house of reason dimmed and died.

Stuffed up there in the forward cabin, unmoved for a week now, his slack body conforming to the contours of the hull, Felix resembled nothing so much as an obscenely tumorous outgrowth of wood, a soggy burl. Fittingly, his last days' thoughts were dreamlike but opaque, the color and tone of wood. Only when a main clutch of cortex rebelled before it died did a thought become lucid, a pocket of profundity sparking once as a dying ember does.

The noises Kirk Morgan made did not penetrate much into the fog of the fat hermit's dull death.

Disguised as a marine mechanic, Morgan had exited stage north by seaplane from his role in the twins' comedy to enter now onto a stage of the cheapest, most sordid tragedy. At least, one could only hope this was going to be tragedy: that is, that Felix d'Amboise would somehow triumph as he died, as his own body's poison killed his spirit.

Morgan had boarded the chartered plane five minutes after the hearing, and it dropped him twelve minutes later around the bend from the cove and its cluster of boats and shabby buildings that made up Bob's Lowtide Motel and Resort. It was now or never. The debt would be paid. Within the hour he'd be back in Vancouver, lunching with the prosecuting attorney. What better alibi? For after his foolish, undisciplined outburst in court, his hatred would be known and he would be suspect.

He jimmied the *Mary Del*'s door with ease, walked briskly in, and plopped a tool box down. Shaking his head, he wondered how that Baal creep could have been so stupid. Morgan was a little disappointed. He almost hadn't looked here. Yet here the boat was, docked in its usual place, painted over and with the name changed. It would take more than some clumsy paint job to foil the aim of a trained detective.

Morgan opened his tool box and took out a flashlight. He pivoted and flashed it around the dim interior. God, how this rat's nest smelled. He shone it into his box, then lifted out the dynamite: five pale yellow sticks of it, taped neatly, a stiff twenty-second wick. This bundle he laid gently on the counter. Pursing his lips, he cooed low to it and ran his fingertips over it with wonder and something like lust, as if over the firm legs of a tiny girl. Taking up his light again, laughing deeply, he spun and shone it around. It stopped on an open cupboard door, catching the glint of a bottle. He pulled out the sake, read the label, winced, but twisted off the top. He raised the sake above his head.

"To one burned-out rat's nest," he said.

He shuddered after his short swallow. Setting the bottle down, he picked up the dynamite. He produced a lighter. He scanned the boat's interior once more. When he lit the wick, the cabin shone with the frantic light of a birthday cake sparkler. In this light, Kirk Morgan did not see the door of the forward berth toeing slowly open.

The act of sitting up took a torturously long time, and during the slow-motion rise, Felix's cartilage popped and clicked, his blood roared like mad surf, and a noise like the scream of a lobster being boiled escaped one nostril. The effort of this monumental journey upright is what killed Felix in the end.

It took the Frenchman about five more seconds to die, and during this time the bell of his consciousness rang with a last series of acute but disconnected thoughts.

"Frank is not blond, *non*."

"Make a wish, blow out the . . ."

"*Boomp*, boomp, boomp, oh Indians drums, *boomp*, boomp, boomp . . ."

"*Non*, it is not my birthday."

"*Dead horse in the rain, I'm afraid of blue veins*—Yes, that is one line of Frank's that exemplifies his awful humanity."

"Emptiness invites the Three Powers."

"*Non*, it is *not* my birthday . . ."

This last thought prompted Felix's last word. It took his remaining energy to hiss: "*Pourquoi?*"

As he died his eyes stayed open and his word tailed off in sibilance, as though he was telling the noisy Kirk Morgan "*Shhhhhhh* . . ."

Morgan dropped the lighter, grabbed up the flashlight, and whirled. Felix's body remained upright, for his fat had shifted and propped him like sandbags. The light fell full on the grand face of Felix d'Amboise. Morgan did not have a chance. Though dead, in Felix's eyes the genes of centuries of bombastic-souled French philosophers burned still, and Kirk Morgan met in them exactly what he had always imagined to be the spirit of a cruel and judgmental God. His jaw dropped.

Four seconds of wick was left when he spun for the door. He tripped on the frame, fell, and rolled out onto the deck. It was all he could do to throw the dynamite straight up.

CHAPTER THIRTEEN

The Toe

*People resort to extremes to make grand what they
sense to be a sad little life. They picture themselves a
book that deserves a special ending. Whether they are
artist types or wild socialites or wooden stoics,
extreme people are pathetic. Their eyes looked pursued.
They act as though an unseen tormentor is giving
their bottoms a switching.*

*J'accuse moi-même and cannot escape. For to
become ordinary—I, Felix d'Amboise—would be too
extreme for thought: the Titanic raised to become a
floating pasta bar in Maine.*

—Felix's last jot

Del's day unfolded as colorfully as any during the past week.
It was as if the wild special effects that had begun the movie
had become a fantastic sameness.

He'd been in jail but two days and two nights when he was
freed. Told of his release, he felt no surprise, no relief, nothing.
He concluded they'd caught Frank, or Frank had surrendered
and explained, and now that was that. And it didn't matter. Del
had decided it no longer meant dick where he spent his life, or
how.

Nor was he startled at the sight of his wife, who waited for
him outside the jail. There she stood, chastely made-up, wearing
a smile held on by a hair. He decided he was neither outraged nor

overjoyed to see her. No, he felt both. And that meant they canceled each other out.

Mary held out a travel bag.

"Your razor and things," she said. "Will you let me drive you up to Frank's boat? Frank wants to see you badly."

"He's not in—?" Del jerked a thumb behind him.

"There's been an accident of some sort. It's all confused. All they know is you're not him. He's out for the moment, though I suspect they'll . . . But he asked me to ask you to come up right away. I owe him. So will you come with us?"

They reached the sidewalk, and Del saw the "us" meant Fraser, who sat in the back seat of the car waving at him like a just-wound toy.

Nor did it startle him when, halfway there and at a gas stop with Fraser busy in the bathroom, Mary told him he was legally a father. Unless they discovered the switch there too. Mary explained Frank's good deed. Del turned his face from hers to stare out the window. It was going to rain.

"Before all of this happened," Mary said, "you would have liked the idea. Don't you think?"

His wife was waiting for him to say something. He would not be trapped so easily.

"We can have it annulled if you want. Tell them it was Frank. Or we can just leave it. It doesn't have to decide anything for you." She paused, and now Fraser was fumbling at the door handle. "Or for us."

They continued the drive, in rain, snaking along the base of mountains hugging the coast. Fraser slept. The sun broke through clouds and the wet green beside the road seemed to swell, as it does at such times, with fresh color. Del found it painful to look at.

Mary, nervous, said: "Looks like it might turn out to be a nice—"

"*Jesus*," Del cut her off and turned away.

He fiddled with the radio. He ran his hand up and down his beard. At one point he grabbed the rearview mirror to pivot it and see Fraser. Asleep, he looked almost normal. Del watched

Fraser's arm jerk in sleep and his mouth quiver as if to proclaim something. The hint of a smile.

"He's exhausted," Mary whispered.

Del stared at Fraser a minute more.

"Everybody's tired, I guess," he said. And if Mary wanted to think he had meant that as some sort of apology, she could go ahead and think it.

Frank's movie was equally colorful.

Having gone more than two days without sleep, having entered the lion's den to play a fraudulent part in adopting a retarded man, he returned, an exhausted fugitive, to his boat. He passed the police cars in the parking lot, not caring if they got him at last. But then he smelled the gunpowder and charred wood, and he trotted up to a bunch of cops subduing a deranged and injured man. Several boats close to his had their glass blown out. *Tammy*—or the *Mary Del*—was in worse shape.

"I shouldn't have done *that*. Didn't wanna do *that*," the man was whimpering. He looked blinded and confused. He clutched himself around the ribs but still fought their hold on him. He looked strong. Behind them, an ambulance pulled into the parking lot.

Frank recognized him then. The jerk who had arrested him. The hard-head hanging around the cop station. The punter in the drunk tank.

"Who's this guy?" Frank asked a cop.

"This your boat?" The cop cocked his head suspiciously at the *Mary Del*. The flying bridge was a blasted ruin, windshield gone, seat cushions smoldering, and compass dangling—as Frank described it to himself—like a piece of black snot. Frank nodded.

"Name's Morgan. Seems we found where the dynamite from Highways went missing. Says he's a cop. Seems the guy tried to sink a boat or two. Yours, anyway. Know why?"

"He doesn't like me."

The officer studied Frank closely, but then said, "Go see what's missing or destroyed. File a claim at the station."

Frank nodded again, whispered "Felix" under his breath, and leapt aboard. He ran forward and pulled on the little door, which the blast had wedged closed. After a mighty heave it came free.

"Felix?"

The Frenchman sat there still, and Frank saw the same eyes Morgan had.

He didn't know why the idea of reporting Felix's death repelled him. He kept meaning to. For all he knew, Morgan's prank might have killed his friend; Morgan could quite rightly be charged with murdering his friend. But it seemed irrelevant. Or perhaps he didn't want Felix tainted by the law. In any case, the longer Frank waited the more difficult it was to explain. So he didn't.

Acting the citizen, he did go to the station to cooperate, and there he heard the facts. He learned that a witness had heard a scream, seen the suspect tumble out onto the deck, fall, and then, maybe thirty feet overhead, the blast. Morgan had been blown down hard. He was now almost deaf, with broken ribs and concussion. While listening to all this, Frank expected at any time to be seen and arrested. It felt absurd and a little depressing to find himself in the shadow of so many corny movies where criminals put themselves under cops' noses because that was the last place they'd look.

Frank spent time on the phone. From Mary he learned what Del had done. From Wally he heard about his friend's TV-drama attempts to get Frank off due to "mistaken identity," but that so far the crown prosecutor was laughing at him. He would continue his search for precedents, though all he'd found thus far was Shakespeare. Wally's excitement at finding himself in the criminal corner of this profession reminded Frank of his old eagerness in the dressing room. C'mon, guys.

He even talked to Kirk Morgan. From his hospital bed the Californian got through to him via Bob's Lowtide Resort. Frank heard a sedated, hollow voice, sounding as though it issued from some dull cave in the center of the earth. Morgan said he'd drop the vandalism charges if Frank would do the same. Then they'll just deport me, Morgan said, and maybe I won't lose my job. He sounded like a little kid.

"We've both committed felonies," Frank said, surprised by his fatherly tone. "We can't just shake hands and go free." Frank knew this to be the strangest, most civilized statement he'd made in years. And that was all he said to this blond man, his nemesis and the bastion of all he hated in the world. Felix's death had put things into perspective. Lately a lot of things had taken a different shape.

And what a loony joker his brother had turned out to be.

"*Ahoy, Titanic.*" Fraser, shirtless, wore a battered old captain's hat of Frank's and was shouting at a small runabout with four Chinese fishermen putting by. To a man they smiled and waved.

"*Prepare to board, Dick,*" he shouted at them, looking hostile now. He hunched back, then made as if to hurl a grappling hook at them. Then he dropped the rope and saluted. The fishermen turned to each other, conferred briefly, and the driver edged his throttle up a notch.

"*PT 109!*" Fraser yelled after them.

Frank squatted on the burned cushions of the bridge, dinkering with the broken compass. On deck in a folding chair, Mary flipped through the photo album on her lap, pausing longest at shots showing both brothers together. For the most part these were of the twins hoisting aloft huge salmon, Del delighted, Frank unmistakably bored.

Del appeared on deck wearing Frank's clothes. He had shaved, but still had the look of the habitually unshaven man. Frank descended the ladder, sighing, " 'Nother write-off," and stood beside Del. Both watched Fraser, who was pretending to pull in an anchor and growing exaggeratedly tired. Mary watched the two brothers. Back and forth her eyes went, from Del to Frank and back again. She looked for a moment confused, and about to say something.

But with all of them there on deck, no one knew what to say.
Fraser, because he had given up trying to figure out who to call
Dad or Uncle. Mary, because now was not the time. Frank,
because things were pretty touchy all around, so he would just
hang out in the background. And Del, because even though he
had started to feel by turns forgiving and at times even embarrassed, his anger still rose quickly and deliciously, and this made
it an easy matter simply to say nothing.

Del wandered over to where Fraser tied knots now, turning
an old rope into a tortured ball.

"We going *fishing*?" Fraser looked up at him, his eyes huge
and lively. Funny how when excited he seemed ten years old, and
when depressed, forty.

"No, Fraser. Maybe sometime this summer. Today Frank and
I are going on a cruise, just the two of us. Mary's going to drive
you home in a few minutes. That okay?"

"Sure." Myopically, Fraser bent over his gigantic knot and
began to untie it. He murmured, "When are you coming home
. . . *Dad*?" The off-grin told Del he'd said this word half-
humorously. But only half.

"I . . . sometime soon. A day or two. How's that sound?"

"Sounds okay to me."

"Good lad."

"Now I can enroll in college." Still the half joke.

"Right, Fraser."

"I'm going to grow up like you and have a tall life."

"Sounds just right, Fraser."

Well, he'd decided, then. Home. But it meant nothing. Fraser
had to live somewhere, and so did he. Simply a case of a roof and
food. Mary could . . . do what she wanted. He would be perfectly
detached. He would give her nothing.

Del heard Frank and Mary talking. Funny. Enemies only a
few weeks ago, these two seemed now to be the only friends
onboard. He heard Frank say: "And I'm in *love* again, I don't
believe it. I phoned Laura five times, she wouldn't talk to me. I
sent her money for her work, she wouldn't take it. She pretty
well *hates* me. So I love her again. Isn't that the way?" Mary was

nodding. "She'll come around, I know that. But I'm excited. I feel like a teenager. It's great."

God, he sounded almost sincere. He'd never seen Frank like that. Smiling. Bubbly. It was a bit pathetic.

They hadn't really discussed it, but Del knew what Frank had in mind today. The dire nature of the cruise. Ten minutes before, carefully avoiding his brother's eyes, he'd followed Frank into the cabin to get some clothes. As Frank tossed things out of the locker at him he noticed water seeping out from under the forward berth door over the cabin floor.

"Got a leak or something there, Frank."

Frank looked at Del carefully for a moment.

"Guess I'll tell you now," he said. "Need your help, Beaker. But you can't tell Mary or the kid, okay? What we're going to do is highly illegal."

"What is it?"

"Remember how Felix was sick?"

"No."

"Well he was. And now he's dead."

Frank wrenched the door open. The eyes had been taped shut, but Felix still sat up, a stiff buddha. He was draped in an oilskin, the hood up, and blocks of ice were packed around him. An old ice-filled headache bag sat atop his head. The day was hot, and ice dripped quickly in the silence. Puddles had formed, rivulets ran.

"I want to drop him at sea," Frank said.

The *Mary Del* pulled slowly from the dock. Up in the parking lot Mary and Fraser stood waving. Frank, one hand on the charred wooden wheel, waved back from the bridge. An observer would have seen a family-picnic sort of scene. Del stood on deck, his back turned, catching his breath, having just sprinted back from the car.

He wasn't sure why he'd suddenly decided to escort them to the parking lot. The boat was ready to go, goodbyes had been done. Mary, pained, had said goodbye to Del's knees. Then she'd turned with Fraser and walked up the dock.

He caught up with them halfway to the car. He didn't have a clue what he was doing. His stomach was a mess of contradictions. He put an arm around Fraser's shoulders to give a visible reason. At the car, Fraser got in. Then Mary turned to Del, still looking down.

Look at her in those shorts. It's only goddamned physical, he thought, as he pulled her to him. Then he was leaning down to kiss his wife. As he did so his stomach became a bag of random magnets, some joining absolutely, others kept perfectly apart. Ah Mare. Oh bitch. He was a father. But look at his son. He was a martyr. He was a fool.

The thought that last struck his mind as their lips pressed together was: I am free to do what I want. Which was maybe why Del, who whenever he kissed Mary did so with nothing but softness and desire, did what he did next. Pressing harder, making as if to open his lips with passion, as if a tongue and an outpouring of soul was forthcoming, he suddenly pulled back, grinning. And there was Mary caught with her eyes closed, her mouth open and her tongue partly out, quivering. She was pink in the face and lonely. There, Del saw, was a being at her most vulnerable. He had played with her.

Del spun around and ran back to the boat. He would play with her again. Why not?

About a mile out on Georgia Strait, Del joined Frank up on the bridge. They covered the charred cushions with life jackets and sat on them. There was no wind, the sea was glassy, and the heat almost oppressive. Frank pointed and both men watched a pack of retching gulls chase an old bald eagle holding a cod in its claws. Such was the contrast between the gulls and the noble brown bird that the eagle seemed of a higher order, a kind of graceful mammal.

They cruised without speaking for about an hour. At one point an RCMP boat a half mile distant appeared to take on a parallel course, perhaps watching. Frank veered ever so gradually northward. They cruised on and out of sight, fugitive on the vast waters, the sun high in the sky.

At last Frank turned to his brother.

"So why did you do it?"

Del turned to his brother too. He gave nothing away with his face, but he did, finally, look him in the eye.

Both heads jerked back just a little at the shock they'd never get used to. Today, with Del no longer yearning, with Frank no longer denying, the shock went deeper. As deep as a toe bone.

Looking at the two brothers, say below from the deck, it was as if two identical birds that had spent their lives in different parts of the sky had now angled in toward a common branch, one from below, one from above. There they sat, in neutrality, the voices of past extremes echoing all around them; sitting, neither good nor bad, neither hopeful nor fearful, in the silent eye of past and future storms.

Del didn't answer. He didn't have to.

They cruised to the very center of Georgia Strait. To the north and south lay nothing but glassy ocean horizon. In the west distance stood the mountains of Vancouver Island, to the east the dim mountains of the mainland. Not a soul. Not even a bird now. The sun had them in the middle of its magnifying glass. Frank shut down the engine and they drifted.

They rigged an ancient block and tackle from the anchor winch, through impromptu pulleys and the stern railing, in through the cabin door and around the immense rigid torso of Felix d'Amboise. Frank operated the winch. It was Del's job to help the body exit the cabin with a minimum of damage to either. The job was slow, a foot at a time, and at intervals Del had to run back to the deck for fresh air. Frank climbed down at times to assess the progress and make suggestions. For both brothers the Frenchman's bulbous corpse, bent sitting, dressed in its hooded poncho, being inched along the carpeted walkway, past table and fridge and stashed fishing poles and ukulele, was the most frightful cartoon that life had shown them since the death of their mother.

Once, as Del went out for a breath of air and Frank descended the ladder to help, a funny thing happened. It had never happened before. They stumbled into one another, and as they grabbed each other's arms to keep from falling, their bare left feet rammed together at the toe. At first there was nothing, or rather a kind of inverse force, like a beach wave receding, but then the jolt that entered them, starting at the toe and traveling up the spine, was not only painful but tantalizingly so, as orgasm can be. They stood there, hands locked on each other's elbows, looking down at the joined foot. Then they pulled quickly back from this thing born in the earliest womb, this thing beyond incest, beyond the beginnings of any love known.

It may only have been a case of raw nerve endings.

But now in their toil the brothers began to play. They didn't talk much, and when they did their conversations sounded like:

"Want to—"

"Sure, but let's—"

"And we can—"

"Yeah."

In such a way they agreed to swim. Frank straddled the transom and laughed as he coyly dipped a foot in the water. Though Frank faced prison, Del loneliness, though their friend was dead and their work grim, it seemed perfectly fine to laugh and, once their clothes were ripped off and they stood naked and identically bony, to dive and splash and swim. Heads bobbed face to face above the water. Breathless and grinning, Frank said, "He spent all his life hiding from them. I couldn't stand to see them get him and—"

"Yeah. This is good."

They thought they saw a killer whale roll and breathe mist in the distance, but they weren't sure. They did see a school of salmon go under them, fabulous gliding nuggets, and they laughed.

They set back to work.

And at last Felix was sitting on the back deck. With a knife they stripped the body naked. His gray mass had for some reason turned almost purely white. Not knowing why, Frank removed the tape from his friend's eyes. They rigged the block and tackle off the stern light mast and around Felix again. Inch by inch they maneuvered his huge whiteness up onto the stern railing and balanced him there. With a length of chain, Frank fastened *Mary Del's* anchor to Felix's ankle. Now they had only to cut the rope and shove.

"Bye, Felix," was all Frank said.

"To the god of fish," said Del, though he hadn't meant to.

The knife sawed, the rope popped, the brothers pushed.

The stern rose up mightily as the body fell off. The splash drenched them and the delayed, hollow *Ka. . .BOOSH* echoed across the strait.

They watched the body float down. In the diamond-clear water it was visible for a long time. The anchor appeared to have no effect—perhaps because of the buoyant nature of such a body, or perhaps because even in death Felix defied convention, even the law of gravity. The body seemed to drift in slow motion, its whiteness simply hanging in space, a snapshot of a huge man sitting, pondering the vastness around him. Both brothers watched. They watched as if waiting for the lucid wail of one French horn to sound, or for the white, white body to burst apart into sequins. Nothing of the kind happened. Just a body, gray-green now in the depths, drifting down. Just a man who had tried to explain things, leaving. Nothing else. Not even a meaning to it. They watched, saw clearly, and that was enough.